The Road to Modern Jewish Politics

*Political Tradition and Political Reconstruction
in the Jewish Community
of Tsarist Russia*

ELI LEDERHENDLER

New York   Oxford
OXFORD UNIVERSITY PRESS
1989

Oxford University Press

Oxford   New York   Toronto
Delhi   Bombay   Calcutta   Madras   Karachi
Petaling Jaya   Singapore   Hong Kong   Tokyo
Nairobi   Dar es Salaam   Cape Town
Melbourne   Auckland

and associated companies in
Berlin   Ibadan

Copyright © 1989 by Oxford University Press, Inc.

Published by Oxford University Press, Inc.,
200 Madison Avenue, New York, New York 10016

Oxford is a registered trademark of Oxford University Press

Library of Congress Cataloging-in-Publication Data
Lederhendler, Eli.
The road to modern Jewish politics: political tradition
and political reconstruction in the Jewish community
of tsarist Russia/Eli Lederhendler.
p.   cm.   Bibliography: p.   Includes index.
ISBN 0-19-505891-7
1. Jews—Soviet Union—History—19th century. 2. Jews—Europe,
Eastern—Politics and government. 3. Haskalah—Soviet Union.
4. Soviet Union—Ethnic relations. 5. Europe, Eastern—
Ethnic relations. I. Title.
DS135.R9L33 1989
947′.004924—dc19   88-23832   CIP

2 4 6 8 9 7 5 3 1
Printed in the United States of America
on acid-free paper

STUDIES IN JEWISH HISTORY
Jehuda Reinharz, General Editor

Jacques Adler
THE JEWS OF PARIS AND THE FINAL SOLUTION
Communal Response and Internal Conflicts, 1940–1944

Ben Halpern
A CLASH OF HEROES
Brandeis, Weizmann, and American Zionism

Hillel Kieval
THE MAKING OF CZECH JEWRY
*National Conflict and Jewish Society
in Bohemia, 1870–1918*

Eli Lederhendler
THE ROAD TO MODERN JEWISH POLITICS
*Political Tradition and Political Reconstruction
in the Jewish Community of Tsarist Russia*

Michael A. Meyer
RESPONSE TO MODERNITY
A History of the Reform Movement in Judaism

New York Public Library
A SIGN AND A WITNESS
*Two Thousand Years of Hebrew Books
and Illuminated Manuscripts*
Edited by Leonard Singer Gold

Jehuda Reinharz
CHAIM WEIZMANN
The Making of a Zionist Leader, paperback edition

David Sorkin
THE TRANSFORMATION OF GERMAN JEWRY,
1780–1840

Michael F. Stanislawski
FOR WHOM DO I TOIL?
Judah Leib Gordon and the Crisis of Russian Jewry

In memory of my grandfather, Moishe (Morris) Chinsky
(Yendzhev, 1890–Tel Aviv, 1981)
אין אנדענק פון מיין זיידן,
משה טשינסקי (חנצ׳ינסקי)

Acknowledgments

It is a pleasant duty for me to express my gratitude to those who have made it possible for me to write this book.

Of critical importance in enabling me to proceed with this work, which began as a doctoral dissertation at The Jewish Theological Seminary of America, were generous grants I received from the Charles Revson Foundation, the Memorial Foundation for Jewish Culture, and the National Foundation for Jewish Culture. During the 1984–85 academic year, I was fortunate in being awarded a junior fellowship at the Oxford Centre for Postgraduate Hebrew Studies, where I was able to pursue my work undisturbed in the serene setting of the Centre's Yarnton Manor and amid the inspiring surroundings of Oxford itself. I would like to express my gratitude to the Centre's president, Dr. David Patterson. My stay in Yarnton was also generously supported by the Matvei Guinzbourg Fund.

Research was conducted at The Jewish Theological Seminary of America, where I studied for ten richly rewarding years, as well as at the Jewish National and University Library, Jerusalem, and at the Bodleian Library, Oxford. I remember with great appreciation the efforts of the librarians at the Seminary, the Jewish Studies Reading Room in Jerusalem, and the Oriental Reading Room at the Bodleian, all of whom invariably fulfilled my every request with professional care. I still marvel at their ability—especially the staffs at the Hebrew University and at the Bodleian—in matching up a new reader's name and face after only a few encounters.

Although I take full responsibility for what I have written, the ideas developed here grew from seeds planted earlier by a number of extraordinarily dedicated and gifted teachers from whom it was a privilege to take instruction. My first teacher of Jewish history, an authentic *maskil* and master pedagogue, was Moshe Goldstein (of blessed memory) who taught his students to address him as Haver. It was he who awakened my love for Jewish history and then helped set me on the path I have since followed when he presented me with a set of Heinrich Graetz's *History of the Jews.*

To Ismar Schorsch, now chancellor of the Seminary, with whom I studied modern Jewish history throughout my undergraduate and graduate years, I owe profound thanks. Whatever I know of historical inquiry as a discipline I have learned from him, and his views on the need to reexamine Jewish political history are directly reflected in much of this book. Perhaps above all else, it was his own commitment to the highest standards of scholarship, coupled with his warm and genuine encouragement at each step of the way, that made my decision to remain at the Seminary for my doctoral work one of the easiest I have ever made and also made my stay so worthwhile.

I never took formal instruction from Jonathan Frankel, but it was after reading his doctoral dissertation on Jewish socialism and nationalism in Russia, some fifteen years ago, that I began to think in terms of the similarities of both movements and to wonder about their possible common roots. The thesis I present here is, therefore, intimately connected with what I learned from him. Since I moved to Jerusalem in 1981, he has become more than an intellectual inspiration: I have had the benefit of his counsel, friendship, and help in countless forms. Both he and Professor Schorsch gave me valuable suggestions on the structure and scope of this study.

There have been others among my teachers who have, unbeknownst to them, made vital contributions to the way I set about writing on Jewish political history. Henry Feingold taught me about the centrality of power in political analysis, and Edward Allworth introduced me to the literature on political modernization.

My parents not only created a home environment that resonated with Jewish awareness and content but also equipped me with that sense of attachment to East European Jewry (as well as linguistic skills for apprehending its culture) without which I would not have embarked on this study. I count them among my most successful teachers.

Steve Zipperstein has been a loyal friend and was instrumental in helping me to bring this work to completion. It was he who encouraged me to spend a year at Yarnton and did so much to facilitate my family's stay there. He and his wife, Sally Goodis, provided close friendship, intellectual stimulation, and social diversion. Steve has read, reread, and made insightful comments on the manuscript. He has also given me the opportunity of discussing his own work with him. In both cases I have been the chief beneficiary.

Shaul Stampfer's warmth and generosity of spirit have made life at The Hebrew University all the more pleasant and rewarding. He has shared unstintingly his fund of bibliographical knowledge, as I have had occasion to remark in my notes.

Jehuda Reinharz's experience, good sense, and wise criticism have stood me in good stead as I prepared the manuscript for publication. As for those who worked to put this book into print, I would like to especially thank Nancy Lane, Senior Editor at Oxford University Press, who supported the publication of the book; Henry Krawitz, who shepherded it through the editing and production process, and Andrew Yockers, for his conscientious and thorough copy editing.

The Institute of Contemporary Jewry of The Hebrew University has provided me with a congenial professional niche during the last few years, one where I have had the flexibility to complete my research. I particularly value the working relationships I have formed there with Ezra Mendelsohn and Peter Medding as well as with other members of the Institute.

Rachel Schwartz of the Institute's Bibliographical Center helped me with typing a preliminary draft, as did Kerry Druk. My mother, who helped with typing, also contributed her expert skills as a proofreader. Maciej Jachimczyk of the Institute of Polish-Jewish Studies at Oxford assisted me with translating Polish documents.

The idea for this study germinated simultaneously with the birth of our daughter, Adina, who had to share her father's preoccupations and erratic hours for her first six years. She and Aryeh, who was born three years later, in Jerusalem, have also had to put up with a great deal of moving around and with the necessity of having to learn to speak Hebrew not just once but twice.

Amy, my wife, has shared with me all the woes and joys connected with this book. Her steadfast moral support kept me at it over several difficult periods. Moreover, she twice postponed the next step in her own career—once in New York and again when we went to England—in order to enable me to go on with my work. I hope that the finished product serves to vindicate her faith in me and to express, if only in part, my deepest thanks.

Contents

The Road to Modern Jewish Politics

Introduction

Toward the end of the last century, nationalism and socialism—between them they would determine the subsequent course of world history—were being offered in Hebrew and Yiddish garb for consideration by the Jews of Russia. After the turn of the century, growing movements that embodied these ideologies in a variety of permutations became characteristic features of Jewish life in Russia, Poland, and wherever the East European Jewish diaspora put down new roots. Despite the differences in their various programs, they shared certain basic values and assumptions. With certain exceptions, they were led by men and women who had broken with traditional religious life. All preached that the wretchedness of the Jewish condition was a product of political causes and therefore required a political solution. All propounded a rather awkward combination of two legitimating principles: the will of the people and historical destiny.

Their obvious break with Jewish tradition—in which such immanent and political forces had never possessed autonomous value or authority—was one reason why they remained minority movements in Eastern Europe. (Their rejection of nineteenth-century liberalism's optimism and progressivism made them an even smaller minority in the West.) Yet, though many of their members were culturally or intellectually alienated from the majority of their nation, they aspired to the status of national movements. Each regarded itself as the unique voice of the Jewish future and the vanguard of the Jewish present.

The movements identified with Jewish socialism and Jewish national-

3

ism took organizational form in the two decades that followed the wave of anti-Jewish pogroms in Russia in 1881–82. In both Zionist and Jewish labor-movement lore, the pogroms and the concomitant reactionary turn of tsarist government policy figure as the precipitative events that led certain Jewish liberal and radical intellectuals to reject their old liberal assumptions and formulate new solutions.

The liberals who, since at least the time of Alexander II, the tsar-emancipator, had placed their trust in the emergence of a tolerant Russia that would emulate the liberal West were brought face to face with a reality that was brutally different from their expectations. Some, such as Dr. Leon (Lev) Pinsker of Odessa, now turned to nationalist solutions, calling on the Jews to emancipate themselves rather than wait for the Russian state to bestow equality upon them.

The radicals, who had put their faith in the Russian peasantry and in the Russian radical intelligentsia, now faced the bitter fact that, far from being welcomed as brothers in distress, the poverty-stricken Jewish masses encountered hostility and even violent hatred among those who were meant to serve as the bearers of the revolution. Some of the Jewish radicals, therefore, began to rethink the formerly accepted proposition that Jewish workers had no particular group interests beyond overthrowing the system that oppressed their class. This process led them to address the Jewish working class as Jews as well as workers and to insist on a particularist Jewish agenda within Russian socialism.

This analysis is true on a certain level that is, indeed, borne out by contemporary statements. For a variety of reasons, however, it remains an unsatisfying explanation. It addresses only one aspect of the emergence of modern Jewish political movements: the process of self-criticism that took place among certain intellectuals in the wake of the pogroms. What it does not adequately explain are structural issues: How could political movements spring up, as it were, overnight in a community that presumably had no political institutions or political leaders? Why did intellectuals who were culturally estranged from most Jews believe that they had a leading role to play in the Jews' political development? How did they neutralize the opposition of the traditionalist and conservative elements in the Jewish communal leadership? Why was the "God of History," as Jacob Katz has put it, "on their side"?[1] Are purely external factors—such as government pressure, persecution, economic and social discrimination, and political alienation—sufficient to induce the creation of political movements if there are not some internal developmental factors at work in a society as well?

In other words, can ideological change really be best understood as a self-generating and self-explaining process or ought one look for underlying structural changes in the political life of a society to which ideological change may be related? To explore the latter proposition—that ideological change reflects deeper political change—what must be sought is an analysis of Jewish political development in the period that led up to 1881.

That is what this study aims to do. It proceeds from an assumption: If modern Jewish political movements emerged from a historical big bang, then some account must be taken of those elements existing prior to the explosion that might have contributed something to the shape of the post-1881 responses. By shape I mean the common elements of their political activism, their definition of Russian Jewry as a political community, and their democratic and secularizing thrust. If one understands the kind of political perceptions and political culture that existed in the Jewish community of Russia before the last twenty years of the nineteenth century, one is likely to arrive at more satisfying answers to the questions of causality just outlined.

The Study of Jewish Political Development

The subject of this study, then, is modern Jewish political development in Eastern Europe. It focuses mainly on the period from the 1760s to the late 1870s and is based on a conceptual analysis of the transition from traditional to modern Jewish politics.

The main theoretical problem is that of defining political change in the Jewish historical context. Change implies the existence of a basis for comparison—that is, a baseline situation from which change may be measured. The central methodological problem is that such a baseline has first to be established. Only in the last few years have scholars begun to consider the place of politics in premodern Jewish society, and I know of only one sustained attempt at a theoretical examination of the problem.[2]

What this study offers in the first instance, then, is a working definition of premodern Jewish politics. Where Jewish historiography has dealt with political history in the past, this has generally been restricted to the external aspects: the attitudes and policies of specific rulers and states vis-à-vis their Jewish populations and the responses of Jewish communities (or of sectors within those communities) to particular events or crises. Although certain general assumptions about what was typical in Jewish political history inform such studies, they do not raise the issues of internal change and development or advance a general theory of Jewish political organization.

Others offer impressionistic statements about the ostensible *lack* of Jewish political development. Thus, Hannah Arendt speaks of the Jews' political "ignorance," "innocence," and existential alienation from the political world.[3] David Vital sees Jewish society prior to the late nineteenth century as "washed clean" of the political instinct.[4] Raul Hilberg offers a rudimentary typology of medieval Jewish reactions to persecution—"alleviation, evasion, paralysis and compliance"—in which he sees the direct antecedent of Jewish behavior during the Nazi era.[5] These are generalizations that appear—in light of the historical data to be examined—to require modification.

The dearth of political studies in Jewish historiography owes something to the way in which Jewish history was traditionally conceived and written—primarily as intellectual or legal history and only since the First World War as social history—and to the way in which political studies were originally defined as relating to states and empires, warfare and diplomacy.

With the worldwide social and political upheaval of the last half-century, however, and with the influence of sociology on the scholarly agenda of historians and political scientists, the relations between ethnic groups, between socioeconomic classes, between colonized societies and their colonizers, between government and interest groups of all kinds are widely studied today as political phenomena.[6] The applicability of this genre of political study to the history of Jewish communities lies precisely in its focus on the political behavior of groups within a larger society.

The scholarly reassessment of the political has made it possible to redefine Jewish corporate life as it was historically embodied in the *kahal* (or *kehilla*), the legally autonomous premodern Jewish community. Many Jewish historians in the past, in fact, dealt with political aspects of Jewish communal life but preferred to call them something else, given the prevailing identification of *politics* with *state*. Thus, to give one clear example, Salo W. Baron's history of the Jewish people[7] is replete with informed discussions of the Jews' political relations. Yet Baron is also prepared to state, "Long before the full evolution of its diaspora community the Jewish people had become a basically non-political entity. Indeed, in its long diaspora career it had demonstrated the independence of the essential ethnic and religious factors from the political principle."[8]

In this assessment, Baron was following in the path of Simon Dubnow, the great Jewish historian and ideologue of diaspora nationalism, for whom the Jewish people, with its autonomous but extraterritorial corporate life, represented a "spiritual people," as distinguished from political, territory-bound nations.[9] Baron similarly speaks of the Jews' "emancipation from state and territory."[10]

Although Dubnow, writing in 1898, and Baron, writing in 1942, could still speak of Jewish history as one of transcendence of state and territory, of "independence from the political principle," after 1948 such statements risk a certain loss of authenticity. Without falling into the trap of anachronism—of viewing the reestablishment of Jewish sovereignty as the inevitable end of an eighteen-hundred-year hiatus—it behooves the historian of today to give the political aspects of the past their due.[11]

A move in this direction has been taken in recent years by Daniel Elazar and a group of other scholars associated mainly with Bar-Ilan University. Concerned about the ambiguous relationship between traditional Judaism and the modern state of Israel, they have begun a search for a usable political past, focusing on issues of constitutional theory and political thought as reflected in rabbinic literature. This group has produced valuable studies on the rights of majority and minority, the public and the individual, and on monarchy and theocracy.[12] Members of this group have also produced a schematic outline of the structural elements of Jewish communal government from the ancient through the modern period. The aim of that project is to demonstrate how successive developments in Jewish communal government may be interpreted as the evolving expression of one guiding principle: the contractual or covenantal relationship that bound all Israel together under its sacred Law, without granting exclusive sovereignty to any one part of this religio-political system.[13]

But this leaves us in the realm of pure theory. Even if one agrees with the underlying postulate, it is clear that such a treatment of Jewish political life does not concern itself with the success or failure of institutions in specific historical circumstances. Neither does it relate to the questions of conflict in the community, the mobilization of resources to meet external threats or to defend vital interests, nor, indeed, does it define what those interests were. In short, the superimposition of an ideal prototype is unhelpful when what we want to look at are the historical dynamics of political survival rather than at the theology of Jewish self-government. This problem demands a different angle of inquiry, one that asks how the Jewish community actually functioned in its power relations with the gentile state, on the one hand, and its own Jewish citizens, on the other.

In addressing the problem of Jewish political development and modernization, I propose a theoretical approach that is specifically formulated to suit the Jewish historical context. One difficulty with general theories of political modernization has been precisely that they are overly general: They are based on universal criteria for measuring political change that are not, in fact, universally applicable or that do not carry the same implications in different cultures. Mass literacy, to cite but one example, is not an effective measure of modernization in the European Jewish context.

The approach to Jewish political modernization used here is not based, therefore, on the application of a universal developmental model. Instead, I attempt to look at Jewish political development from within and to identify factors intrinsic to, and characteristic of, the particular Jewish experience. Substantive change in the operation of these culture-specific features may then be taken as the test for modernity.

The most important of these specific features is the dependence of the premodern Jewish community on the influence, power, and active intervention of the non-Jewish state in Jewish politics, especially with regard to external defense and the internal balance of power in the Jewish communities. Accordingly, recourse to gentile political authority for the purposes of defense and the resolution of internal conflict becomes one of the major criteria for measuring continuity and change in Jewish politics.

The problem of conflict, in particular, is one that is rarely, if ever, treated in its own right in Jewish historiography.[14] And the practice of making use of outside political force to resolve an internal Jewish dispute (informing) is normally relegated to the footnotes of Jewish history. Placing conflict in the center of my theoretical model was dictated both by the particular aptness of analyzing conflict resolution for the measurement of Jewish political development and by the nature of political study in general.

East European Jewish Historiography

Many of the issues taken up in this study were dictated by problems raised because East European Jewish historiography is relatively young. This is a field, moreover, that has suffered the loss of a generation of scholars and their students, cut off by the Holocaust. It is for these reasons that certain issues—mainly those related to the ideological biases of historians who were themselves participants in, and leaders of, political movements—were left unresolved.

Thus, the central question of this study, that of the origins of modern Jewish politics in the period before 1881, is one that presents itself today because a balanced assessment of nineteenth-century Russian Jewish social movements has rarely been conceivable before. Portrayals of the politics of the Russian Jewish modernizers of the mid-nineteenth century (the "Enlighteners" [*maskilim*]) that one encounters in a variety of contexts tend to be negative.[15] In the more extreme versions, the maskilic approach to questions of Jewry–state relations and Jewish social integration is characterized as naive, obtuse, assimilationist, and oppressive (toward other Jews). A similar problem of perspective is encountered in historical assessments of the Jewish lobbyists and notables (*shtadlanim*) of the premodern and modern periods.

Nonetheless, as will be apparent, it would surely have been impossible to undertake the present study had it not been for the work of historians of past generations and, indeed, that of several of my own contemporaries. I have been influenced in particular by their probing for the underlying social significance of Jewish communal and literary activity.

My own treatment of the subject is not meant to be a definitive history of Russian Jewry in the nineteenth century. Thus, the reader will not find here a general overview of Russian Jewish life; an overall analysis of cultural, social, religious, and economic trends within the Jewish community; or a chronological survey of Russian government policy on matters related to the Jews. Rather, I seek to provide explanations for several outstanding historical issues and to build a conceptual model of Jewish political development. Throughout, it is the political aspect that remains the focus of this study, and within this political context, I will deal chiefly with the internal dynamics of Jewish development and the mutual relationship between the Jewish community and the state.

For the period up to the nineteenth century, I have been able to rely on previously published primary research and compilations of documents, applying to these materials the particular questions that my own study generates. For the period from the end of the eighteenth century until the end of the 1870s, I have, again, made use of published documents as well as works based on archival sources now destroyed or closed (Russian and Polish materials in particular). Fortunately, a fair amount of the relevant documents were published between the 1890s and the Second World War. Memoirs and literary works, as well, served sometimes as primary source material. The Russian Jewish press was a particularly vital resource for the last period covered in this study (1860–81), as was the published correspondence of leading personalities and that of the Society for Promoting Enlightenment Among Jews in Russia.[16] Again, the insights of other scholars have been invaluable, even (or especially) where we might differ in interpretation.

Although I hope that I have retrieved much historical detail and fleshed out certain less widely known aspects of nineteenth-century Russian Jewish history, my primary aim has been to synthesize an interpretive framework that will encourage others to apply similar methods to other Jewish communities. The pursuit of such a framework for the study of Jewish political development requires that the Jewish community's internal and external politics be examined and portrayed, warts and all. For this purpose weaknesses sometimes count as much as, or more than, strengths; conflict, more than unity. The result may be something less than recognizable to those who would idealize the image of East European Jewry. I would like to hope that, for all that, it would be recognizable to those who participated in the events described.

A note on place names and dates: Most geographical terms have been standardized according to *Webster's Geographical Dictionary,* even though this may sometimes result in cases of anachronistic usage. Dates cited in chapters 3 through 5 follow the old-style Russian calendar.

1

The Medieval Legacy of the Polish-Lithuanian Kahal

Power and the Jewish Community

The Jews of late eighteenth-century Eastern Europe were the heirs to a political legacy whose roots lay in the medieval era. This had been the formative period of Jewry's life in dispersion, in which mastery of the art of endurance was painstakingly—sometimes painfully—acquired. The Jews found a place in the corporate structure of European society as an autonomous social, religious, economic, and political entity.

During this period, Jewish communities were able, by and large, to exert social control internally through the application of religious sanctions and to achieve many of their goals through the mobilization of their economic resources. The question of whether medieval Jewries possessed political power is a difficult one. One may speak of the Jews' economic power and of their political alliances. Jewish communities certainly did not have the kind of sovereign power associated with states, but in medieval times few if any political entities were able to claim unlimited sovereignty.[1]

Power, in any case, is a relative category. The power of one state, class, or ethnic group exists in relation to the greater power wielded by others. The relativity of power is the basic fact underlying Jewish political history, and it determined the course not only of Jewry's external relations but its internal politics as well. On the external level this relativity enabled the Jews to maneuver for allies and security among rival centers of power (the royal court, the nobility, the city burghers, and the

Church hierarchy). Very early, the Jews also came to appreciate the way the division of the world into rival empires enhanced their own chances for survival.[2]

On the internal plane the political viability of the Jewish community depended on its ability, on the one hand, to minimize interference in communal affairs by the greater power of the state and, on the other, to secure state sanction for the community's corporate privileges and governmental functions.

The dependence of Jewish self-rule on the consent of the gentile state and the Jewish reliance on the state's enforcement powers as the ultimate coercive force available to the community held true throughout the medieval period, beginning in late antiquity and continuing in many respects into the modern era.[3] Although it may be argued that the ban (*herem*) was an ultimate sanction, it is true, too, that the ban subjected the target not only to social and ritual ostracism but also to confiscations by the state. Dissidents who might disregard purely ritual or social coercion would probably find it harder to cope with this kind of enforcement. On the other hand, a ban imposed by the Jewish community could also be nullified by the government—once again indicating the potential weakness of the ban.[4] The power exercised by Jewish communities was, therefore, *derivative power*.[5]

According to Baer, the medieval kehilla was dependent on outside authority (for enforcement as opposed to protection) mainly in the early phases of its development.[6] This is a conservative assessment, no doubt accurate for the normal state of affairs in the Jewish community; but it may be questioned when we turn to the admittedly exceptional but persistent—and in our context, crucial—phenomenon of conflict within the kehilla. It is precisely the recourse to gentile authority by both the dissident members of the community and by the community itself in the effort to reimpose its discipline that demonstrates the ultimately decisive political fact about Jewish self-government in the medieval diaspora: its contingent basis.

Informing: Recourse to Gentile Authority

Given the need to defend the prerogatives of communal self-rule against encroachment by outside authority, it was essential that conflict be resolved within the kehilla's own judicial and administrative institutions. The greatest political crime was informing, a concept that extended not only to the revelation (or fabrication) of information potentially damaging to Jewish interests but also to the citing of fellow Jews before non-Jewish tribunals or otherwise bringing the pressure of gentile power to bear in communal affairs. Thus, according to Moshe Frank:

> There are no definite distinctions between recourse to gentile courts and betrayal by informing, since anyone citing a fellow Jew before a gentile court caused him loss or injury through illegal means and even endangered his life. That is why according to Jewish law handing over a Jew to a gentile court was equivalent to informing, . . . in all of the rabbinic literature of the Middle Ages.[7]

Among the earliest recorded provisions for Jewish self-government in Europe is the strict prohibition of recourse to gentile authority. The regulations (*takanot*) attributed to R. Jacob Tam of mid-twelfth-century France forbade summoning a Jew before a gentile court as well as intimidation of the community through gentile offices.[8] What is ironic is that these very provisions were backed up by the following appeal, "We the undersigned request all those who are in touch with the government to coerce through the power of the gentiles anyone who transgresses our commandments."[9]

The exclusive right of recourse to gentile power that the kehilla arrogated to itself may be analogous to the monopoly of violence asserted by the state and, as such, a basic constitutive element in the traditional Jewish political structure.

The invocation of strict measures against informers occurs repeatedly in halakhic literature, communal regulation, and charters granted to the Jewish communities throughout the later Middle Ages.[10] Nevertheless, informing continued to bedevil Jewish life, both in the sense of malicious betrayal of "the secrets of Israel" and in the sense of resorting to gentile courts ("handing over the property of Israel").[11] Recourse to gentile authority also continued through seeking the support of, or the official appointment to communal office by, powerful rulers.[12]

The settling of individual scores through defamation or through litigation in gentile courts indicates an acute sensibility in Jewish society of the relativity of power in the Jewish situation—that is, the constant temptation to pass over the heads of duly constituted communal authority and go directly to the source of power. That such direct recourse was also routinely used by those vested with authority—whether to confirm their office, to coerce recalcitrant taxpayers, to broaden the scope of their jurisdiction, or to punish violators of communal discipline—shows that the medieval kehilla, even in its mature developed stage, could not function as a closed system.

The severe limitation of available power was most radically felt when conflict based on social or ideological differences broke out between entire factions. The resolution of such conflicts was often impossible, given the limits of Jewish power, without the intervention of outside authority. Each side invariably tried to outflank the other by winning the support of one or another powerful ally.[13] Of relevance here are the campaigns of Rabbinite Jews and Karaites to gain jurisdiction over each other or to secure government intervention against their opponents.[14]

Another case in point is the Maimonidean controversy that split the Jewish intellectual world into two bitterly opposing factions (in 1180, between 1230 and 1232, and again from 1300 to 1306). The controversy involved substantive issues (the legitimacy of philosophical study and of allegorical interpretation of the Bible) as well as procedural political issues (the binding nature of a ban pronounced by one faction seeking to exert a centralized authority that is then invalidated by their opponents, claiming intellectual and jurisdictional autonomy). Although seemingly an internal, ideological, and philosophical affair, the appeal to gentile authorities by the anti-Maimonists on several occasions gave it an external dimension as well.[15]

Both informing and resorting to gentile authorities by the community itself followed logically from the scarcity of power within Jewish society and the derivative nature of the power that was available. Although such methods of conflict resolution seemed to contradict the normative values of the community, the consistent pattern of such incidents leads one to suspect that recourse to outside centers of power was an important defining attribute of traditional Jewish politics that reveals the limits of intracommunal authority. The internal political features of the kehilla regime were shaped to a significant extent by its external relations.

The Politics of Survival: Quietism, the "Royal Alliance," and *Shtadlanut*

Jean Juster, writing in 1914, recalled the opinion of Vespasian (9–79 C.E.) that the Jews were "a seditious people." This impression is certainly borne out by a review of the numerous Jewish revolts during the first and second centuries.[16] Yet most historians agree that the hallmark of subsequent Jewish policy was deference to authority. This change is undoubtedly what Isaac Abravanel had in mind when he wrote, "The three curses of the Exile are . . . lack of courage . . . lack of honor . . . and lack of government."[17]

Abravanel's sentiment aptly illustrates one of the main difficulties faced by the historian in attempting to analyze the patterns of Jewish political behavior: the difficulty of separating facts from their evaluation. The Jews in Exile were not totally bereft of government and Abravanel, of all people, was himself a paragon of political courage and honor. In the wake of the disaster of Iberian Jewry, however, his intimate knowledge of the Jewish political machinery was overwhelmed by his perception of its (and his) patent failure. Almost all subsequent views of Jewish political history have persisted in taking symptoms for causes and in giving way to the temptation of stereotypical thinking.[18] Indeed, they have dismissed Jewish political strategy as nonexistent (Vital), a blunder (Arendt), or a "strait-jacket" which led the Jews to their doom (Hilberg).[19]

Arguing against this view of Jewish political "passivity," Ismar Schorsch contends that "survival as a dynamic, creative, and cohesive minority evokes a presumption of political sagacity of a fairly high order," and that "Jews have displayed over time an unusual ability to identify their collective interests, to assess the possibilities for action, to locate allies, to organize and deploy their resources, and to learn from their failures and mistakes."[20]

He urges the use of the term *political quietism* to describe Jewish strategy, a term, he argues, that leaves room for the elements of "consciousness and initiative . . . a calculated policy of cooperation with established authorities on the basis of utility." A similar view has been taken by David Biale, who notes that "[t]he Jews possessed an extraordinary ability to maneuver between the extremes of a quest for full sovereignty and a state of political passivity. . . . Jewish history continued to be characterized by a wide spectrum of persistent and ongoing political activism."[21]

The Legitimacy of Gentile Rule

The Jews of medieval Europe were hardly the first Jews to be subject to gentile rule; certain formulaic guidelines had been laid down for Jewish political obedience by the Talmudic sages and, even earlier, by the governing authorities of Greco-Roman Judea. It remains unclear just when a prayer for the well-being of the gentile king was introduced into synagogue ritual, but the text is included in the earliest medieval manuscript and printed editions of the prayerbook, both North European and Mediterranean.[22] What seems most probable is that the liturgical practice was both an evolution from preexilic conventions of the Temple cult and early synagogues in which prayer was offered on behalf of the emperor of Rome, and a political necessity in Christian Europe—where Catholic liturgy also had prescribed forms for recognizing the temporal sovereignty of kings and emperors.[23]

We can be more certain about the origins of the rabbinic dictum *dina demalkhuta dina* (the law of the kingdom is law [for the Jews]). Attributed to the leader of Babylonian Jewry in the mid-third century C.E., Samuel Yarhinai, it is at one and the same time an expression of the Jewish *modus vivendi* with the gentile state and an assertion of the autonomy of Jewish law.[24]

This legal principle provided a mechanism by which the state's tax laws, tolls, and property deeds registered in non-Jewish courts might be upheld as valid in Jewish judicial proceedings. It did not, however, imply a wholesale acceptance of a foreign legal system. (As already noted, recourse by two Jewish parties to a dispute to a gentile court was not considered to be legitimate.) The *dina demalkhuta* principle was applied and interpreted selectively, and it was considered valid in very limited spheres. It did not apply, for example, to special state taxes on Jews or property confiscations, which the rabbis considered to be "illegal." A Jew who was the beneficiary of "illegal" state actions could not use *dina demalkhuta* as a defense if a Jewish victim of state confiscations sued him for damages before a Jewish court. Similarly, Jews who evaded payment of a discriminatory or extraordinary tax (i.e., imposed only on Jews) were immune from damage suits based on *dina demalkhuta* brought before a *bet din* by other Jews who did pay the tax.[25]

In this way a rudimentary theory of monarchic legitimacy began to develop. The right of the king to impose laws and taxes for the general welfare was understood in one of several ways by the rabbis who grappled with the *dina demalkhuta* issue. In the first instance, it was explained that the "natural" consequences of God's subjection of the Jews to gentile rulers entailed the king's right, in principle, to impose his will on them (within certain bounds). Second, the king was considered to be the agent of customary law and the executor of that law by common consent and therefore empowered to levy customary taxes. Third, the king was described as owner of the land and hence permitted to impose conditions on the inhabitants. Fourth, the gentile kings were (at a stage relatively late in the Middle Ages) seen as analogous to the kings of Israel, with the same prerogatives and limitations. The tendency, in most cases, was to limit the king's absolute prerogatives by reference to custom, consent, and equity.[26]

Indeed, as Baron has pointed out, the theoretical implication of *dina demalkhuta dina* is that state law is subject to review and recognition by divine law (i.e., Jewish law)—an inherent "clash of sovereignties" that was avoided by compromise on both sides.[27] The state generally did not interfere in internal Jewish legal affairs; the rabbis applied their strictures concerning "illegal" uses of royal power only within Jewish jurisprudence.[28] This would appear to testify to a certain finesse on the rabbis' part in simultaneously safeguarding both political security and jurisdictional autonomy. The preservation of a dynamic equilibrium between these two motives, Baron argues, "constitutes much of the political history of the medieval Western Jewries . . . [in which] perseverence of Jewish leaders and the active or passive resistance of the masses always salvaged a broad range of communal autonomy."[29]

Another way of understanding this is in terms of the Jews' general inability to do anything but acquiesce in royal demands—manifested in their quietism, or deference to the power of the state—while refusing to crown the superior power of the gentile state with true legitimacy. This mask of submission is deeply embedded in the medieval Jewish worldview, which has its roots in late antiquity.[30]

As we shall see, Jewish reservations as to the limits of gentile laws and their applicability to Jews had significant political ramifications. The refusal to abide by the "law of the kingdom" would at times take place in the context of defending a matter of the Jewish interest and at other times simply in the evasion of tax or customs regulations. Suffice it, now, to say that any broad assertions about Jewish loyalty to kings and quietism within the law must be qualified: These were tactical positions that did not elevate the legitimacy of gentile rule or gentile law to a matter of principle.

The "Royal Alliance"

What is noticeably absent from theoretical rabbinic considerations of *dina demalkhuta* is any reference to the kings' prerogatives by virtue of the contractual relationship between Jewish communities and medieval rulers as embodied in the Jews' charters or "privileges." The rabbis are also seemingly oblivious to the medieval concept of the Jews as servitors of the royal chamber.[31] Yet the political status of the Jews was based precisely on their charter-bond with the royal or imperial court.

The chief feature of these charters was the exclusive protection of and jurisdiction over the Jews by the crown in return for the Jews' financial obligation to the royal treasury.[32] The first explicit enunciation in a charter of the principle that the emperor was "responsible for the peace and well-being of all his Jewish subjects throughout the empire" occurs in 1182; but the principle was affirmed much earlier in practice.[33] The principle was put to the test particularly in times of mass violence, such as those associated with the Crusades. That the Jews came to depend on royal and imperial guarantees of safety was based on such successful instances as the forceful protective measures adopted by Frederick I in 1188 in response to a plea by Jewish representatives in Mainz. Between the twelfth and the fifteenth centuries, the Jews also looked to bishops and popes for similar protection.[34]

Thus, there is no confusion about how the Jews came to identify their political interests with strong royal, Church, or baronial government, despite Hannah Arendt's peculiar formulation that "they had *somehow* drawn the conclusion that authority, and especially high authority, was favorable to them." Even Arendt admits that this "prejudice" reflected "a historical truth."[35]

The pragmatic and utilitarian aspects of the Jews' primary political orientation to the ruling powers of their society were dictated not only by the problem of security but also by the overall dependence of the kehilla system (discussed earlier) on the active or tacit cooperation of the state.

Indeed, the "alliance" of the Jews with kings and emperors has become one of the truisms of Jewish historiography.[36] It is attested to in a variety of contemporary sources and is summed up succinctly by Abravanel, "Be the servants of kings and not servants to the rest of the people. This in truth is what the Jews have been throughout the Exile: the special possession of kings and lords, and not slaves to the rest of the people."[37]

Yet what has been insufficiently noted is the fact that this tactical alliance was embedded in a matrix of other ideas, some of which were rather reserved about the legitimacy of gentile rule. The most important of these, of course, was the messianic tradition, of which Abravanel was an important exponent. Messianism was the way in which Jews expressed the conviction that their own survival as a distinct group was both foreordained and ultimately meaningful and that they were destined to be liberated from their Exile. At bottom, messianism challenged the supremacy, durability, and historical significance of gentile rule.

Thus, although the Mishnaic tractate of *Avot* enjoined the Jews to "pray for the welfare of the kingdom," the original, unexpurgated formula of the grace recited after meals included the plea, "And free us from the yoke *of the gentile nations,* raise us up higher and higher in everlasting time and bring our enemies lower and lower. . . . May the

Merciful One avenge the blood of His servants and send us a redeemer to build the walls of the sanctuary, and gather the dispersed of Judah and Israel.[38]

To be sure, the two ideas could be balanced; indeed, they often were. The best illustration of this lies in the text of the traditional prayer for the welfare of the gentile ruler.[39] The difficulty of reconciling the two positions does come through, however, in the works of those Jewish thinkers who took a more clear-cut position on one side or the other, in favor of messianism or of conservative quietism. It was also expressed by the antiestablishment and antinomian tendencies that surfaced in radical messianic movements, such as that of the messianic pretender of the seventeenth century, Sabbatai Zevi.

The threat that these represented to the stability and security of the communities was generally recognized by the religious and political leadership, who preferred to leave redemption to God. It was precisely moderate, legitimate messianism—incorporated into the liturgical and ritual cycle of Jewish life—that encouraged a political pragmatism over the indeterminate short term. As long as the timetable for divine salvation remained vague and indefinite, all feasible means necessary for survival might be taken without infringing on divine prerogatives in the overall scheme of earthly and cosmic salvation. Separating God's sphere of responsibility from man's allowed for a certain qualified autonomy for the human sphere.[40]

It was not only radical messianism, however, that discouraged an unqualified "alliance" with royal power. As already noted, the halakhic (legal) traditions helped to perpetuate such reservations. We also have evidence of temporary alliances by Jews and municipalities against royal or imperial edicts as well as explicitly antimonarchical sentiments expressed by chroniclers and philosophers.[41]

Therefore, to be accurately understood, the concept of the "royal alliance" cannot be taken in a strictly literal sense. It must be carefully qualified to stress the idea's tactical, contingent quality; and, in addition, it must be amended to refer, as Baron does, to "the Jews' attachment to the ruling power of the state, be it imperial, royal, episcopal, ducal or municipal."[42]

Shtadlanut

Largely taken for granted and rarely spelled out in Jewish historiography is the emergence of *shtadlanut* (intercession by individuals with the powers-that-be) as the main vehicle of Jewish political activity on the external plane. Given the usually confidential nature of such activity, the documentation here is relatively sparse. At the same time, it was so ubiquitous a feature of traditional Jewish politics—and, as we shall see in the Polish case, quite systematically developed by the seventeenth century—that its roots in medieval Jewry are worth a brief examination.

The word *shtadlan* was apparently not coined earlier than the mid-fourteenth century, although the functions of lobbyist, petitioner and spokesman were certainly filled in earlier times by those who were not given any terminological designation. Indeed, the entire medieval background of shtadlanut, as of Jewish communal activity in general (including the rabbinate), is one of nonprofessionalism.

Shtadlanut was a necessary concomitant of the Jewish political condition in the Middle Ages. Dependence on a ruling figure or figures, often not located in the immediate vicinity, required the intermediary activity of someone with ready access to the court. Second, as the Jews' political status rested to an overwhelming extent on their fiscal bond with the feudal treasuries, political activity was virtually synonymous with handling the communities' or private assets judiciously and to the public benefit. This required trustworthy persons of experience, tact, judgment, and, usually, wealth.

It was in 1354, at a meeting of Jewish communities of Aragon, in Barcelona, that the term *mishtadlim* was applied to such spokesmen. The word connotes assiduous application and acquired particular meaning only in the context *mishtadlim ushluḥim,* (intercessors and agents).[43] The Aragon decision represents a stage in the routinization of Jewish lobbying efforts.

A remarkable centralization of Jewish political representation took place in sixteenth-century Germany, where the Jewish communities departed from their individualist tradition to elect Josel of Rosheim as their "leader and commander."[44] Josel began his career in 1510 as leader of the Jews of Lower Alsace, and his journal records events until 1547 in which he was personally involved as intercessor and petitioner. Further evidence shows that he was politically active through 1554. He negotiated the terms of Jewish charters and tax obligations, interceded for communities threatened with expulsion, charges of ritual murder, and accusations of treason. He was also involved in efforts to reform Jewish moneylending practices and in a campaign to counter Martin Luther's anti-Jewish propaganda.[45]

Josel of Rosheim was apparently an intrepid man of great ability. Although he described in some detail the measures that he took in interceding on German Jewry's behalf, he did not take the credit himself for his successes. These he attributed to God:

And God caused the Count of Anjou and the Bishop of Strasbourg to hearken to my cries. . . . With God's help I persuaded the king until the expulsion decree for Kaysersberg was nullified, just as the expulsion from Rosheim was never implemented; for with great effort each time, and under great stress, we won postponement after postponement, though until today we are still uncertain. Thus we can depend on none but our Father in heaven. He is our savior who rescues us from our enemies. . . . Praise God who saved us from their hands and from evil designs, long may He continue to protect us, Amen.

. . . I brought the old documents from the popes and emperors to the city of Günzburg, where I copied them together with some words of defense into a special booklet which I sent to the king and his officials . . . and God counted in our favor the merit of those holy martyrs whose souls achieved perfection in dying for the sake of God's name.[46]

This is not surprising in an age of faith. The point here is twofold. Josel needed to view his own activities as the secondary or dependent element in an equation in which God alone was truly autonomous as an actor in history; yet his belief in an active Providence did not absolve him from taking the most pragmatic and carefully planned steps possible in pursuit of defined goals.

In this he was a typical, even paradigmatic, figure in traditional Jewish political life, as we will see confirmed in the case of Polish-Lithuanian Jewry. Because Jews tended to view the continued survival of their people as a sign of divine favor, practical efforts to maintain communal life were invested with religious justification and purpose. The scope of such efforts was limited only by the belief that God Himself would ultimately provide the definitive vindication of Jewish steadfastness, so that the Jews themselves need not orient their political activity to the goal of final redemption.

As considered from within this point of view, a temporary and tactical alliance with gentile power did not contradict the belief in Divine Providence, in the chosenness of the Jews, or in a messianic restoration. It followed naturally from the idea that a remnant of Israel must be preserved in order finally to merit redemption from the "yoke of the gentile nations."

The Polish-Lithuanian Kahal (Until 1764)

Polish Jewry from the sixteenth to the eighteenth centuries was an authentic incarnation of the religious, social, and political legacy of medieval European Jewry. Its communities were founded upon the rule of rabbinic law and on Jewish traditions of civil administration. At the same time, the specific context and conditions of Jewish life in Poland-Lithuania necessitated the development of new adaptations of general patterns. In the political realm there were several features that became characteristic of Polish Jewry.

As had been the case elsewhere, Jews in Poland sought and received the protection of the crown and the royal courts. Again, as elsewhere, the crown viewed the Jewish population as an asset of the royal treasury.[47] Exclusive jurisdiction over Jewish matters was in principle reserved for the crown, but, in fact, it had long been entrusted to the regional governor, or palatine (*wojewoda*), and his deputy, who, though appointed by the crown, were in most respects representatives of the nobility.[48]

The jurisdictional and political powers of the Polish nobility were broader than those exercised by noblemen elsewhere in Europe of that time, and this constitutional difference contributed to the greater influence in Jewish affairs wielded by the Polish gentry of the sixteenth to the eighteenth centuries. By 1539, the noble landowners were granted formal legal authority over Jews living on their domains and private urban enclaves (*jurydyki*). As royal authority waned, particularly after the end of the Jagiello dynasty (1572) and as the city burghers increasingly challenged the residence, trading, and manufacturing privileges of Polish Jews, the importance to the Jews of noble patronage was enhanced. By 1764–65, between half and three-fourths of Polish Jewry lived under nobles' jurisdiction.[49]

A second characteristic feature of Jewish life in Poland was the free scope given to the concept of Jewish autonomy. Contemporary observers of the Polish-Lithuanian kahal of the seventeenth and early eighteenth centuries believed that its authority and power compared favorably with the communal authority's status in medieval Western Europe.[50] Polish Jewry developed a nationwide network of super-kehilla provincial councils (*va'adim*) and a supreme consultative and judicial council, the Council of the Four (Polish) Lands (*va'ad arb'a aratsot*), later to be paralleled by the analogous *va'ad medinat lita* (Lithuanian Council).

Having evolved over the period of some four decades, these provincial and national bodies are certain to have existed formally from around 1580 (the Lithuanian Council from at least 1623). Although divided over whether it was primarily the wishes of the state's fiscal administration or the Jews' own desire for a ramified system of communal government that led to the establishment of the councils, most historians generally concur on the advantages of the system for both the state and the Jewish communal leadership.[51]

In fact, the question of whether it was the state's requirements or the Jews' needs that produced the va'adim structure becomes far less problematic when seen from the political perspective stressed in this study. It was precisely the link between the two factors that here, as always, determined the course of Jewish political development. Clearly, the va'adim could not have come into existence without a context in which both the Jewish communities and the state had an interest in erecting such formal political structures.

King, Gentry, and Burghers

Although ultimately depending on the royal charters ("privileges") obtained by Jews in Poland since the thirteenth century, the Jews found that these were never sufficient in practice. They were routinely supplemented by specific privileges obtained by individual Jewish communities. These often contradicted more general provisions of charters granted by the same king to the municipalities and guilds.[52] Jewish communal leaders found, in any case, that exclusive reliance on the central authority of the crown was ineffective and, in many instances, not as beneficial as maintaining good relations with powerful local figures. To a certain extent, the nobility became the Jews' main point of political orientation.[53] But recent scholars caution against the automatic equation of gentry and Jewish interests and stress instead the relative independence of Jewish political strategy.[54]

In general, the Jewish communities' main interests—apart from security—lay in maximizing residential and occupational rights and maintaining or expanding communal jurisdiction (fiscal and judicial). These goals were often pursued against the resistance of other actors in the political arena: gentry, clergy, merchant and craft guilds, and municipal councils. What often resulted was a semipermanent contest in which first one side and then the other resorted to both legal and extralegal means in order to gain the upper hand.

In Lvov (Lwów), for example, the Jewish community and local authorities fought continuously for extended periods over matters of residential and occupational freedom. Resisting city ordinances enacted in the late 1480s, the Jews of Lvov turned to the king and, in 1493, obtained a royal decree permitting them greater occupational diversity. This had to be confirmed in 1499 and again in 1503. The conflict was renewed repeatedly over the course of the following two centuries.[55] In the area of residence rights, the Jews persevered through lengthy court battles and negotiated a series of compromises with the city between

1581 and 1635. As late as the mid-eighteenth century, however, the issue remained essentially unresolved.[56]

In Poznań between 1532 and 1628, the town authorities obtained successive and increasingly stern court orders and royal decrees forbidding the Jews to move outside their assigned street, requiring them to sell all Jewish-owned houses outside the permitted zone, ordering thereafter the Jews' eviction for noncompliance, and finally, directing the Sejm (Diet) to launch an investigation—all to little or no avail.[57]

In Lublin the struggle lasted from the mid-sixteenth century to the 1780s, during the course of which the balance finally tipped against the Jews.[58] In Pinsk in the 1660s, the burghers and the Jewish community charged each other with acting illegally in a protracted court battle over residential and occupational rights.[59]

The case of Vilnius (Wilno, Vilna) also illustrates that neither burghers nor Jews were willing to accept legal orders as binding and that both repeatedly appealed to other jurisdictions in addition to taking unilateral action. In the course of seventy years (1713–83), the two sides alternately agreed to and rejected arbitration by the bishop; were summoned before the royal courts but failed to appear or otherwise obstructed litigation; ignored warnings, refused to pay fines, and disregarded explicit stipulations in signed agreements. Finally, in 1783, the Jews won much of their case.[60]

In each instance the Jewish community sought recourse to royal charters and decrees but also played one authority against the other. Individual nobles, clergy, the Sejm, or the royal bailiffs could be persuaded to block action by the municipality.[61]

A document has been preserved that not only supplies information about events in the city of Kaunas (Kovno) around 1783 but also gives us a rare insight into the way in which Jews perceived such struggles. The motif of Purim, the archetypical "miraculous" salvation wrought through the success of shtadlanim in gaining the favor of the king, is evoked by the author in a celebratory "new *megilla*":

> Had not God been with us . . . our ancestral home would have passed from our possession. . . . We put our hope in the Lord and He inclined toward us His favor and caused us to find mercy in the eyes of the illustrious and pious King, Stanislav Augustus . . . and his compassionate viceroy . . . who gave us a portion in this happy city, where our fathers' fathers have lived from time immemorial. . . . We were twice expelled from it. The first time, thirty years ago, it was less difficult [to bear], since we were not expelled from all [of it] but only from a part ruled by the wicked men of the place [i.e., the burghers] and we settled in the suburb

called the King's Court. . . . Eighteen years later, the decree was turned against us and we were forced to leave. Nothing was left to us there and our holy house [*beit kedosheinu,* (the synagogue)] was burned; [the sacred scrolls] that we held most dear were destroyed . . . and mocked by the impudent ones. We prepared to remove to the other side of the River Viliya, [now Neris, ed.] where a few [Jews] had settled after the first expulsion, under the government of the Vilna wojewoda, Karol Stanislav Radziwiłł . . . but even there, we had no rest from the people of Kovno, who sought to have us removed further . . . God spared us this, until the time of the coronation of our lord, the gracious and pious king [*hamelekh hehasid*]. Then we arose and strengthened ourselves to supplicate him and seek relief from the anger of the wicked ones . . . and our suit was success-ful. . . . And God moved the heart of the gracious king, to so order that the Jews who were expelled might return to their patrimony.[62]

The crown and the higher nobility, therefore, were perceived as the mainstay of the Jews' security vis-à-vis the burghers—and, of course, the peasantry, who normally did not figure in the political process. This pattern of tactical alliances was not essentially altered by the massacres during the Cossack uprising of 1648–49 and the ensuing period of war and instability. The experience, albeit shattering emotionally, seemed rather to confirm than to shake conventional political wisdom in the Jewish community. If anything, suffering at the hands of insurgents and foreign invaders tended to reinforce traditional views about the impor-tance of stable and friendly government.

Thus, we find that during a peasant uprising in White Russia (in the area of Mstislav, Mogilev province) in 1744 in which Jews were again singled out for brutal treatment, killings, and forced conversions, they looked for protection to the provincial governor, who, indeed, sent his own troops as well as the militia of one of the local nobles to put down the rebellion. The governor himself reportedly supervised the restitution of plundered Jewish property and permitted those forcibly converted to revert to Judaism.[63]

Jurisdictional Prerogatives

The Polish-Lithuanian kahal, in keeping with inherited traditions of communal policy, sought to maintain and, if possible, to expand the reach of Israel's law and enhance its independence and enforceability. Both independence and enforceability, however, could not be maxi-mized at the same time. A case in point was the authorization or ap-proval by gentile authority of appointments within the communal apparatus. This tended to enhance the enforcement powers available to the Jewish authorities but also tied them closer to outside influence.

The Jews' privilege of internal self-rule and judicial autonomy was a basic component of all privileges obtained by the Polish kehillot. Thus, the earliest royal charters (thirteenth to fifteenth centuries) already incorporated recognition of the competence of Jewish courts and successive privileges amplified this, with provisions for the enforcement by state power of decisions of the community executive and rabbinical tribunals—as in the charters granted in 1551 by Sigismund II, in 1576 by Stephen Báthory, and in 1592 by Sigismund III.[64] Individual communities and even individual rabbis found it useful to obtain royal patents confirming their authority and imposing punishment for breaches of discipline and obedience (including, of course, matters of taxation).[65]

The same provisions appear in authorizations granted locally by the wojewoda or the noble landowner. It was customary for rabbis and kahal officers to obtain from the wojewoda written confirmation of their office, and thus political protection, generally in return for a handsome fee.[66]

The renewal of his official appointment, which R. Haim Rapoport received from the Lwów wojewoda, Prince Czartoryski, in 1763, read:

> This will inform all who need to know, to wit, the noble deputy wojewodas and judges in my courts, that the rabbi, Chaim Szymchowicz [Haim b. Simha], who has served here with distinction in the city of Lwów and the province of Rus and whose selection is approved by the communities of the Jews . . . will continue to serve in his office as before, since I desire no disruption in the legal affairs of the Jews. . . . Out of my wish to make him secure and confident in his office, I have given him the power to judge the Jews in every matter of the law and to institute proper order in their communities. I have granted him the particular privilege of being free from tax obligations, both to the Treasury and to the kahal. . . . Indeed, by this writ, I take him under my personal protection and he shall not be answerable to any complaint [of another authority]. I command all Jews of Lwów and the Rus Province and its cities to bring their suits only before this rabbi.[67]

Gentile authorization was also granted to the Jewish community board and its court. In 1741, the Dubno kahal recorded the following resolution in its minutes:

> Inasmuch as our lord the prince has commanded that all civil suits between Jew and Jew be brought before the *bet din* and damages cases shall be brought before the judgment of the chiefs of the kehilla, sitting together with the rabbi . . ., anyone who refuses to submit to judgment by the Law

of Israel is liable to the coercion of the castle [i.e., the civil authority]. Those who violate and weaken the law have multiplied; they even evade taxes and bring their meat from outside our community. . . . Therefore, we have decided that this shall not be done any longer and all shall be enforced according to the points in the prince's charter. Anyone in violation of this, who does not go before a Jewish court in the first instance, shall be excommunicated . . . and pay a fine of fifty zlotys to the prince, in addition to a fine to the community chest.[68]

As was the case in earlier centuries, the kehilla or the rabbi enjoyed in this way a measure of coercive power beyond what they could command by virtue of their own socioreligious legitimacy and authority. By the same token, this enhanced power was always derivative in nature, as is revealed by the way in which individuals and kehillot had recourse to gentile courts for particularly contentious lawsuits.[69]

Conflict over jurisdiction was a significant element in the intramural relations of the wider Jewish community. Growing communities sought the right of self-administration and larger kehillot routinely disputed with each other regarding jurisdiction over smaller provincial settlements. Such battles, waged largely over tax revenues, came before the regional and central councils as well as the gentile courts.[70]

A major controversy of this kind embroiled the major Lithuanian Jewish community of Brest Litovsk (Brześć nad Bugiem) in running litigation with the other three Lithuanian centers—Grodno, Pinsk, and Vilna—and against the Jewish community of Minsk, from 1681 to 1685. In the first dispute, which was ended only after a royal decree ordered the Jewish communities to resolve their differences through an arbitration procedure, the jurisdiction of Brest Litovsk over smaller settlements and the apportionment of taxes to be collected from these communities were at stake.[71] The final decision of the case, which was reached by the rabbinic panel prescribed by the king's order, reprimanded all four communities for improper conduct of their suit and in particular for taking their case to gentile courts.[72]

A celebrated jurisdictional controversy took place earlier in the seventeenth century (1627–28) between the Polish and Lithuanian councils over the town of Tykocin (and thereafter between Polish Tykocin and Lithuanian Grodno over smaller satellite communities). It demonstrates that a case did not necessarily have to reach a gentile court for the authority of the state to be invoked. In a remarkable application of the principle of *dina demalkhuta,* the Polish Council, meeting in Lublin, wrote to the kahal of Tykocin, urging it to resist any efforts by the Lithuanian Council to subjugate the kahal to its authority:

This is only right, for the law stipulates that "the law of the kingdom is law" and the king has ruled that your district be attached to [the jurisdiction of] Poland, in all civil matters. Who, then, shall presume to contradict that which the king has determined? The word of the king is law and who may tell him what to do? It is fitting for us all to obey.[73]

Recourse to Gentile Power: Influence, Intimidation, and the King's Law

Although the community had mechanisms of its own for settling disputes and conflicts of interest, for disciplining offenders, and for apportioning power and influence, it was only natural that intense competition or unresolvable differences would become the occasions for the appeal to outside forces (i.e., gentile authorities). Reliance on powerful nobles or officials to guarantee or to undermine the position of rabbis and communal leaders was often decried as a blemish on Jewish public life, but it was, nevertheless, part of the system. The popular preacher and social critic R. Ephraim of Luntshitz reported, "I have seen many among us who expend all their wealth on gifts to 'princes,' out of ambition for office and envy of the high station of others."[74] Payment to noble landowners and governors to secure rabbinical office was widespread, despite repeated condemnations of such actions and attempts to resist such appointments.[75]

The hand of gentile overlords was felt not only in the realm of communal appointments but also in the ability of some Jews—generally the very wealthy and the well connected—to defy traditional restraints and communal discipline. A proclamation issued by the Polish Council in 1676 was severe in condemning "those people who do their wickedness or intimidate [the public] through the 'authorities.' "[76]

But the communal authorities were not often able to face down such challenges easily. One community that found itself in conflict with its shtadlan found him a dangerous adversary, indeed, and only succeeded in driving him out of town after informing against him to his gentile patrons.[77] The Lithuanian Council, meeting in 1700, was able merely to condemn the outrage committed by a group of prominent kahal members from Minsk in filing a highly damaging accusation against the Minsk kahal before the Treasury Court at Grodno:

[A]nd because time is short and we cannot deal properly with this matter before it comes to trial, let it [in the meantime] be set down in the records of the province [council. We give warning that] those who resort to the fist will surely fall in the end and, at that time, we will see that justice will be done in every particular.[78]

Later in the century Judah b. Mordecai Hurwitz commented acidly that "[w]hen 'influential' men arise, men of the fist multiply. They inform against their people but none dare call them informers or sycophants but only 'influential' with the gentry."[79]

A sensitive issue, informing was not likely to have been dealt with openly except on rare occasions and, thus, there is no reliable way of measuring how pervasive a phenomenon this was. Nevertheless, it was apparently necessary, from time to time, to reinforce the age-old prohibitions with explicit warnings. The councils and communities prescribed courses of preventive action and threatened to punish treasonous behavior with excommunication and expulsion.[80]

The reliance on gentile authority by opposing factions within the kahal, by communities in dispute with each other, and by dissident or deviant members of the community was matched by the recourse kahal rulers had to royal or manorial power for the enforcement of taxation procedure and the control of illegal activities.

The frequency with which the kahal had to invoke state authority for the collection of taxes in times of economic crisis (e.g., in the mid-seventeenth century) indicates that the community was sometimes simply unable to function in this realm unaided. One community, indeed, gave up all semblance of independent action and asked treasury officials to send troops to collect the taxes by force if necessary. In other cases the kahal and the wojewoda cooperated in efforts to apprehend and return to their local jurisdiction Jews attempting to evade their tax obligation.[81]

The state, in its turn, expected the kahal to help enforce the laws against dealing in clipped or otherwise counterfeit coinage and against the purchase of stolen goods. The Polish Council declared those who violated these laws to be outside the umbrella of protection normally granted to Jews in trouble with gentile law, and it authorized the communities to inform the authorities about such activities—even to the point of supplying an appropriate bribe to insure that action was taken to "burn out the thistles of God's vineyard."[82]

Violations of a less serious nature, by contrast, were not condemned so severely. Smuggling or evasion of customs duties was included in this category. Those who failed to make an accurate statement of the value of their merchandise were admonished that they would pay a heavy fine. On the other hand, the Lithuanian Council offered those who reported the worth of their goods honestly the opportunity to pay Jewish customs- and toll-lessees only half the officially required amount.[83]

It is clear that the king's law was invoked when serious Jewish interests were at stake. Serious interests included jurisdictional prerogatives, the defense of the good name of the entire community, and the ability to fulfill the collective tax obligations of Polish Jewry, on which the Jews' political security ultimately depended.

Political Self-defense in Poland-Lithuania

The ability of the Jewish community to achieve any of its political objectives hinged not only on a workable system of intelligence gathering, lobbying, and bribery, but also on the effective use in litigation of charters and privileges. The simple requisite for all these activities was money—an effective tool of political persuasion. Its handling was entrusted by the communal and super-kehilla authorities to their appointed negotiators and representatives: the shtadlanim, or syndics. Intercession with the authorities required expertise in the political and legal intricacies of the majority society as well as knowledge of the language and skills of diplomacy. The Jewish communities often turned in these matters to non-Jewish agents, especially prior to the seventeenth century. Even when Jewish shtadlanim were active, however, it remained a basic ploy of Jewish political efforts to persuade (or pay) influential non-Jews to speak in behalf of Jewish interests.[84]

The diligence of the kehilla administration in buying influence and seeking out allies generally is reflected in both Jewish and non-Jewish sources. Among the latter we may cite the opinion, tending surely to the hyperbolic, of a deputy at a regional nobles' assembly (Dietine, *Sejmik*) in 1669, that "in practice, Jews do not let any law materialize that is unfavorable to them."[85] Similarly, the records of the Polish and Lithuanian councils bear out that constant attention was paid to the responsible selection of shtadlanim and their posting at all tribunals, at regional assemblies, at royal coronations, and at the national Sejm.[86] A central committee of shtadlanim of the councils was maintained in Warsaw from the mid-seventeenth century.[87] From the same period, we also know of a chief syndic of the Polish and Lithuanian councils, who was chosen by the communal representatives and approved by the king as Jewish plenipotentiary.[88]

The sources present a consistent picture of a well-regulated system, in which shtadlanim received official appointments, were given a salary, tax exemptions, and an expense account in addition to the large sums that they conveyed to the proper destinations. The shtadlan was responsible to his kahal or council.

A number of contract agreements between the communities and their agents have been preserved. From these we learn of the terms of their employment, the dignity of the office, the care taken to ensure account-ability, and the sense of grave responsibility attached to the office. Two examples may be cited here, the first coming from the 1690 agreement of the Poznań kahal with Abraham "Shtadlan":

> [H]e shall faithfully serve the heads of the kahal, he shall be constant in his work, alert to his duty in serving the community faithfully and in doing God's work honestly. He must not fail to obey the heads of the kahal in all matters regarding missions on which he is sent, whether here in our com-munity or abroad in the province [and] in other places, far and near. He is to serve vigilantly, to perform all that is required of him by the heads of the kahal. Let him act with all speed and with all due deliberation and in his mission never falter.[89]

A second example is the 1730 agreement reached between R. Nissen b. Yehuda (Nissen Judowicki) and the Lublin community:

> In view of the great abilities of the noted scholar, R. Nissen b. Yehuda, shtadlan of the holy congregation of Chechanoptsy [Ciechanówiec] . . . , a man adept at his sacred task, who speaks before kings with great wisdom, lucidity and a command of words and tact. . . . We therefore have agreed to appoint him as shtadlan for the [Polish] Lands Council . . . in addition to the office of shtadlan of the holy congregation of Lublin. . . . May he maintain a holy vigil and perform every mission entrusted to him as a faithful representative of those who send him, in true, pure and holy service . . . to seek the welfare and salvation of Jewry, both at the Sejm in Warsaw . . . and before state commissions. He is to turn over to the royal treasury the yearly tax. . . . He is to receive a salary of eight zlotys each week. . . . He is granted power of attorney to act in all matters of the law and in all other pertinent matters, with all the means at his disposal. God Almighty be merciful and stand by those who speak for Israel.[90]

By virtue of his position of trust, his supervision of Jewish affairs, and his connections with powerful political figures, the shtadlan also exer-cised a degree of internal authority in the communities. In 1623, the Lithuanian Council directed that any Jew seeking to become involved with the royal mints must seek the permission of the Warsaw Commit-tee. Similarly, the Warsaw shtadlanim were directed to enforce strict supervision of any individual Jew arriving in the city without written permission from his kahal.[91]

The care that was taken by the agents of the communities to protect Jews summoned to testify or to answer charges before non-Jewish courts is evident in the following complaint of one rabbi, who felt that such protection could be taken too far: "I must protest the practice of our leaders, who seem to intercede on behalf of every arrested thief or criminal, to try to have him released through bribery. This practice only leads to greater thievery; there is no curb to people's actions and law-breakers multiply, for our many sins."[92]

The fact that the kahal might, nevertheless, choose to withdraw its protection from individual Jews by forbidding shtadlanim to intervene in their behalf was itself a weapon of social and political control. Thus, when the Lithuanian Council prohibited unauthorized individuals from traveling to Warsaw to pursue a personal suit, it put teeth in this provision by empowering the kahal to detain them, and it warned that no intercession would be made for them, "should [they] encounter any mishap, Heaven forbid," while on their journey.[93]

Cases of an emergency nature that required *ad hoc* measures were handled by the community closest to the scene:

> Where the [Lithuanian] Tribunal is sitting, should a case arise of saving the life [of a Jew] . . . requiring some intercession and if the man who has been arrested is of some other community, the kehilla is to spend up to 100 zlotys to win a delay of the trial, so that word can be sent to the head of the rabbinical court in his home community. Action should then be taken in accordance with the directive of the rabbi there and the expenses incurred, the 100 zlotys and the cost of the messenger, are to be borne by the man's home community; but if the matter is very urgent and it appears that the man's life is in danger and that no postponement is likely, then it is the obligation of those leaders [at the site of the tribunal's sessions] to save his life and, according with their discretion, to spend up to an additional 500 zlotys. At the next council of the province, it will be determined how to divide the amount between the home community, the community where the trial took place and the council itself. . . . In these matters, the leaders must act and not hesitate for any reason.[94]

Such exceptional cases highlight the importance attached to consultation, proper organization, and the equitable sharing of the financial burdens of self-defense, all of which was the expected norm.

When Jews could, they took legal action to protect their interests and their safety. For the troubled period between 1645 and 1680 alone, Lithuanian court records provide numerous cases in which both individual Jews and kehalim sought restitution from non-Jews for breach of contract, assault, illegal arrest and seizure, and violations of trade privileges.[95] The thrust of Jewish political activity, however, as revealed in the elaborate network of shtadlanim, lay not so much in reactive litigation, as in a preventive strategy of forestalling adverse legislation and forming advantageous alliances.

The chief instrument of this type of political action was money. Expenditure of this kind typically accounted for the lion's share of the annual budget of a Jewish community. Comparing five communities in the seventeenth century, Weinryb showed that gifts to city, ecclesiastical, manorial, and royal officials and dignitaries accounted for 85 percent of reported expenses.[96] In 1774 Poznań, less than one fifth of the budget of the kahal was used to fund internal communal services; the rest represented gifts to officials.[97] Debts owed to individuals or to communities or owed by the latter to the central councils—the result of money spent in lobbying efforts—figure frequently in the records of the councils. We find the matter of apportioning the burden of these expenses to have been the occasion of disputes among the communities, between the councils, and between the Karaite communities and the councils.[98]

Intercessions for which funds were raised often involved defending a community against restrictions, oppressive taxes, expulsions, collective accusations and the like, but routine expenses were directed toward safeguarding the general interests of the community through obtaining or retaining the favor of officials, Sejm delegates, monastic orders, and bureaucrats of state offices.[99] An illustration of how this applied on the local level is provided in a decision of the Poznań kahal in 1639:

> It has been the long-established practice of the kahal to pay the lord general each year a sum of 200 zlotys, in order that he cast his vote for burgomaster in accordance with our desire. But he has three times failed to keep his agreement and this year, in particular, he favored the candidate whom we opposed. . . . Therefore, let the arrangement be [altered so] that he will no longer be paid the 200 zlotys until after the election.[100]

Mahler reaches the plausible conclusion that the constant payment of exorbitant sums by the collective organs of Polish Jewry was a form of extortion by Polish nobles and officials and, thus, a symptom of the asymmetrical relationship between the powerful and the powerless.[101] However, as the last-quoted document suggests, the initiative did not always proceed from the powers-that-were to the Jews. The latter could reasonably assume that the payment of protection money introduced a certain element of reciprocity into these relations. Indeed, it is the logic of such fee taking that the exchange is of mutual benefit to the payer and the recipient.

Jewish political behavior in the medieval European diaspora exhibited a certain pattern of regularity. This pattern had a structural, a tactical, and an ideological component. Structurally, the configuration of Jewish politics was defined by the dependence of the Jews on gentile sources of power. Tactically, political activity focused on the drive to achieve, enhance, or use to best advantage a direct relationship with those in power. Ideologically, Jews viewed pragmatic efforts to maintain the security and stability of their communities as consistent with, and therefore legitimized by, their belief that their own efforts mirrored a divine plan for their people.

The careful course plotted by medieval Jewish communities set the pattern for Jewish political behavior in sixteenth- to eighteenth-century Poland-Lithuania. A minority group of limited political means, the Jews turned their past experience to good account in determining the strategies of internal governance and external defense. Experience had taught them the value of sound information in contingency planning and had demonstrated the paramount importance of maintaining channels of influence with those in power. This lesson was also not lost upon those in the community who wanted to pursue their own private interests or to challenge the authority of those in control in the kahal.

The decentralization of the Polish state and the diffusion of authority in Polish Jewry meant that contact between Jews and their rulers existed at many levels. The importance to the Jews of gentile political support and the economic significance (whether welcomed or not) of the Jews in Polish society insured that a lively political discourse would develop at each point of contact.

For the Jews, external relations and internal social control were enmeshed with each other. Neither the ability to govern effectively nor the freedom to criticize those who governed or to oppose their authority could ever be entirely disengaged from external political ramifications. In traditional Jewish terms, this was an aspect of exile and of the "yoke of the nations." Put differently, this was a situation that naturally adhered to the public life of a minority group.

Despite its flaws and vulnerabilities, the system of Jewish political practice in the Polish setting was coherent and, in times of relative stability, could be highly successful. It provided mechanisms for the defense of interests and for the resolution of internal and external conflicts. In times of instability and stress, these mechanisms proved less adequate. But, even then, avenues of defense or redress remained open. Few of the internal conflicts ever threatened the integrity of the community as such, and few of the external difficulties—legal restrictions, threatened expulsions, violent outbreaks, or hostile incitement—ever threatened Polish Jewry's tolerated status on a national scale. When a crisis of national scope did occur in the mid-seventeenth century, it was the state as such that was endangered, so that the upheaval could legitimately be understood as something other than a failure of Jewish policy. It is instructive that when proposals to expel the Jews from Poland were bruited about the Sejm and the royal court in the wake of the Swedish occupation (1657) and in the years of turmoil from 1665 to 1670, these ideas came to naught. Although an expulsion order was decreed against the small Arian sect, the Jews were both too numerous and too well placed economically for the same treatment to be applied in their case.[102]

Jewish politics continued, then, to pivot around the foci of power in gentile society. As long as the institutions of Jewish public life remained intact, they consistently tried to regularize contact with gentile power and to control it for their own benefit. As we have seen, in this they were partially successful. Coordination of shtadlanut stands out as one area of success in this regard, as does the reinforcement of kahal and rabbinical authority by the central regime and by local overlords. On the debit side, the strict prohibitions against seeking independent access to gentile authority only impeded but could not wholly prevent individuals, rival factions, and competing communities from gaining such access. In deviating from prescribed norms, such Jews undoubtedly helped to weaken the political position of the kahal and to facilitate gentile interference in Jewish affairs.[103] What they did not do was to effect a basic change in the structure of Jewish political relations. Gentile tutelage continued to serve the malcontents, the ambitious, the kahal, and the national Jewish community alike as the most important political resource.

2

The Breakup of the Super-Kehilla System in Poland

Traditional Jewish societies developed certain patterns of political activity and political attitudes that became so typical that we may be entitled to call them a Jewish political tradition.

The terms *tradition* and *traditional,* implying continuity and regularity of overall features, do not imply the absence of dynamic factors of change. Indeed, in discussing the case of Poland, we saw that within the traditional framework itself, historical circumstances and social trends produced adaptations and refinements of older techniques, changes in emphasis, and realignments of relative position in the interrelationships of the various active political factors. Thus, in Poland-Lithuania the nobility assumed a greater role in Jewish political affairs than was the case elsewhere, and the national and regional institutions of the Jewish communities became very highly developed.

Nevertheless, it is true that until now we have been chiefly concerned with defining common elements that reappear continuously (or at least regularly). As the discussion now shifts toward the examination of the crisis of Jewish politics in Eastern Europe, which lasted roughly from the 1760s to the 1880s, the role of change will become more central to our analysis. It was in these hundred-odd years that Jewish politics in all its dimensions—structural, tactical, and ideological— gradually ceased to adhere to the traditional typology. The conditions were thus created for the emergence of new patterns of Jewish political organization and behavior.

But we shall see that even as change became more rapid and more far-reaching in its implications for the basic structure of Jewish politics, not only did elements of the old system continue to function but political roles defined by that system also appeared to be created anew by those in Jewish society who were most caught up in the process of change. What should be clear, then, is that no implication of absolute stasis is intended in referring to tradition, just as modernity is not used here to describe a complete break with the past. Rather, modernization will be presented as a process of accelerated change in which traditional structures lose their compelling character and their integrity. But those structures nevertheless linger on, at least in memory, and some of their distinctive features are reconstructed in new form.[1]

The first symptom of major change in Jewish politics in Poland-Lithuania was a process of decline and disintegration that weakened both the individual communities and the coordination of political activities (both internal and external) that they had achieved under the system of the va'adim. The most important factor in this process was the pressure brought to bear from without, first by the Polish Commonwealth and afterward by tsarist Russia. Internal factors in the Jewish community played a role in the process of decline as well. But because premodern Jewish politics were built on the premise of derivative power and external tutelage, the impact of external factors in political development were of special importance.

Dismantling Jewish Self-government: From the Abolition of the Councils to the Four-Year Sejm

The sole surviving page of the *pinkas* of the Jewish council of the Lwów province contains a document from 1746 that illuminates the early stages of Polish Jewry's political fragmentation.[2] The representatives of the district's kehalim agreed to allow the offices of council chairman (*parnas hagelil*) and trustee (*ne'eman*) to remain vacant for two years in order to allow the council to save the significant expense of maintaining these executive positions. This, in turn, would allow the council to concentrate its fiscal efforts on repaying its debt to the royal treasury, a debt that had been accumulating for several years. Any kahal that violated the agreement by appointing someone to these offices would be subject to the strictest religious ban and, in addition, a large fine would be imposed, payable to "all the ruling lords of the province." The fine itself was to be executed by a gentile court if necessary and was to be enforced by the authority of the magnate. The decision was witnessed by the two chief rabbis, R. Haim Rapoport of the city of Lwów and of Lwów province, and R. Yitzhak Landa of Żolkiew.[3]

The provisions for enforcement through gentile authorities should not surprise us. Their involvement was likely to have had some connection with the fiscal difficulties referred to in the document. The magnates' local economic interests were clearly going to be hurt by the excessive drain on Jewish capital of the efforts to defray the mounting tax payments, and they would hardly countenance unnecessary Jewish expenditures.

It is unclear when or if conditions in the Lwów area changed, but the chairmanship was restored after several years.[4] The important features of this episode—the dissatisfactory fiscal performance of the council and the apparent desire of the local Polish authorities to impose a modified administrative regime—were to have far-reaching implications in the light of later developments. If left in place, the interim plan for the Lwów council would have emasculated the super-kehilla system in the province and placed the individual communities under the more direct control of Polish authorities. Although we can only speculate on the reasons why none of this was carried out, we do know that in 1764, eighteen years after the Lwów agreement, the same set of considerations produced more definitive action at the national level.

On 1 June of that year, the Sejm took up a proposal to abolish the Polish Four Lands Council, the Lithuanian Council and the regional councils and to impose a direct poll tax on the Jewish population in lieu of the collective tax that the councils had apportioned and collected for the treasury on an approximate per capita basis (last set by the Sejm in 1717 at 220,000 zlotys). On 6 June, the proposal was approved and a mechanism was worked out for the liquidation of the councils and the establishment of Jewish (and Karaite) tax rolls based on a new census. In justifying its decision, the Sejm noted that the councils collected revenue from the Jews far in excess of the poll tax itself and charged that this money was being used improperly. The state, it argued, could reap greater fiscal benefit by levying the tax itself.[5]

Although the abolition of the councils left the status of the individual kahal intact (the kahal remaining responsible for collecting the Jews' poll tax for the treasury), the jurisdictional power of the local community came under attack from a different quarter. The Jews' judicial autonomy, partly undermined by increasing Jewish recourse to the magnate and wojewoda courts, was challenged in principle by a number of local overlords. An early example (1725) was the removal of exclusive Jewish judicial privileges in Shklov by the local magnate, Sieniawska.[6]

Similarly, Jan Branicki, seigneur of Bialystok, empowered his city governor in 1759 to exercise complete judicial authority, including cases arising among Jews and therefore initially within the jurisdiction of the
rabbi or kahal court.[7] Although such declarations did not abolish rabbinical courts, they removed from them the full recognition of autonomy
that they had long enjoyed. By providing an explicit formula that encouraged Jews to pursue civil litigation in gentile courts, these powerful
regional landowners threatened the political integrity of the Jewish community that was based, in significant measure, on the communal authorities' asserted monopoly over recourse to gentile power.

After the abolition of the va'adim, the viability of the local kehillot
was challenged not only by magnates intent on maximizing their own
direct control over judicial and municipal matters but also by newer
political forces, intent on reforming the state and Polish society in a
modern spirit, that emerged during the last thirty years of Poland's
independence. They were joined by those among the Jews who sought
to reform Jewish life along West European lines and foster Jewish-
Polish social integration.[8]

One of the focal points of the various projects of Jewish social reform,
proposed by both non-Jewish political figures and by several Jewish
dissidents, was the strict limitation or the outright abolition of kahal
autonomy. Thus, in the opinion of the anonymous author of a pamphlet
"On the Necessity of Jewish Reforms in the Lands of the Polish Crown"
(1782), the kahal was to be restricted to the supervision of purely religious matters.[9] Shimon b. Ze'ev-Wolf (Szymon Wolfowicz), spokesman
for the opposition faction in Vilna Jewry in the 1780s (see later discussion), submitted to the Sejm a pamphlet in 1789 in which he urged the
abolition of the kahal. More than a proposal for administrative change,
Shimon b. Ze'ev-Wolf's address was a bitter polemical denunciation of
the kahal as a form of institutionalized tyranny and corruption, a "state
within the state" that would never pay its debts or properly tax the
Jewish populace and that engaged in criminal subterfuge to avoid its
obligations under the law.[10]

Under the newly constituted permanent Sejm that sat from 1788 to
1791, these and many other proposals for Jewish social and economic
integration formed part of the general discussions of fiscal and political
reconstruction and became the basis of a legislative initiative undertaken
in a special Jewry-law commission established in the summer of 1790. Its
deliberations sparked such great controversy that its report was not
ready before the promulgation of the state constitution of 3 May 1791.[11]
This turn of events saved the Jewish communities from having to come

to terms with a far-reaching curtailment of their prerogatives. The reprieve lasted thirty years in the central Polish Crown territories. (In that period, these passed through successive Prussian, Napoleonic—Saxon-Polish—and Russian administrations.)[12]

In the Austrian-annexed area of Poland, on the other hand, the state seemed determined to turn the Jewish communal structure to use for its own purposes. The Austrian Jewry law of 1776 called for the appointment of regional chief rabbis and a consistory of twelve lay representatives (divided evenly between six district units, on the one hand, and the city of Lwów, on the other). The communal board was to exercise civil judicial powers under state supervision and was to oversee the appointment of rabbis and local kehilla officials.[13] In the parts of Poland that remained independent until 1795, however, and in those portions annexed by Russia, the local kehillot continued to function without any formal unifying structure.

Effects of Structural Decentralization on Conflict Management at the End of the Eighteenth Century

It was in the absence of a prestigious intercommunal regulatory body, then, and in an atmosphere of growing uncertainty about the future of Jewish government even at the local level that two major controversies and several brief local conflicts agitated the Lithuanian and White Russian Jewish communities in the last quarter of the eighteenth century. The most important of these controversies was the battle surrounding the burgeoning pietist movement known as Hasidism, which began to make inroads in the northeastern provinces of Poland-Lithuania at this time. The second, both in terms of duration and substantive implications, was the conflict between the kahal of Vilna, the rabbi of Vilna, R. Shmuel b. Avigdor, and a large section of the Jewish public of that city.[14]

The Hasidic Controversy

At the heart of the historiographical debate over the social impact of Hasidism on traditional Jewry in Eastern Europe lies the question of its effect on the strength of the local kahal organization.

The vital connection between the decline of the kahal and va'ad system and the rapid spread of Hasidism was remarked by such students of the subject as Dubnow and Dinur.[15] In the same vein, Jacob Katz has argued that the rise of Hasidism ought to be seen as one major component of the great crisis of traditional Jewish society in late eighteenth-century Europe.[16] These and other historians differ over the question of cause and effect—that is, whether Hasidism hastened the decline of the kahal by posing an alternative form of community to the traditional geographic-jurisdictional kahal or whether it established itself only because the kahal had already ceased functioning as an effective governing apparatus and thus actually played a rather positive role in communal reconstruction.

Critics of the thesis of extensive damage to the structural integrity of East European Jewish society—whether prior to, concomitant with, or as a result of the breakaway of the Hasidic groups—tend to deny that socioreligious radicalism in the teachings of early Hasidism had any lasting or practical effects in terms of the normative functioning of the local community. There was a great deal of continuity, they argue, between pre-Hasidic and Hasidic-dominated modes of socioreligious self-regulation.[17] Although the Hasidim at first posed a serious separatist challenge to the authority of the kahal and the rabbinate, economic and social interdependence eventually brought the Hasidim recognition within the general community.[18] Hasidic leaders are known to have signed kahal regulations along with local communal authorities and to have maintained the system of kahal taxation when they themselves attained representation on community boards.[19]

A more recent study that examines Hasidic conduct manuals suggests that, in religious behavioral terms, there was an early appreciation on the part of Hasidic leaders of the need to restrain antinomian tendencies.[20]

Yet, Hasidic religious-behavioral conformity did not preclude the perception on the part of Hasidism's antagonists in the traditional kahal and rabbinic elite that the new group constituted a sectarian phenomenon and that it was detrimental to the stability and welfare of the community. The challenge of separate Hasidic conventicles and religious leadership, even if no actual sectarian schism was involved, was revolution enough, in traditionalist terms, to warrant a vigorous reaction.[21]

The emergence of Hasidism is significant for the study of Jewish political development for two reasons. First, the sprouting of Hasidic master-disciple communities—alongside or displacing the older noncharismatic forms of communal organization—played a major role in the fragmentation of Jewish leadership and political representation. The parallel Hasidic courts and dynasties were not organized in hierarchical fashion, nor did the personal authority of any one leader normally receive widespread recognition as sometimes occurred in Mitnagdic circles. This had important repercussions for the coordination of political activity and representation. The Hasidic-dominated provinces were rarely to supply nineteenth-century Russian Jewry with prominent shtadlanim (as we shall note later).

Second, the Hasidic-Mitnagdic controversy can serve as a barometer of change and continuity in the behavioral modes of conflict resolution. One may say, in fact, that it was the last great ideological dispute affecting a traditional Jewish society in Europe to be carried out entirely within the inherited parameters of communal conflict.

The first round of what was to be a thirty-year war took place in 1772—after Hasidism was firmly entrenched in the southern communities where it originated but coinciding with the more recent percolation of Hasidism into White Russian and Lithuanian communities. Friction with the more well-established rabbinic leadership was inevitable in such places. A writ of excommunication against the "sect" was issued in the spring of 1772 in Vilna, followed by letters circulated to other major communities, where similar bans were pronounced.[22]

The proclamation issued in Brody is particularly instructive as to the Mitnagdic camp's feeling of weakness in the face of a concerted opposition:

> Some years back there arose just such evildoers.[23] Then we had eminent sages and leaders, and the parnasim of the Four Lands Council, who repressed them and made the public aware of their wickedness, until we were finally rid of them. Today, alas, the crown is removed from us,[24] we are poor in men of true faith who would stand up to the wicked ones, and so they have sprouted again.[25]

The political efficacy of the national councils and their leaders is contrasted here with the sense of disorder and disorganization in the absence of such institutions, thus making the proper enforcement of communal sanctions difficult.

The fundamental weakness of the Mitnagdic position in the absence of a state-sanctioned, nationally authoritative body was underscored when Hasidim in Grodno burned copies of the collection of anti-Hasidic pronouncements, *Zamir 'aritsim veḥarvot tsurim,* later that year. In the absence of such an authority, the ban was only effective in certain communities. The Hasidim flouted it openly where possible. The Vilna kahal, in a letter to its counterpart in Brody, noted further that little could be done to avenge the "blasphemous" act in Grodno, "They [the Hasidim] are unscrupulous criminals, with wily tongues that they put to use in the courts of governors and rulers, so that we risk, God forbid, all of our communities being placed under restraint."[26]

The struggle was renewed in 1780–81, in the wake of the printing of the militantly partisan Hasidic tract, *Toledot Ya'akov Yosef,* that openly defied the authority of the traditional rabbinate. In response, the major Lithuanian and White Russian communities' representatives met at the Zelva fair in 1781 and, following the lead of Vilna's kahal, proclaimed a new and more stringent herem against the nonconformist conventicles.[27]

Yet what is most striking about the successive attempts to cow the dissidents and purge the community is, of course, their ineffectiveness— this, despite the cooperation within the Mitnagdic community leadership. When pronounced, the bans were already too late to matter. The challenge posed by the Hasidim offered a variation on the old recurring theme of jurisdictional exclusivity and autonomy, in which the demands or sanctions pressed by one community ceased to be regarded as authoritative by a second community once it asserted its right to preside over its own affairs.

In the past, intramural jurisdictional disputes had been resolved in one of two ways: Either the conflict was submitted for arbitration by the court of the supercommunal va'ad or else one (or both) of the sides sought recourse to gentile courts or protective patronage.

As long as R. Elijah, the Gaon of Vilna, was alive (he lived until 1797), the conflict was waged with weapons of ideological deterrence and social ostracism. R. Elijah's preeminent reputation substituted—for the moment—for the older institutionalized forms of supercommunal authority. Moreover, Hasidic leaders themselves apparently entertained the hope that R. Elijah might be persuaded to reconsider the schism.[28] This turned out not to be the case.

On the death of the Gaon, given the absence of any other supercommunal authority, it became virtually inevitable that recourse to gentile power would be the next step. In the early months of 1798, the Vilna kahal embarked on a forceful campaign to break the back of the semiclandestine Hasidic following in that city. In response, a leading figure among Vilna's Hasidim lodged a complaint with the provincial administration, protesting illegalities and improprieties in the kahal's persecution of the dissidents (excessive corporal punishment, illegal entry, economic boycott) as well as in the kahal administration (misappropriation of funds). This was a temporary victory for the Hasidim, who were granted protection by the Russian administration while the kahal's powers were curtailed.[29] A month later (May 1798), militant Hasidim handed over to the government a secret letter, signed by

seven members of the Vilna kahal, that called eighteen other communities to an urgent conference on the impending expulsion of Jews from
villages in Minsk province, with a view toward sending a joint delegation of shtadlanim to St. Petersburg.[30]

The Vilna kahal in its turn sent an informer to the capital to implicate
the White Russian Hasidic leader, R. Shneur-Zalman, in antistate activities. After a month-long investigation, R. Shneur-Zalman was released
in late November.[31]

Once again, at the beginning of 1799, Hasidim informed against the
kahal of Vilna, alleging falsification of population records, evasion of
taxes, misuse of funds, and manipulation of the communal financial
records. In the ensuing seizure of kahal books and their investigation, it
was clear that the state officials received the fullest cooperation of the
Hasidim.[32] In February, they staged a coup with the help of their patrons
in the administration and voted into office a Hasidic kahal board. Its
legitimacy was immediately challenged by the ousted, Mitnagdic board
in a petition to the tsar. The Hasidim remained in office, however,
blocking the kahal election of 1799 (the elections were generally held
during Passover) and succeeded in retaining an influential role in the
kahal board elected in 1800, despite their minority status in the city.
During this time the rabbinical court was unable to function normally
and the civil administration was often called upon to shore up the authority of the Hasidic kahal by dispatching soldiers.[33]

The Vilna Rabbinate Controversy

At the same time that the Lithuanian and White Russian communities
were plunged into this pitched battle over authority and autonomy, they
were drawn into a more local dispute that—before it finished its rather
squalid course in 1791—involved several central Jewish communities,
two rival Lithuanian magnate houses, the Lithuanian courts, the Polish
king, and the Sejm. This was the power struggle within the Vilna community between the kahal and R. Shmuel b. Avigdor, and their respective
supporters. In terms of conflict in a traditional Jewish society, the Vilna
rabbinate affair presents us with a classic case that illustrates what we
have observed before regarding the inseparability of Jewish external and
internal politics and gives us a convenient baseline (together with the
Hasidic schism) for measuring continuity and change in Jewish political
conflict during the following century.[34]

In its barest outlines, the affair concerned the decision of the kahal to
alter the terms of the rabbi's lifetime contract in the wake of the latter's

independent behavior, his penchant for currying favor with local authorities and with the community's artisan and middle classes, and his attempts to pack the kahal administration with relatives and supporters. Repeated initiatives (beginning in 1762) to alter the balance in the kahal board, to rewrite the contract, and to intimidate the other side by means of appeals to outside courts finally led to a compromise of sorts, effected through the involvement of the Slutsk and Grodno communities (1777).[35] However, in 1781, the dispute broke out again over a failure to adjudicate compensation claimed by R. Shmuel. This time, the kahal resolved to break its contract with the rabbi entirely, on the grounds of conduct unbecoming his office. This they succeeded in doing in 1785 with the help of the Vilna wojewoda, Karol Radziwiłł. R. Shmuel, for his part, won the support of the bishop of Vilna, Ignacy Massalski, whose private domain included the suburb of Antokol, where the Jewish community had always generally chafed at its subordination to Vilna.[36]

In deposing R. Shmuel, the kahal of Vilna explicitly rejected the right of any other Jewish jurisdiction to interfere. It maintained that the regulations of the defunct Lithuanian *va'ad hamedina* under which Slutsk and Grodno (in concert with Pinsk and Brest Litovsk) had summoned Vilna to an arbitration were no longer in force. The Vilna kahal judged its own position with the wojewoda to be strong enough to sustain its unilateral action in the face of open opposition and discontent within the community. R. Shmuel, with recourse to other Jewish courts blocked to him, found that his only option lay with the bishop and with litigation in various Lithuanian and Polish courts.[37] Thus, a dispute of seemingly little consequence rapidly took on regional, even national, proportions.

During the first week of April 1785, the artisans and small merchants of Vilna, many of whom sympathized with R. Shmuel, were increasingly alarmed by the high-handedness and extravagant expenditures of the kahal as it proceeded to press its case. Therefore they named seven representatives to speak in their behalf before the special tribunal set up by Radziwiłł to untangle the various legal claims.[38] Of these seven, one who was to achieve a great deal of notoriety was Shimon b. Ze'ev-Wolf.[39] The battle was thus joined over which social element would control communal affairs, a battle in which the division between Hasidim and Mitnagdim also played a complicating role.

Failing to win their case before the wojewoda's commissioners, a court of three rabbis appointed at Mir, or Radziwiłł himself, R. Shmuel's party and the leaders of the social opposition moved into neighboring Antokol and prepared to file suit in two other courts: the

Treasury's legal commission, charged with overseeing the liquidation of Jewish communal debts, and the Crown Court. They also secured a letter from King Stanislaw II Augustus Poniatowski of Poland who promised them protection against arbitrary and coercive acts committed by the kahal.[40] In the course of the following episode, that was not resolved until 1791, the pro-rabbi party and the communal dissident faction charged the kahal with illegal taxation, misuse of public funds, and improper coercion.[41] Both sides resorted to such other means as lay within their grasp. The opposition published advertisements in Polish urging that no credit be extended to the kahal, brought about the secession of the Antokol community from the kahal of Vilna, and was also apparently involved in kidnapping (or planning the escape of) the seventeen-year-old son of the kahal strongman, Abba b. Wolf, who was then secretly baptized at the Dominican monastery and spirited away to Prussia.[42] The kahal trumped up criminal charges to bring about the arrest and imprisonment of its three principal opponents (including Shimon b. Wolf), placed the dissidents under a ban, and published counterpolemics in Polish. Most important, the kahal canceled elections for three years (1787–89) with the help of the wojewoda administration.[43]

The aftermath of the affair included Shimon b. Wolf's radical attack on the kahal system as a "state within a state" (1789); his suit for damages against the Vilna kahal and its leader, Abba b. Wolf (1790); the election of a new kahal that included both factions and also two Hasidim; and the virtual abolition of the office of community rabbi (*av bet din*) in Vilna.[44]

The conclusions drawn from this episode by historians are unequivocal: The kahal in Vilna and the kahal system, as such, in the Lithuanian territories (soon to be annexed by the Russian Empire) were "shaken to their foundations" and never recovered.[45] Together with the Hasidic controversy and with other more localized conflicts over kahal powers (in Minsk, Vitebsk, and elsewhere),[46] the Vilna rabbinate affair demonstrates not only the level of civic demoralization in Jewish politics at the end of the eighteenth century but also the structural inability of a Jewish community shorn of supercommunal restraints to maintain even that precarious balance between internal control and external interference that had been maintained during the previous two centuries.

From Community to Communities

The edifice of Jewish self-government in Poland, already partially dismantled in the closing decades of the eighteenth century, was to be demolished almost entirely by the middle of the nineteenth century in the Russian Pale of Settlement. The regional and national councils had been the first to go; the local community was to be next—a step already foreseen in the Four-Year Sejm and in the first years of the nineteenth century.

The new circumstances could not but profoundly alter the political relations between the Jews and the state, and, indeed, relations among the Jews themselves. The traditional political basis of the kahal was its reciprocal relationship with the ruler: The kahal had been the guarantor of civil order in Jewish society and of effective fiscal administration in the state's behalf; the state, in return, had often protected Jewish interests and had stood behind the kahal administration and its courts. If the traditional Jewish approach to the state had contained elements of loyalty and quietism and had focused to a considerable extent on maintaining conduits of influence and information to the sources of effective political power, this was but an indication that tactics and attitudes were reflections of structural realities.

Once the key element of state recognition and support was withdrawn—as it was in stages between 1764 and 1844—the Jews of Poland and Russia faced two essential political problems. First, in the Jews' inner, communal life, no single agency could claim an exclusive relationship with the state. And, second, in their external relations, they no longer had any expressly sanctioned basis for collective representation. There was no ecclesiastical hierarchy that might take on this function.

If the traditional reciprocal structure had led to certain orientations in the Jews' understanding of ways, means, and goals in politics, one might expect some changes in approach to have occurred once the reciprocal structure was undermined and, finally, removed. Together these structural and orientational-behavioral changes constitute political modernization in the Russian Jewish context.

Official Status of the Kahal Under Russian Rule (Until 1844)

The Russian state did not define its policy toward the Jewish communities in any precise manner until well into the nineteenth century, but certain trends were consistently pursued.[47] The first set of laws meant to deal with Russian Jewry in a coherent fashion was promulgated in 1804.[48] A clearer Jewry law was deemed necessary, however, within two decades, and successive state commissions took up the issue until a new law was passed in 1835.[49] Very soon thereafter, the government embarked on a new policy initiative that brought in its wake the formal abolition of kahal autonomy in 1844.[50]

Paragraph 49 of the Jewry statute of 1804 stated, "because justice should be uniform for all subjects of the state, the Jews, too, must in all lawsuits have recourse to the general courts," adding that the Jews might also have minor courts of voluntary arbitration, in line with the general provisions in the laws for such courts.

Paragraph 50 established that kahal officers, to be chosen for three-year terms, would represent the Jews before the provincial administration, from which they would receive their confirmation and official status. The obligations of the kahal included ensuring that taxes were correctly paid and the rendering of an annual account of the kahal's income and expenditures (par. 54). The kahal was also obligated to help regulate the travel of Jews from place to place by furnishing proof that travelers had no outstanding tax liabilities (par. 46).[51] Each town was to have but a single kahal, though different "sects" (i.e., Hasidim and Mitnagdim) might have their own synagogues and choose their own rabbis (par. 53). Although the kahal remained a state-sanctioned local authority side by side with the municipal administration, it was not entitled to impose new or unauthorized taxes (par. 54) and rabbis were forbidden to impose the ḥerem or similar coercive measures (par. 51).

The statute of 1804 was the product of two years of work that included the summoning of Jewish representatives before the commission responsible for drafting it.[52] The measures incorporated in the statute were aimed at achieving the maximum of state control without actually abolishing the kahal—a proposal that had, in fact, been strongly recommended by some members of the commission. The prohibition of new taxes and of effective judicial power (i.e., the power of rabbinical and kahal authorities to summon Jews to answer charges) and disciplinary sanctions (i.e., bans, boycotts, etc.) reduced the kahal's prerogatives vis-à-vis its constituents and hence increased its dependence on the Russian authorities.

A considerable degree of official concern and effort was expended to assure the Jews that no substantive interference in their religious life was intended, apparently in response to reports of great turmoil among the Jewish population. The little evidence we have suggests, however, that it was the economic and residential restrictions in the statute (pars. 34–41) aimed at rural Jewish distillers and innkeepers as well as rumors of the intention to conscript Jews for military service that principally exercised the Jews.[53] Because these provisions of the law threatened the livelihood and the homes of about one third of the Jewish population[54] and were based on what seemed to be a broad consensus of provincial administrators, there was ample and just cause for worry. The arrangements for kahal administration, on the other hand, were of concern only to a small group of top Russian and Polish policymakers; local officials, at this stage, were not overactive in their supervisory duties unless particular complaints were brought to their attention. The examples of direct interference of government officials in internal Jewish affairs in the first quarter of the nineteenth century generally grew out of either routine involvement in the confirmation of kahal elections or Jewish appeals to gentile courts and the state administration in cases of internal conflict. Such cases of open conflict and opposition are recorded in this period for the towns of Keidan (1815),[55] Vilna (1819), Wobolnik (Vilna province, 1820), and Brest Litovsk (1823).[56] In this category, too, we should place the harassment and (second) arrest of R. Shneur-Zalman (1800–1801).[57]

Paradoxically, the recurrence of resistance to entrenched kahal elites indicates that internal social control was still strong enough in this period to become a public issue, despite the formal restrictions on kahal autonomy.

The kahal was also perceived by Polish leaders after the Congress of Vienna as more than a vestige of Jewish autonomy. Indeed, a wide-ranging debate over the issue took place in Poland at the time, reminiscent of the polemics that took place during the tenure of the Four-Year Sejm (1788–91). When Nikolai Novosil'tsev, adviser to Grand Duke Constantine and to Alexander I, presented to the Polish Council of State a blueprint for the reform of the Polish Jewish communities that included a hierarchical bureaucracy of Jewish communal authorities (not unlike the French Jewish *consistoires*), the Polish political leadership objected strenuously. To them, this was tantamount to a state within the state, and within several years they had succeeded in abolishing the kahal system in Poland altogether (1822).[58]

The theme of kahal power—tendentiously portrayed as overbearing greed and misused authority—furnished the basic material, as well, for Jewish social criticism of the period. It occurs in the works of such writers as Isaac Erter (across the border in Habsburg Galicia), Isaac Ber Levinsohn, and Avraham Ber Gottlober, and it is present as well (although with a withering contempt rather than a righteous indignation) in Israel Aksenfeld's work.[59]

The state itself relied on the efficacy of kahal and rabbinic authority, first of all in enforcing the collection of taxes and the registry of the population but in other areas as well. The kahal of Vilna, for example, was expected to act as a censorship board for a proposed Yiddish newspaper in 1813—no official censor being available to check Yiddish material.[60] Another task assigned to the kahal was the reinforcement of antismuggling laws. The assumption was that the Jews, who were endemically (and justifiably) suspected of playing an important part in the contraband trade (of which more will be said in a later context), could be expected to heed their own rabbis and leaders even when they disregarded the laws of the Christian state. To this end the state was even willing to countenance official rabbinic discipline against violators. This was conveyed to representatives of the Jewish communities in 1817 in an audience with Alexander I. Although the communities of Volhynia, Minsk, and Courland declined to impose such a ḥerem, the Vilna kahal did so at the state's urging in 1820.[61]

In the second quarter of the nineteenth century, coinciding with the reign of Nicholas I (1825–55), we have the clearest example of the way in which the discretionary powers of the kahal were given extraordinary latitude when it came to executing state policy. This was, of course, the conscription of Jews for the Russian army (instituted in 1827) that the local kahal administered by means of a quota. The *rekrutchina* (conscription regime) had an enormous impact on Jewish social and political development, with lasting negative implications for the legitimacy and authority of the kahal in the eyes of the Jewish public, as well as for Jewish attitudes to the Russian state.[62]

Furthermore, the record is clear enough on the abuses of the quota system for the purposes of social control by the kahal leadership throughout the period from 1827 to the 1860s. This was a highly charged emotional staple in the literature of Jewish social protest, starting from Shlomo Isaiah Landsberg's *Megilla 'efa* and Isaac Ber Levinsohn's *Di hefker velt* and continuing long after the *rekrutchina* itself had faded into history. It was also the occasion for a great deal of informing, either against kahal officers or by these officers against their opponents.[63]

In the present context, however, it is essential to separate these issues from the question of the political status of the kahal as a social agency granted derivative powers by the state. As in the case of smuggling control, the communal conscript-quota obligation illustrates the state's intention to harness the Jews' self-administration to a narrowly defined sphere of executive duties.

The Jewry law of 1835 reaffirmed this position.[64] Paragraph 67 specifically obligated the kahal to insure the Jews' obedience to the laws of the state. The officers of the kahal and the rabbis were required to take an oath of loyalty to this effect, pledging themselves to police their fellow Jews.[65]

What was emerging most clearly was the lack of reciprocity in the state's relationship to the kahal. Although it had the effect of enhancing the power of those in a position to determine how the conscript-quota would be filled, the delegation of this onerous duty to the kahal was not accompanied by an enhanced degree of jurisdictional autonomy in other spheres—the Jewish courts, Jewish schools, Jewish printing presses, and the rabbinate. Quite the contrary, imperial decrees would soon subject Jewish communal life to ever-greater controls and supervision in each of these areas. All Jewish printing presses but two were shut down by the censorship law of 1836 (see later discussion). All Jewish schools were placed under the supervision of the Ministry for National Enlightenment in 1842. The assignment of police duties and other government responsibilities to rabbi-registrars began at the latest in 1812 and was reinforced in 1835. In 1844, the kahal itself was formally abolished. In 1847, government-sponsored rabbinical schools were opened in Vilna and Zhitomir, where Russian-educated rabbis were to be trained for this office. In 1857, selection of rabbis from among seminary or other government-school graduates become mandatory.[66]

The result was an aggravated imbalance in the kahal-state relationship that not only did not halt the previous trends of decline and disintegration in the Jewish political system but, in fact, hastened these trends immeasurably.[67]

With its effective power limited to specific functions as the state's fiscal and conscript-recruiting agent, the kahal itself came to be perceived as dead weight by some who were active in communal affairs. The rabbi of Shavli, R. Yitzhak-Ayzik, testified (around 1843) that leading members of his community openly and wantonly flouted the regulations of the kahal. He lamented: "If only they might pause and reflect where this is likely to lead, . . . for in our times the honor of Israel is cut down and the dignity has been removed from the *bet din*. The *bet din* is an object of mockery. . . . And if prominent and educated people also hold it in contempt . . . [there could result,] God forbid, an irreparable disaster for Judaism as a whole. All the ordinances of the community will be null and void, may God preserve us, and everyone will do as he pleases."[68]

Others, more well placed, did not content themselves (as did those whom the rabbi was criticizing) with sniping at authority in their own local communities. Like Shimon b. Wolf during his period in the communal opposition in Vilna, they took a public stand against the existence of the kahal, as such, and recommended its abolition to the government. Such, for example, was true of state contractors H. Markevich (in 1820) and Litman Feigin (1830).[69]

Thus, when Count Pavel Kiselev (minister of State Domains) recommended in 1841 that the kahal be abolished as a governing agency with

autonomous privileges, and that henceforth essential administrative functions in the Jewish communities be handled by individuals appointed for
these specific tasks by the state administration, it was something of an
anticlimax. Nicholas approved the decree in 1844.[70]

The result was somewhat ambiguous. The law did not affect the existence of the Jewish community, as such, and it has been argued that the
kahal—the communal administration—continued a twilight existence in
the period after 1844 at the state's own behest.[71] Indeed, as we shall see,
both communal institutions and the positions of communal officers
(chiefly rabbis) maintained their existence, at least in sub rosa form, so
that to the average Jew little seemed to have changed. Although there
may be some merit from the sociological point of view in judging this
issue by the realities of everyday life in the decades following 1844, when
we approach the question from the political-development point of view,
we must assert the essential change that took place with the move to
abolish the autonomous kahal organization. We are clearly no longer
dealing with a state-sanctioned corporate body on the traditional, medieval model. Communal discipline, where it remained strong, depended
on more informal arrangements: the prestige and authority of a rabbi or
tsaddik, or the coercive domination of local strongmen.[72]

Moreover, the idea that the Jewish community remained essentially
unchanged after 1844 rests on a purely local definition of community.
The historical kehilla, or kahal, was not, however, simply an instrument
of local self-administration. Its legitimacy was founded for the most part
on its place as the basic unit of the Jewish community at large in a given
region or country—and ultimately as part of all Israel. Morally and
politically, collective values and mutual responsibility among kehillot
were what made each community a legitimate part of the system. For
that reason it is not enough to analyze the local Jewish community as an
isolated phenomenon and to draw conclusions about its institutional
stability based on local continuity alone. Along with the steps taken to
ensure the existence of local communal life, which we shall note in a
later context, we must take even greater notice of the impact of the
fragmentation of the national community to assess the subsequent political development of Russian Jewry.

The Problem of Jewish Political Representation (Until 1825)

The abolition of the national and provincial va'adim in Poland-Lithuania
and the division between Hasidim and Mitnagdim made all but impossi-

ble the kind of policy coordination and collective political activity that we saw in chapter 1.

In the field of policy coordination, we know of few, if any, instances when chosen representatives of the communities met on a regional basis to determine a course of action on a range of issues. When they did occur, these meetings were usually motivated by the need to deal with a specific problem arising from government actions. Thus we find that Jewish communal representatives met in late 1791 to draw up a plan to counter the proposals for the new Jewry law being promoted in the Polish Sejm.[73] The conference, however, took place half a year after the proposed law began to be discussed and was only convened at the eleventh hour. This is an early indication of the inability of the communities to respond promptly and effectively to a threat to their interests.

The piecemeal incorporation of the White Russian, Lithuanian, Ukrainian, and Polish provinces into the Russian Empire certainly militated against cross-provincial communal coordination, and this difficulty was only accentuated by the divisions between the Hasidic-dominated south and the northern bastions of anti-Hasidic conservatism. Levitats makes the further point that it was the Lithuanian super-kehilla tradition that was the direct and dominant influence in the areas annexed first by Russia—a tradition far less centralized than the Polish tradition in which certain important communities and regions had been independent of the Lithuanian *va'ad hamedina*.[74]

We get one view of the general state of Jewish communal politics around 1804 in the following assessment by R. Hillel b. Ze'ev-Wolf. The va'adim of the past, he states, and the rabbis and communal leaders, had had the power to discipline their communities, and they took the responsibility for "directing the affairs of the province in accordance with the way of the world, by collecting treasure with which to gain the favor of the rulers." He continues:

> Not so today, woe to such a generation, that since the borders were divided and the frontiers closed[75] . . . there is no [central] council and the provincial council is no more. With no conferences of elders, there is no one to plan ahead and to go before the officials or petition the king. . . . [N]or is there proper law and judgment, seeing that authority and governance has been impoverished along with the leadership. . . . Today transgressors have multiplied . . . and each one builds his own altar, conspiring [against the whole community] in separatist gatherings. . . . Each one is for himself, so that no common counsel is taken to find a remedy in the face of harsh decrees.[76]

The absence of a regular intercommunal forum was partially offset by the growth of regional political nerve centers like that of Yehoshua Zeitlin's court in Ustiye near Shklov.[77] But here the pattern of individual and local efforts at dealing on a one-to-one basis with officials of the government tended to replace the vestiges of the previous era. Zeitlin, who enjoyed the patronage of Prince Potemkin, was a free agent who held no communal position. It was his prestige and his influence alone, rather than the combined efforts of the Lithuanian and White Russian communal leadership, that enabled an unofficial regional network to function.

Zeitlin's informal methods came into conflict with a community-based collective representation in the years from 1802 to 1804, when the Jewry-law commission in St. Petersburg invited the Jewish communities to send their own delegates to the preliminary discussions. Such delegates were sent from the provinces of Mogilev, Minsk, Podolia, and Kiev. Vilna was also represented by two shtadlanim in St. Petersburg during this time. They came with little if any previous experience in the capital and their requests that key provisions of the proposed Jewry law be suspended for twenty years were rejected. In general, the effect of their activity appears to have been negligible.[78]

On the other hand, Zeitlin's son-in-law, Avraham Peretz, his protégé Judah-Leyb (Lev) Nevakhovich, and another prominent merchant at Shklov and would-be reformer of Jewish socioeconomic life, Neta (Note) Notkin, played a far more active role in the Jewry commission discussions. Apparently, too, their approach was more cooperative and supportive of the government initiative.[79] Nevakhovich composed the first Russian work in favor of toleration of the Jews in 1803 and dedicated it to Internal Affairs Minister Count Viktor Kochubei.[80] The pamphlet included a paean to Alexander I as a worthy heir to Peter the Great and Catherine the Great.[81]

Given their position in St. Petersburg and their favorable response to some of the state's proposals on reforming Jewish society (particularly in the realms of education and occupational diversification), the three independent shtadlanim tended to undermine the status and the positions of the official Jewish delegates.

In 1807, a year before the Jews were to be expelled from villages where they had been long-established as distillers and innkeepers,[82] Count Kochubei began campaigning for the postponement of the order and for a new discussion of the issue. In putting his case he urged the convening of another group of Jewish representatives as a counterweight to the Jewish Assembly of Notables (1806) and Sanhedrin (1807) convened in Paris under Napoleon's orders.[83] He may have referred to the danger of war in Russia's western provinces and the need to insure Jewish loyalty merely as a tactic to persuade the tsar, as Gessen suggests; but the fear of Jewish loyalty to Napoleon was quite real in high government and church circles (see later discussion).[84] A postponement of the mass expulsion was ordered by Alexander in 1808 (with the process to be phased in over a three-year period); early in January 1809, a new commission to study the issue of the Jewish liquor trade in rural areas was set up under Senator V. I. Popov.

Prior to the constitution of this commission, however, a modified version of Kochubei's proposal to win Jewish cooperation through a conference of delegates was put into effect. The Jewish communities of eight provinces were asked to elect representatives who would present their views on the "best means of implementation" for the 1804 statute. Rather than calling the delegates to St. Petersburg, the tsar instructed each provincial governor to convene them in their respective provincial capitals.[85]

Here, again, the initiative was that of the state, and the representatives' brief was strictly defined. Once they rendered their opinion, the delegations were disbanded.[86]

A major effort to restore a system of intercommunal coordination was undertaken in the years between 1815 and 1818. During the war against Napoleon, two Jewish contractors to the Russian army, Zundl Sonnenberg and Eliezer Dillon, had transmitted Jewish petitions to the highest government circles, and, at an audience with Alexander I in June 1814, were referred to officially as the "deputies of the Jewish people." It remains unclear just who sent Sonnenberg and Dillon their instructions. It is, however, improbable that Sonnenberg would have drafted on his own initiative the detailed memorandum that he submitted in 1813 asking for the abrogation of restrictions against Jewish trade in the Russian interior, the restoration of the herem, and other privileges.[87]

Both men, it should be noted, came from communities in Lithuania and White Russia, and it is likely that they maintained links chiefly with the communities of Vilna, Minsk, and Vitebsk. It was, in fact, at a meeting of the main Lithuanian and White Russian communities at Zelva in 1815 that the delayed response came to the tsar's proposal of 1814 that a permanent Jewish deputation be sent to St. Petersburg. Nothing, however, was done for an entire year, and the rabbinical and communal leaders of the northern provinces met again in Minsk in 1816 to attempt to put the idea into practice. The resolutions adopted at this conference, which referred to itself as a *va'ad hamedina*—a term that had last been used officially in 1764—show that the communities' leaders aspired to a more formalized political mechanism. The operative section of the Minsk resolution not only called for the raising of a special fund throughout the Jewish communities but also assigned officers in each province to supervise the collection and to serve as the communication link between local districts and the provincial and superprovincial leaders. At the district level chosen officers were to apportion and collect the deputies' tax and to forward to the provincial center their list of grievances and instructions as well as formal accreditation for a representative to St. Petersburg.[88] The leaders at Minsk clearly had in mind a hierarchical structure reminiscent of the Lithuanian and Polish va'adim.

The resolution invoked the tsar's instructions to Sonnenberg and Dillon in 1814, no doubt to lend weight to the authoritative character of the project. In fact, the government had no intention of recognizing any collective representative body on the va'adim model and quickly stepped in to ensure that the collection of funds be controlled by the local administration. Moreover, although it was prepared on this basis to accept a Jewish fund-raising campaign, it stopped short of actually mandating the execution of the plan,[89] and the 1816 resolution clearly reflects the fact that the entire effort to win general cooperation was to be based solely on moral suasion. The conference members, headed by R. Haim of Volozhin, pleaded with the local communal leaders not to take their instructions lightly. "We have," they said optimistically, "complete faith in our brothers of the people Israel, children of compassion and performers of righteous deeds, that they will certainly rouse themselves to collect the necessary funds out of their own good will—for Israel can surely not be accused of breaking ranks."[90]

The letters of Dillon and Sonnenberg from St. Petersburg in the latter part of 1816 and the first part of 1817 make it abundantly clear, however, that they were left to their own devices and reduced to pleading for funds and the assistance of other deputies.[91] By this time plans were being circulated by the Internal Affairs Ministry to the provincial governors, and by Sonnenberg to the communal leaders, for an election of Jewish deputies to take place the following year in Vilna, where each province was to be represented by two delegates. This time almost every province participated, resulting in the selection of three official deputies and three designated alternates who were sworn to keep the communities informed of their activities and to obtain prior instructions before proceeding with any official action.[92]

During the ensuing four years, however, the deputies operated with little financial or political backing, and there is no evidence that intercommunal consultation was maintained once the deputies were elected. By 1823, the deputation had all but ceased to function, and in 1825 it was formally abolished.[93] There were some local efforts to coordinate political action only in connection with *ad hoc* contingencies. Such an instance was the appeal by the Tykocin kahal in 1822—sent to Lublin and several other communities—to convene a conference of delegates and to send a committee to Warsaw in an effort to reverse an order to expel Jews from Polish villages and towns close to the Prussian, Austrian, and Russian borders. It is not known whether such a meeting took place.[94] In a memorandum of 1833, the kahal of Vilna proposed to Nicholas I that a Jewish representative body be reestablished—if only consisting of four men—to advise on projects concerning Jews and to serve as a means of communication between the government and the Jewish population.[95] This may or may not have been a regional initiative, but in any case it was not heeded.

The inability of the Russian Jewish communities to act in concert to defend common interests (for both intrinsic and external reasons) indicated that the kahal as a system and as a concept had been weakened at a very basic level. The fact that, despite the government's conditional approval, the communities themselves could not bring to fruition a plan for sustaining a collective, responsible deputation shows that the kahal had already lost a great deal of its political and moral stature by 1815 and that the fault for this did not entirely lie with the state. The public character of traditional Judaism insured that the local Jewish community would retain its importance as the context of religious and social activity; but the signs of its political demoralization were quite clear by the time Nicholas I came to the throne. For our purpose the most crucial transformations in the Jewish community were those that separated the communities one from the other and thereby promoted a sequence of structural disintegration and reconstruction.

3

The Mask of Quietism and the
Politics of Survival

Although structurally weakened, Jewish communal life could not but retain a political aspect. With diminishing resources and suffering from a fragmented leadership, Jewish communities continued to confront political issues out of their perception of where Jewish interests lay. Among the tactics used to safeguard and defend these interests were both a willingness to bend to the "law of the kingdom" when necessary and a conscious ambivalence toward that law. Loyalty and obedience could be given a decidedly liberal interpretation and were not elevated to the status of a sacred principle. We saw how the Jews applied this policy with some success in Poland-Lithuania.

The partition of Poland and the incorporation of its eastern portions into the Russian Empire (and the subsequent rule of the tsar of Russia over central Poland as well) did not by itself present particular difficulties either to Jewish communal spokesmen, who commissioned poets to compose odes to Catherine the Great[1] or, it would seem, to most Jews. One exception was an active member of the Vilna kahal and one of its important spokesmen in dealings with gentile authorities, R. Haim "Shamas" b. Yehuda Groysdorfer. R. Haim was on his deathbed in 1794 during the Kosciuszko revolt against Russian domination when he reportedly confided the following to his good friend, Mikhl Gordon: "I should like you to hear the good feelings I have for the Polish state before I die, and let them be my comfort in the grave."[2] The actual participation of Jews in the Kosciuszko revolt was extremely marginal, however, and ample testimony by Russian military commanders attests to assistance by Jews to the Russian forces.[3] It is true that later on, during the War of 1812, some Polish Jews sympathized with, aided, or fulfilled administrative and supply tasks for the Napoleonic forces.[4] In 1806 (before the Treaty of Tilsit ended the first phase of the war against Napoleon), at the time of the Paris Sanhedrin, a proclamation of the Russian Church's Holy Synod unequivocally identified all Jews with Napoleon.[5]

Most Jews in Lithuania and White Russia, however, appeared to be rather neutral and uninvolved, or pro-Russian.[6] As Jews did not serve in the armed forces, their involvement in the war in any capacity was numerically quite small. The noncombatant population was only directly affected when their towns and villages became battlegrounds or lay in the path of troop movements. The Jews were suspected by both sides of aiding the enemy. Yet no less a figure than the future tsar, Nicholas Pavlovich, wrote in his journal in 1816 that the Jews had "surprisingly" been "very loyal" in 1812, sometimes risking their lives.[7] He was later to be reminded of this by the Jews of Vilna in their petition of 1833. The Jews, they insisted, had demonstrated their loyalty not only in 1812 but also quite recently as well, during the Polish sedition of 1830–31.[8] This claim, of course, was not accurate as an unqualified statement of fact with regard to either 1812 or 1831, but it was more than a half-truth.[9]

It should be clear that what motivated Jews and especially their leaders to demonstrate obedience to one or another side was not, generally speaking, what would be associated with the word patriotism. As members of a nonsovereign group, they saw it as their duty to accord to whomever was the sovereign what was legitimately his due in terms of subservience, and they recognized in the sovereign the proper address for petitions. Thus, just as Polish Jewish communities had dealt with the Polish regime in Warsaw in defense of group interests in the years 1807–13 (the tenure of the Duchy of Warsaw under French-Saxon rule), their representatives adjusted rapidly to the change in regime as Tsar Alexander pushed the Napoleonic forces westward out of Poland. Although certain polonized members of the Jewish upper class (who did not regard themselves as communal spokesmen) continued to turn to the Polish political leadership (notably to Prince Adam Czartoryski), the Warsaw kehilla opened negotiations over the relief of Jewish disabilities with the tsar's representative, Nikolai Novosil'tsev. In August 1814, the tsar received their delegation in St. Petersburg. A similar episode took place in the aftermath of the Polish uprising of 1830–31.[10]

Of much greater import for the Jews' attitudes to the Russian state were the facts that (a) as time went on the Russian authorities did not permit the continued exercise by the Jewish communities of a relatively untrammeled jurisdictional and judicial autonomy; and (b) the Jewish communities, through the loss of their roof organizations, were no longer in a position to maintain an ongoing political presence close to the seats of imperial power. Both of these elements had in the past played important functions in determining the character of Jewish reliance on, and sense of direct access to, gentile rulers and their high officials.

Moreover, certain internal changes in Jewish society during this period had a significant impact on the attitudes of Jews toward the government. One of these was the rising influence of Hasidism with its socioreligious units that cut across kahal lines. Shmuel Ettinger has noted that this "independence" from the old geocommunal structures (that remained tied to the state through fiscal obligations and, later, military conscription) militated against dependence on the state, with the result that "hasidic communities and the courts of the hasidic tsaddikim became cells of opposition."[11] This opposition, to be sure, was not manifested in overt political acts, but was hidden by a mask of quietism.

The other important change within East European Jewish society that was to have an impact on Jewish relations with the tsarist state was the slow but steady growth of the number of Jews whose lifestyle was oriented toward nontraditional, urban, European models. This was true both of individuals scattered throughout the areas of Jewish residence and of those communities of Jews that began to develop where no Jewish community had previously existed and where European influence was particularly strong: the towns of New Russia, Riga, and the capitals, St. Petersburg and Moscow. Such Jews aspired to move closer to the aristocratic and bourgeois culture of modern Russia and consciously or unconsciously distanced themselves from the traditional sociocultural patterns of most of their fellow Jews. They tended to view gentile society in general and the Russian state in particular from a new and different perspective as well.[12]

This process—involving economic and occupational change, linguistic adaptation, acculturation, and elements of what Milton Gordon called "behavioral assimilation"[13]—has generally in the past been subsumed under the cultural-intellectual rubric of the Haskalah (the Jewish Enlightenment). It is clear, however, that much more is involved here than the development of Hebrew, Yiddish, and Russian Jewish belles lettres, as Zipperstein points out.[14] The vocal and literary Jewish intelligentsia of the Haskalah, the maskilim, were neither the only advocates nor the sole products of social change in Russian Jewry. Nonetheless, because of their awareness of, and greater access to, the newest currents in Russian political and cultural opinion and because they became the source of a new political elite in Jewish society, they remain of primary concern in our study. The role played in 1803–4 by Lev Nevakhovich is indicative of the direct involvement of maskilim in politics that was to leave a permanent imprint on Jewish political development.

The Limits of *dina demalkhuta dina*

In his book *Ruaḥ Ḥaim,* R. Haim of Volozhin (1749–1821) included a gloss on *Avot* 3:2 ("Pray for the welfare of the kingdom") in which he stated the traditional position vis-à-vis Jewish obligations to their gentile rulers. Noting that the dictum in *Avot* was said at a time when Israel was ruled by Rome, sacker of Jerusalem's temple, R. Haim stated, "it is all the more incumbent on us, who live in peace, thank God, under our glorious government's protective wing, to seek its peace and welfare with all our ability and conscious thought."[15]

However, his son, R. Yitzhak, pointed out the equally traditional caveat that in Jewish law, "the tsar's will is as holy as that of God, as long as it [the tsar's law] applies equally to all his subjects."[16]

Finally, we have the testimony of Jacob Mazeh that by the early 1860s the prayer for the king, *hanoten teshu'a,* had long since fallen into disuse by common, tacit agreement in Russian synagogues. It was considered a sign of boorish ignorance not to know that this prayer (along with certain liturgical poems) was not to be actually pronounced. "A prayerbook that didn't include the prayer didn't exist, but neither did a single synagogue where the prayer was said."[17]

The classical injunctions to heed the word and law of the king had never been accepted unqualifiedly or absolutely literally. In the context of diminishing reciprocity between the state and the Jewish community, how loosely did Russian Jews interpret the available leeway? We shall use two specific areas of tension in Jewry-state relations in this period—smuggling and military conscription—to make some observations on this point.

Smuggling

The partition of the former Polish-Lithuanian lands among three major trading powers did nothing to discourage a large-scale contraband economy along major trade routes in frontier areas.

It has been reported that contraband supported a significant part of the economy of Shklov, for example, in the last years of the eighteenth century when that city was one of Russia's most important commercial depots, with a Jewish population of some twelve hundred. Local Russian officials openly connived at this lucrative trade.[18] The Vilna ḥerem against smuggling, imposed at state insistence in 1820, aroused serious concern in official Prussian circles in Königsberg and Berlin until they were reassured that no permanent damage to Prussian exports would result.[19]

The identification of Jewish merchants with the contraband trade led to the government's determination to prohibit further Jewish settlement within 50 versts (about 33 miles) of the frontier and in some areas ordering the expulsion of Jews already settled there. Orders for such expulsions and restrictions were given in 1816 (for Volhynia), in 1825, 1839 (Bessarabia), 1840 (100 versts), in 1843–44, and in 1852 (Poland), but various extensions and exceptions were made, so that they were never fully executed.[20]

According to a later memoirist, Jews were forced into a life of risk and criminality because of mounting economic pressures and discriminatory restrictions, even though smuggling was clearly considered to be theft and hence forbidden by Jewish law.[21]

Contemporary maskilic writers were not as generous, however, or else not averse to employing any weapon that came to hand in denouncing what they considered to be wrong with Jewish social and religious life. Both Isaac Ber Levinsohn and Israel Aksenfeld condemned smuggling in no uncertain terms, arguing that it grew out of the greed of dishonest merchants who filled the coffers of corrupt Hasidic rebbes with ill-gotten gains.[22] According to Levinsohn, it was not religious hatred that motivated the government's restrictions on Jews, such as the prohibition against settlement within 50 versts of the border; rather, it was due only to the greed, sinfulness, and criminal behavior that characterized "most of our petty trade."[23]

Much less ideologically tendentious (and more informative) was the view taken by a group of Jewish merchants in Kishinev in 1864 in their petition to the Ministry of Internal Affairs asking that recently renewed restrictions on Jews in frontier zones be rescinded. They denied that all Jewish merchants dealt in contraband or that Jews were the only ones to do so. Yet they also argued that forty-five years of government efforts to combat smuggling had been in vain because (a) the trade in smuggled goods would continue as long as customs taxes were set at unrealistically high levels; and (b) smugglers were too sophisticated to be stopped by

50-verst limits and were able to ship goods 100 and 200 versts into the interior.[24] The implication clearly was that government trade policies had been pushing importers into illegal trade for at least half a century and that the merchants themselves, Jews and non-Jews alike, should hardly be blamed for the state's economic shortsightedness. Keeping Jews 50 versts from the border had not had any impact on smuggling in the past, and it was unlikely to have any in the future.

There was no doubt in anyone's mind that Jewish merchants (among others) routinely evaded import regulations. This fact even served the Hasidic rebbe, R. Levi-Yitzhak of Berdichev, as material for one of his homilies on the holiness of the Jewish people. The tsar, with all his soldiers and inspectors, could not prevent Jews from dealing in forbidden goods; yet, on Passover, you could not, he asserted, find a speck of bread in a Jewish home for all the money in the world, though there were no government inspectors or soldiers forcing the Jews to do God's will. Here was proof of the Jews' absolute devotion to God.[25]

Smuggling was at the center of an affair that at one time generated a fair amount of scholarly attention: the so-called Jewish revolt of December 1843 in Mstislav.[26]

The affair began as an inspection for contraband that indeed turned up quantities of nontaxed merchandise in the warehouse of a prominent Jewish merchant. The goods were ordered seized, and the district police chief ordered his soldiers to commandeer a nearby horse and wagon over the wagoner's protests. A melee ensued in which a crowd gathered and numerous Jews were beaten, some returning the blows as they attempted to stop the soldiers from taking the wagon. The chief of the gendarmes, one Bibikov, charged the Jews of the town generally with treasonous assault, accusing them of beating his men and breaking several of their guns. The report rendered to St. Petersburg by the civil governor of the province, Engelgardt, prompted the tsar to order the conscription of 10 percent of the male Jewish population as punishment.

After a lengthy investigation by the Internal Affairs Ministry, Bibikov was himself charged with falsifying the evidence and using false testimony in the initial investigation. In the end only four Jews were found to have struck one of the soldiers. The Jews contended that their intent had been solely to defend the poor wagoner's only means of livelihood in response to the improper actions taken by Bibikov's men. This argument along with the sympathy of Count Aleksandr Benckendorff, head of the Third Section of the Imperial Chancellery (i.e., the secret police), apparently helped to clear the Jews from charges of mutiny.[27]

Simon Dubnow's grandfather, however, one of the kahal leaders involved in the investigation, confided to his historian-grandson in later years that the Jewish defense was a fabrication. It was not the wagoner whom the Jews were summoned to defend, but the goods about to be seized from the merchant, Neta Frumkin, that they apparently hoped to spirit away.[28]

The story possesses numerous important features for the purposes of our discussion. No one, for example, challenged the claim that large-scale marketing of contraband was taking place on a continuing basis. A significant section of the town's Jewish population was in some way dependent on this trade, to the extent that they were willing to go to considerable lengths to oppose what was clearly a highly unusual confiscation. They not only risked an open confrontation with gendarmes and the provincial administration, they also dispatched an important shtadlan, Yitzhak ("Itchele") Zelkind of Monastyrshchina, to St. Petersburg to take their case beyond the local level.[29] The security and economic interests of the community took clear precedence over qualms concerning smuggling and *dina demalkhuta dina*.

Military Conscription

The Jews of Russia, with a good deal of justification, viewed the imposition of military service on their sons as a national catastrophe. Coming as it did (in 1827) in the absence of any amelioration of other restrictions against Jews, the conscription decree was a very serious blow. In time it became clear that the *rekrutchina* threatened not only the well-being of the individual draftees and their families but the very fabric of Jewish communal life as well, for it was the community that was to administer the recruitment procedure and swear those drafted to absolute loyalty and obedience to the tsar.

This was a severe test indeed of the *dina demalkhuta dina* concept that for so long had operated in the context of a corporate society where the Jewish obligation to the ruler was mainly fulfilled through the royal treasury.[30]

In the Habsburg Empire, where conscription of Jews was decreed in 1788, the highly regarded rabbi of Prague, R. Yehezkel Landau, formulated a response to the new situation that tried to accommodate both the tradition of compliance with the king's law and the requirements of the Jewish religious conscience. In an emotional address to Jewish conscripts about to leave their homes, Landau exhorted them to pray daily whenever possible, to avoid the consumption of meat, and to be true to their heritage. It was, however, to perform God's will and "the merciful emperor's" bidding that they had been chosen for service in which he hoped they would take care to obey their superiors.[31]

This, of course, took place within the framework of Habsburg Jewry's civil emancipation. In the Polish Duchy of Warsaw, where emancipation failed to take place, Jewish negotiators won for the Jews (in 1811) an exemption from military service on payment of what was meant to be an annual tax.[32] But in Russia, Jewish efforts to avert the "evil decree" through negotiation, influence, and bribery came to naught.[33] As late as November 1833 the kahal of Vilna was still trying to persuade Nicholas I to return to a system of exemption taxes and release fees. In a surprisingly strongly worded memorandum, they spoke of the "unbearable hardship" of personal military service introduced so suddenly. The Vilna spokesmen boldly pointed out that in other countries where Jews were personally liable for army service, they were also equal to non-Jews in civil status.[34] There can be no doubt that the Jewish leadership had sought to avoid conscription; when it did come, however, they were faced with a different problem, that of implementation. This was an internal problem in that it was the kahal's responsibility to administer the recruitment rolls.

Resigning himself to the inevitable, the rebbe of the Habad (Liubavich) Hasidim, R. Dov-Ber b. Shneur-Zalman, gave a remarkable talk to his devotees in December of 1827, just prior to his death. In it he demonstrated how a political act of the gentile state, as terrible and fearsome as it seemed, could be reduced from an apocalyptic catastrophe to more manageable dimensions by viewing it as a small component in a cosmic process, a necessary stage in God's plan for the universe.[35]

The rebbe essentially told his listeners that the created world depended for its existence on Israel's proper and sincere fulfillment of God's will, embodied in the *mitsvot*. The Jews, however, had been guilty of performing the commandments without complete spiritual devotion and had thus jeopardized the universe. God had prepared a means to rectify this situation in the form of gentile kings who are empowered to administer the discipline ordained on high. If the king forces the Jew to shave his beard and earlocks and to desecrate the Sabbath (a reference to the fate of army recruits), this oppression leads the Jew to yearn in his heart for true devotion to God. In this way the spiritual balance of Israel—and hence of the universe—is restored.

Second, the weeding out of those among the Jews who are "impure and wicked" must precede the coming of the Redeemer. Indeed, the "mixed rabble" have always been the source of great wickedness, as in the sin of the Golden Calf. They are a danger to Israel as long as they are intermingled with Israel; once identified and separated, they are no longer a threat. Just as the conscription decree would lead some Jews to renew their wholehearted fear of heaven, it would of necessity point up the contrast between them, the "refined silver," and the "dross," "heretics and apostates" (*apikorsim umumarim*).[36]

R. Dov-Ber's formulation provided a religious rationale both for accepting the *gezera* (oppressive decree) as *din* (the law) and for justifying its implementation within the Jewish community. For it was but a small step between acknowledging the theological correctness of "winnowing the chaff" and actually selecting recruits in such a way as to place the burden on the "mixed rabble" and control the damage to the "refined silver." In the rebbe's view, conscription was a trial, ordained in heaven, with potential spiritual benefits for those who survived the ordeal.

That most communities indeed practiced a heavy-handed selectivity in filling conscription quotas—and not necessarily out of theological considerations—is a matter of record.[37] Indeed, a later apologist for the kahal and the rabbinic leadership claimed that weighted conscription procedures combined with a standing policy of nonregistration of young scholars in the kahal's conscription rolls succeeded in "saving more than half of the people, in both quantity and quality." For this purpose, our memoirist explicitly states, it was deemed "absolutely permissible" to violate *dina demalkhuta*.

> [A]ll the pious men of Torah, teachers, slaughterers and the like, as well as every young student of Torah, all of them were hidden from the registry books . . . , and so [the communities] did not have to furnish their full quota of souls. . . . [T]he leaders of the kehillot chose to conceal people of that type because it was easier to hide them than people who frequented public places: tradesmen, shopkeepers, artisans and village peddlers, all of whom must come into contact with non-Jews in their daily work.[38]

The self-interest of the Jewish communal elite was thus justifiable in its own eyes not in religious terms alone; it also coincided with the most expedient means for reducing the overall Jewish quota. If it was necessary to engage in illegal practices, this, too, could be justified by denying the applicability of *dina demalkhuta dina* to an oppressive decree.

With regard to the response of the Jewish rank and file, here again, the record is very clear that conscription was universally considered to be a catastrophe. The implications of this are, however, a matter of controversy. Some historians choose to equate the negative Jewish response to the *rekrutchina* with political, even revolutionary, opposition to tsarist rule, as such, and link this with both contemporary revolutionary trends in Russian society and with the later development of Jewish nationalism and socialism in the 1880s.[39] Yet, as others have argued, escape to the countryside, agony for lost children, rage at the *khappers* (Jewish press gangs) and the kahal, and hatred for Nicholas still did not add up to a political opposition movement with revolutionary overtones. Even physical assaults against kahal officers and the forcible freeing of conscripts awaiting transport did not necessarily constitute acts of violent resistance against the state. This was not revolution, but only *ad hoc* passive resistance against a particular decree accompanied by an inward-turning resurgence of religious fervor.[40]

The question is one of definition, interpretation, and emphasis. A breakdown into specific time periods is likely to clarify some of these issues: The worst excesses of the drafts of the Crimean War years should not be read back over the entire period from 1827 to 1855, for example. Nor is it clear that a strict conceptual distinction is possible between active and passive resistance or between popular anger vented against the kahal leaders and the underlying attitude toward the gentile state. It would appear that at both the leadership and popular levels, a feeling of helpless resignation in the face of the omnipotent state coexisted with a willingness to take certain risks in the cause of self-defense.

Negative attitudes toward the state tell us something of the valence of Jewry-state relations but do not indicate the extent to which Jewish reliance on the state continued to characterize Jewish politics. The structural-analytical scheme that has been advanced throughout this study emphasizes the importance of the ruler as an orienting point in the Jews' inner as well as external politics. Thus, we have seen how in cases of severe internal conflict either the kahal or its opponents—often both—turned to the non-Jewish powers-that-were as a means of defeating the other side and settling the issue. Did the conscription crisis, in this sense, show any alteration in the substructure of the Jews' political orientation? The answer, it would seem, is that it did not.

It was difficult for the Jewish population to look to the state for assistance against kahal conscription officers. It was generally the case that kahal officers maintained a close working relationship with corrupt Russian officials. They utilized this relationship and the power granted to them to fill quotas almost at will in order to continue the policy of selective conscription. Dissidents, under these circumstances, could be dealt with easily through the conscription machinery—a form of executive coercion that far outweighed in severity previously available weapons in the Jewish communal arsenal.[41]

Nevertheless, complaints concerning unfair conscription were made to the authorities. This was done through informing as well as occasional open petitions for redress.[42]

Thus, much of the traditional mechanism of political conflict remained as it had been before, even as the rest of the Jewish political structure was being reduced to only a faint semblance of its former self. The anarchic contention for power that the rabbi of Shavli bemoaned in 1843, though not unprecedented, was at least partly conditioned by this state of affairs. The levers of power were still there to be manipulated, whereas a moderating and legitimating framework was less and less in evidence. The hallmark of Jewish politics in Russia in this period was the fragmentation of the community and of its leadership, particularly on the intercommunal level. This, in turn, had immediate implications for the preservation of standards in Jewish civil life on the local level.

Spokesmen and Intermediaries (1800–1860)

We have already noted that from the turn of the nineteenth century on, political spokesmen tended more and more to be self-directed. It is, of course, true that in the past, as well, Jewish leaders had often dominated public life by virtue of personal qualities: either their moral authority, their charisma, or their social prominence and wealth. But such leaders had always before functioned in a context where a formal structure also existed, with which the exceptional or dominant personality interacted, and from which he derived tacit or explicit approbation.

What was different now, with the progressive disintegration of the Jewish corporate structure, was that no universally recognized mechanism existed any longer for the selection, acclamation, or support of national leaders. Political representation, as such, passed completely into the hands of individuals of local, regional, or sometimes national reputation, almost all of whom acted out of their own sense of civic responsibility or personal capability and ambition, none of whom was accountable to some higher Jewish authority and most of whom defined the Jewish interest in more or less narrowly subjective terms. The field was also open in this period for obscure claimants to the attention of community and government to aspire to a public role.

Rabbis as Political Leaders

When the Lithuanian and White Russian community representatives met at Zelva in 1816 to arrange an intercommunal apparatus to support the Jewish deputies in St. Petersburg, the first signature on the memorandum of agreement was that of R. Haim of Volozhin.[43] According to the account of their secretary, Yitzhak Sasson, in 1818 the deputies Eliezer Dillon and Zundl Sonnenberg, while traveling back to the capital, made a point of stopping at Volozhin to consult R. Haim once again.[44]

Not every rabbi commanded the respect and authority that were accorded to R. Haim, and very many kept aloof from public affairs; but the involvement of rabbinic figures in Jewish politics is one of the characteristic features of nineteenth-century Russian Jewish public life. Their influence was expected—even taken for granted—by most maskilim, let alone more traditionalist elements of the population. Michael Stanislawski speaks of the heightened prestige of the rabbis in the period of Nicholas I's reign as part of "a thoroughgoing religious realignment" that produced a militant Jewish Orthodoxy in Russia, roughly from the late 1840s on.[45] The involvement of leading rabbis in dealings with the state can be viewed as one aspect of this heightened prestige.

The need for a substitute political leadership was certainly acute, particularly on the intercommunal level where no regular channels for consultation existed. Yet the role of political counselor and spokesman was not one that came naturally to, or was expected of, those well-known rabbis who took on such functions. In introducing R. Haim of Volozhin's commentary to Mishna *Avot,* Yehoshua-Heshl Halevi found it necessary to add the following justification for the political activity of the founder of the Volozhin yeshiva:

> In each generation a leader emerges. . . . [In *Avot* we find] what each one said in his own time to repair the breach and be on guard . . . both in religious and civil matters. This shows that in ancient days the one who was chosen to lead the community had to be aware of the affairs of his generation. . . . And in their civil needs, as well, he sought their welfare to the extent of his ability and his means, being faithful to both God and his king. . . . [T]his is his duty, and, this is what is fitting for a faithful shepherd.[46]

That not all rabbinical figures were of the same opinion becomes clear from a report of the efforts of R. Shneur-Zalman, the first Habad leader, to raise funds in the southwestern provinces to aid Jews expelled from White Russian villages in 1808. One of his stops was in Tulczyn to ask the help of R. Borukh (one of the Hasidic dynasts of the Ba'al Shemtov's family). R. Borukh allegedly objected to the campaign on principle, arguing that "God will save us." To R. Shneur-Zalman's counterargument that it is forbidden to rely on miracles and that Israel must seek God's favor with deeds, R. Borukh reputedly replied, "And who asked you to be Israel's benefactor?"[47]—a response that reflects not only the incongruity of political activity and the rabbinic role (even in its recast, Hasidic form) but also the lack of legitimizing mechanisms in the informal political structure of Russian Jewry.

Another Hasidic leader, R. Levi-Yitzhak of Berdichev, made a special point in his sermons of stressing the need for human activity in achieving miraculous escapes from danger. In his sermons for Hanukkah, he spoke of two kinds of miracles—those performed solely by God and those achieved partly through men's actions. In the latter category he placed the Maccabees' war against Antiochus IV.[48] Thus, again, there were supernatural miracles and miracles within natural and historical conditions: the parting of the Red Sea, on the one hand, and the salvation of the Persian Jews through the efforts of Esther, on the other. To save the nation, it is even permitted to commit forbidden acts.[49]

R. Levi-Yitzhak took his own activist advice on several occasions. It appears that he was in Warsaw in 1791 as part of the Jewish leadership's effort to forestall a Jewish reform act by the Polish Sejm, and it was he who convened a meeting of rabbinical leaders in Berdichev in 1809 (1803?) to discuss what they saw as the dangerous aspects of the Russian government's Jewish policy.[50]

The Hasidic rebbe of Rizhin, R. Israel Friedman, was apparently involved in efforts prior to 1821 to lobby against conscription of Jews for military service—something that as early as 1803 had been rumored to be pending before the highest policy-making circles of the government. Friedman sought to make use of his connections with the daughter of a Hasidic family (Leah Rafelevich) who had married the admiral of Russia's Black Sea fleet but who continued to support Friedman's opulent court. He confirmed as much to R. Haim of Volozhin, when the latter sent his grandson, R. Yitzhak Ze'ev Soloveichik, to Rizhin to urge Friedman to use all the influence he possessed to win a reprieve.[51] Friedman was later imprisoned for allegedly ordering the murder of two informers, Oksman and Shvartsman, at Novo Ushitsa (1838).[52]

Less well-known rabbinical figures were also called on in this period to represent their communities in political affairs. When in 1817 the kehalim of each province were ordered to send two delegates each to Vilna the following year to elect the Jews' deputies, several communities sent their rabbis, including R. Leyb Borukh Margolis of Belostok and R. Haim Mordecai Margolis of Dubno.[53] The rabbi of Dubno was particularly prominent in local affairs, partly because he was a merchant himself (before his financial ruin).[54]

In a later period, Dubno was for a time the home of Yitzhak Eliyahu Landau of Vilna, where he served as preacher. His ability to deal with the gentile authorities and his general reputation as a capable and articulate spokesman prompted Dubno's Jews to send him to the Rabbinical Commission convened by the Ministry of Internal Affairs in 1861–62.[55] A fellow member of the 1861–62 commission, R. Avraham Madievskii of Khorol (Poltava province), was a Hasid of the Liubavicher rebbe and served as government (i.e., officially recognized) rabbi of Poltava as well as Jewish advisor (*uchonyi evrei* ["learned Jew"]) to the governor-general of Kharkov.[56]

Another example of a rabbi with a purely local reputation who apparently served as political spokesman was Yehoshua-Heshl Ashkenazi, rabbi of Lublin from 1852 to 1867. R. Yehoshua-Heshl had won the respect of government officials to the extent that he was awarded the distinction of honorary citizenship. Around 1860, R. Yehoshua-Heshl delivered a memorable sermon glorifying Alexander II, a sermon that was orally translated into Polish for the benefit of members of the local gentry and officialdom who were in attendance.[57]

The most important role, however, was played by rabbis of national reputation who were the effective leaders of transcommunal constituencies. In the period of Alexander I, R. Haim of Volozhin and R. Shneur-Zalman of Liady had played this role. In the 1840s, their respective successors—R. Yitzhak b. Haim of Volozhin and R. Menahem-Mendl Schneersohn, heir to the leadership of the Habad Hasidim (after the tenure of "the middle rebbe," R. Dov-Ber)—continued to fill this function. As acknowledged leaders in the Mitnagdic and Hasidic camps, respectively, it was they who took part in the dramatic rabbinical conference in St. Petersburg in 1843.

Participating with them were a number of lay figures representing other constituencies: Bezalel Stern of Odessa, director of the progressive school there and a representative of the "enlightened" sector of Jewish society; Jacob-Joseph Halperin of Berdichev, a wealthy banker, a militant antimaskil and a spokesman for Volhynian Jewry;[58] and Dr. Max Lilienthal, assisted by Leon (Lev) Mandelstamm, designated by Count Sergei Uvarov, the Minister of National Enlightenment, as liaison with the Jewish community.[59]

The choice of the two rabbis was perspicacious and was probably made at the suggestion of Lilienthal (who, in turn, was being coached by Nisan Rosenthal, a wealthy and important communal figure in Vilna). It was Lilienthal who had made a point of seeking R. Yitzhak's approbation while on his second trip through the Jewish communities in the early autumn of 1842, when R. Yitzhak agreed to serve on the planned commission.[60]

The inclusion of the Liubavicher rebbe, whose influence in the Pale was almost as extensive as that of the Volozhiner *rov,* was also probably at the urging of Lilienthal and his associates. Until 1841, Uvarov was not even aware of R. Menaham-Mendl's existence. At that time, reacting to an article by an anonymous maskil (probably from Vilna) that named a certain "Mendl Lobovitzer" as an enemy of Enlightenment, Uvarov asked Count Benckendorff, head of the secret police (the Third Section), to investigate and determine who this person was.[61] On receiving the full report from Benckendorff (June 1841), Uvarov replied:

> One can see, it is true, that the leader of the Hasidic sect Mendl Schneersohn has thus far not behaved illegally, and that, taking into account his [poor] moral [i.e., spiritual] endowments and his limited intellect [!], he is unlikely to be a dangerous person. Nevertheless, I would say that it would not be superfluous to keep him under covert surveillance, particularly as time goes on and the state's plans for Jewish schools will be implemented.[62]

There is no hint here that Uvarov had R. Schneersohn in mind for a central role in the implementation of his scheme, an idea that must have been proposed to him between the summer of 1841 and the fall of 1842.

The results of the St. Petersburg conference, which took place from May to August 1843, are generally known, their most important feature being the introduction of state-sponsored schools for Jewish pupils.[63] The Jewish representatives (Stern, Halperin, and the two rabbis) had been summoned to lend the project some chance of success in the various constituencies they spoke for or at least to minimize, by their imprimatur, the expected opposition to the education reform on the part of the Jewish populace.

The rabbis were under tremendous pressure. They were unable to do anything but accede "voluntarily" to the ministry's plan, lest the Jews be accused of refusing to do the will of the tsar—something that was obviously to be avoided—yet they could also not mislead their own followers.[64] Their position was clearly untenable, as Lilienthal stood ready to argue that the school reform did not contradict the tenets of Judaism.

Subsequent statements by each of them (in R. Yitzhak's case, remarks attributed to him) may be seen as supporting the idea that they both viewed their collaboration as necessary because they had no choice or because their support was some sort of holding action. Thus, R. Menahem-Mendl later reminded Leon (Lev) Mandelstamm, the ministry's Jewish advisor, that certain guarantees had been agreed on regarding the continued operation of private, traditional Jewish schools.[65] R. Yitzhak, stopping at Ukmergé (Vilkomir) on his return trip to Volozhin, was asked by an excited and anxious throng to reassure them, something that, in one account, he grimly refused to do.[66] A different version of R. Yitzhak's return from St. Petersburg describes him as having been quite optimistic about the concessions he felt he had been able to obtain.[67]

The results were apparently quite satisfactory to Tsar Nicholas because the idea of using a rabbinical conference to settle outstanding issues (i.e., to bring the Jewish population into closer conformity with the wishes of the government) was formally enacted into law in 1848.[68] The commission was to be attached to the Ministry of Internal Affairs on a permanent basis and was to consist of four members and a chairman (selected by the minister from among candidates proposed by the Jewish communities and approved by the governors-general). These were to swear an oath of loyalty and faithful service. Sessions were to be held two months out of every year, and the chairman was to be changed annually.[69] The purpose of the commission was "to supervise and render opinion on questions related to the laws and customs of the Jewish faith and affairs of the rabbis." The commission would also deal with any subject laid before it by the ministry.[70]

In fact, however, the Rabbinical Commission did not meet until 1852 and was convened only sporadically thereafter. It met five times during the nineteenth century (1852, 1857, 1861–62, 1879, and 1893–94) as well as a sixth time in 1910.[71] Its members were lay leaders, shtadlanim, and rabbis, and they generally were joined in their discussions by the ministry's Jewish advisors ("learned Jews"); thus, the history of the commission does not entirely lie within the parameters of the discussion of "rabbis as political leaders." Some facts about the commissions are, however, worth noting.

First, the commissions that convened beginning in 1852 tended to include the middle-level local and regional leadership rather than those of national reputation (R. Schneersohn and R. Yitzhak of Volozhin) who were summoned in 1843 by Uvarov. Possibly for this reason, the membership of the commissions changed from one to the next (with the exception of two individuals, R. Dr. Neumann of Riga and St. Petersburg and Yekutiel-Sisl Rapoport of Minsk—both of whom had national visibility as leading figures).

Second, the agenda of the commission tended to be restricted to matters such as divorce law, schools, the synagogue, and the status of the rabbinate.[72] The members did not function as deputies of the Jewish people or as petitioners, but rather as respondents to queries posed by the ministry, that is, along the lines of Napoleon's Sanhedrin.[73] At no time, for example, did they take up sensitive issues such as military conscription, reform of the *korobka* tax, and residence privileges outside the Pale.

Third, the commissions were heavily weighted against Hasidic representation, with the one exception of R. Madievskii of Poltava, who took part in the third commission (1861–62) and who belonged to the Habad group. This lack of formalized access to the highest-level state officials cannot be said to have diminished in any way the influence and authority of the Hasidic rebbes over their own followers; this tends to underscore the argument raised earlier concerning the relative independence of the Hasidic sector from the kahal-state complex.

An important political role was to be played by one member of the commission of 1857, R. Yaakov Barit of Vilna, who figured prominently in the Vilna commission of 1869 (see chap. 5). For the last part of the century, two other rabbinical figures, R. Isaac Elhanan Spector and R. Israel Salanter, were to play important political roles, but they were not among the Rabbinical Commission members.[74]

Thus, the Rabbinical Commissions never became a legitimating force for political activity: the structural looseness of Jewish politics continued to encourage the participation of individuals on an ad hoc basis.

The New Aristocracy and the Rabbinical "Shadow Government"

The story of the men who made it their business in this troubled period to speak for the Jewish interest—whether in accordance with their own understanding and subjective motivations or at the behest of their community—is one that seems hopelessly buried in myth and countermyth and veiled by a general impression that lacks detail.

Brief mention of quite a number of individual figures active in this period does occur here and there in historical and antiquarian studies, in published documents and memoirs, and in the Jewish press of the latter part of the nineteenth century. We have already noted several from the turn of the century: Shimon b. Ze'ev-Wolf, Yehoshua Zeitlin, Avraham Peretz, and Neta Notkin. The most famous of Russian Jewish shtadlanim later on in this period is undoubtedly Baron Joseph (Yozel) Günzburg. Many other, relatively unknown figures were drawn into political activity during the first half of the nineteenth century, adding to the proliferation of spokesmen and intermediaries that was abetted by the political fragmentation of Russian Jewry.

We may divide these politically active figures into two groups:

(a) appointed shtadlanim or communal representatives; and (b) independents and notables (see Table 1).

In the first group are included the few remaining examples of commissioned official spokesmen who held power of attorney from a particular community or communities. In addition, there was the much larger group of local or provincial activists who represented their communities at intercommunal conferences such as the Minsk conference of 1816 or the Vilna conference of delegates in 1818. Finally, in this category we include the "deputies of the Jewish people" in the 1812–23 period.

Table 1. Russian Jewish Representation, 1780–1855

Region (by province)	Appointed Shtadlanim and Communal Representatives	Independents and Notables
North		
Courland,	Leyb Maytes	Neta Notkin
Vilna,	Yirmiah Sarason	Shimon b. Ze'ev-Wolf of
Vitebsk,	Eliezer Dillon[abc]	Vilna
St. Petersburg	Yehuda Zundl	Nahum (Menahem) Mitaus
	Sonnenberg[abc]	(Rivkind)
	Beinish Lapkovsky	Shimshon Hacohen Mazeh
	(Baratz)[bc]	Avraham Peretz
	Yekutiel-Ziskind b. Yaakov	Lev Nevakhovich
	Halevi[b]	Joseph (Yozel) Günzburg
	Shmuel-Haim Klaczko[b]	Israel Salanter
	Shmuel b. David Gordon[b]	Yom-tov Lipmann Seltzer[d]
	Yaakov Barit[d]	Isaac Elhanan Spector
	Hirsh Davidovich	Elya Levinsohn Kratinger
	Shimon b. Ze'ev-Wolf of	Elhanan Cohen
	Vilna	
	Shmuel b. Leyb Epstein[c]	
	Marcus b. Feibush	
	Feitelson[bc]	
	Shimon Markl[e]	
Center		
Grodno,	Mikhl b. Hirsh Eisenstadt[bc]	Yehoshua Zeitlin
Minsk,	Pinhas Genekhovich Schick[ab]	Avraham Peretz
Mogilev,	Leyb-Borukh[b]	Lev Nevakhovich
Smolensk,	Shepsl Bishkevich Kaplan[b]	Hay Danzig (Moscow)
Moscow,		Haim of Volozhin
Bialystok		Yitzhak b. Haim of
(Belostok)		Volozhin[f]
		Menahem-Mendl
		Schneersohn[f]
		Yekutiel-Zisl Rapoport[d,e]

Table 1. (Continued)

Region (by province)	Appointed Shtadlanim and Communal Representatives	Independents and Notables
South		
Volhynia,	Itzik Gelmanovich	Yitzhak ("Itchele") Zelkind
Podolia,	Moshe Bliukhin[b]	Litman Feigin
Bessarabia,	Shmuel Frenkel[b]	Joseph (Yozel) Günzburg
Kiev,	Haim Mordecai Margolis[b]	Jacob-Joseph Halperin
Kherson,	Hirsh Erlich[b]	Bezalel Stern[f]
Chernigov,	Leyb Orshanskii[b]	
Poltava,	Meir Barskii[b]	
Ekaterinoslav,	Yitzhak Rabinovich[b]	
Kharkov	David Herzenstein[b]	
	D. Orshanskii[e]	

Sources: Gessen, "Deputaty"; Levitats 1; Maggid, "Iz moego arkhiva"; Maggid-Steinschneider, *'Ir vilna;* Zitron, *Shtadlonim;* Ginsburg, *Meshumodim;* Lifschitz, *Zikhron Ya'akov* 1; idem, *Toledot Yitzhak;* Dubnow, *History* 1; Barit, *Toledot Ya'akov;* Shimshon Dov Yerushalmi, "Va'adot uve'idot"; Natanson, *Sefer hazikhronot;* Trunk, "Geshikhte fun yidn in vitebsk"; Margaliot, *Dubna rabbati;* Nevakhovich, *Kol shav'at bat yehuda; EE.*

[a] Minsk Conference, 1816

[b] Vilna Conference, 1818

[c] Deputy of the Jewish People

[d] Delegations to Nicholas I, 1850s

[e] Rabbinical Commission, 1852

[f] Rabbinical Conference, 1843

Among the spokesmen who were given official standing or commissions for a specific purpose, we can cite several individuals from the turn of the nineteenth century. Vilna retained an official shtadlan between 1788 and 1807, Yirmiah b. Nahum Sarason. Also active on behalf of the Lithuanian communities from the 1770s to the 1790s was Leyb "Shtadlan" Maytes of Pinsk.[75] In 1803, Vilna sent Hirsh Davidovich (that is, b. David) to St. Petersburg to speak for "all the Lithuanian communities" in the matter of the Jews' voting rights in municipal elections.[76] Into this group we also put the Jewish delegates sent to St. Petersburg during 1802–4 for the Jewry-law discussions (see earlier). In this last case, however, as with all subsequent deputies and delegates, the commission of designated spokesmen came only in the wake of a government summons. This holds true for the Rabbinical Commissions as well.

In any case, as we saw in the case of Zeitlin and his coterie, the official spokesmen were overshadowed by the independents and notables who operated without formal mandate or restraint.

Unlike the communal representatives, the notables were generally in direct contact with high state officials on a regular basis. They were military contractors or liquor-duty lessees, and later, bankers and industrial magnates. The Günzburgs, for example, got their start as leasers of the state liquor monopoly (*otkup*) for the Crimea. After the boom owing to the Crimean War, they parleyed this into an empire that spanned ten provinces.[77] Jacob-Joseph Halperin of Berdichev, as another example, was a banker. These were not intellectual figures, but they were Russian-speaking and generally knew German as well. They paid their taxes along with the rest of the first-guild registered merchants rather than through the kahal.

Three typical examples of notable shtadlan figures in this period (their collective careers span forty to fifty years in mid-century, from the 1820s to the end of the 1860s) are Litman Feigin of Chernigov and Odessa, Yom-tov Lipmann Seltzer of Shklov, and Yekutiel-Zisl Rapoport of Minsk.

Feigin, a first-guild merchant and a government contractor, is noteworthy as one of the few shtadlanim based in the southern provinces. In 1830, Feigin addressed to Nicholas I a detailed plan for reorganizing Jewish life that included eliminating the Jews' anomalous civil status by integrating them with the local administration's public registry.[78] In 1833, he wrote to Count Benckendorff, enclosing a further memorandum on what he called the plight of the Jews of Russia, in which he reviewed the Jews' grievances. The Jewish people, he stated, "cried out" in "sore distress." "Its status, instead of the improvement which [the Jewish people] rightfully expected, has become ever more precarious . . . not only in all civic rights but even in those pertaining to basic living conditions."[79]

Reviewing the hopes of civic advancement raised ever since the 1804 statute and emphasizing the Jews' faithful service to Russia in the War of 1812 and the Polish uprising of 1831, he spoke of the humiliating limitations still placed on Jewish life: on their residence in cities within the Pale such as Kiev, Nikolayev, and Sebastopol; on their trading privileges at markets outside the Pale (such as Kharkov); on their presence for business purposes in the Russian interior generally and in the capitals, St. Petersburg and Moscow; on their employment of Christians; and on their entry into state service. If the Jews were not to be made fully equal with other loyal subjects of their social rank, at least the Jews' progress in thirty years (since 1804) of raising their level of enlightenment should be recognized and measures taken to ease several of these restrictions. This, he concluded, would befit the Russian state in the spirit of the nineteenth century.[80]

Noteworthy here is Feigin's appeal to justice and to the rights of man as well as to the obligation of the modern state vis-à-vis its subjects. This rhetoric of the Enlightenment sets off this petition and others like it from appeals to charter privileges that were made by shtadlanim of an earlier age.[81]

Yom-tov Lipmann Seltzer of Vitebsk was born in Shklov, one of the main nerve centers of Russian Jewish politics, where he quickly made a name for himself as a man of practical abilities. At age 25 he became *parnas* (head) of the kahal, a position in which he remained for seven years.[82] He began to play the role of shtadlan by 1839 at the latest. In that year he composed an ode in Russian and Hebrew to Alexander Niko-laevich, the future Alexander II, and presented it in person when Alexander passed through Shklov. In 1846, he was in St. Petersburg to ask for better conditions for third-guild (the lowest rung) merchants, townsmen, and students seeking entry to St. Petersburg. He claimed to have spoken on these matters with Nicholas's most important ministers—Kiselev, Uvarov, Mikhail Speranskii, and D. N. Bludov.[83]

In 1851, he was involved in an effort to mitigate the effects of the reclassification of Russian Jewry ordered by Nicholas, under which Jews were to be graded as belonging to one of four useful categories or else to a fifth class of idlers (see later). According to a different source, a group of shtadlanim approached the chief secretary of the Ministry of Internal Affairs, who for 35,000 rubles (and a promise of 15,000 more) agreed to make the first four grades as broad as possible.[84] Seltzer was more cryptic about his own activities, stating merely that he had "prayed" and "thank God, my request was granted."[85] It is not clear whether he was involved in the bribe or not.

In 1851, he also submitted an 82-page reform proposal dealing with Jewish agricultural colonies, schools, and the rabbinate. In response to this he was invited by Count A. N. Golitsyn to serve as one of those "appointed by the government in matters of the Jewish welfare."[86] The reference appears to be to the position of *uchonyi evrei* ("learned Jew"): Beginning in the early 1850s, Seltzer was the official "learned Jew" (Jewish advisor) attached to the governor-general of Vitebsk-Mogilev-Smolensk, a position that Golitsyn held at the time.[87]

In 1852, Seltzer was part of a delegation (including R. Yaakov Barit of Vilna, Shmarya Luria of Mogilev, and Yitzhak ("Itchele") Zelkind of Monastyrshchina) that met Nicholas I in Gomel and petitioned him for a reprieve from the higher conscription quota for Jews announced in July of that year (see n. 103).[88]

Seltzer's contemporary in Minsk, Yekutiel-Zisl Rapoport, was a key figure in Jewish politics in White Russia. His career, like that of Seltzer, extended from the 1840s until 1872 (the year in which both men died).[89] Although for Seltzer we have no real information about the extent of his involvement in his local community after his initial stint as parnas, we can definitely point to Rapoport's continued involvement in Minsk communal affairs alongside his broader political interests.

In 1852, Rapoport was already prominent enough to be considered as a possible participant in the first Rabbinical Commission; he did not, in fact, participate, however.[90] Rapoport did join the 1857 and 1861 Rabbinical Commissions, one of the very few men to serve more than once in that body.[91] In 1859, he was one of the leaders of Russian Jewry who received a letter from the editors of the Paris newspaper *Le Nord* when the latter proposed to devote regular attention to Jewish achievements in Russia and to defending Russian Jewry against its vilifiers.[92]

Reports from St. Petersburg in September of that year paired Rapoport with Yozel Günzburg as the two most prominent Jewish notables taking part in birthday celebrations for Alexander II's son Nicholas. Günzburg was styled as "the spokesman and head of our people in this land" and Rapoport, as "the glory of our people and chief of our community."[93]

Rapoport had apparently lent a certain amount of support to Max Lilienthal and to the idea of encouraging Russian education for Jews and, thus, aroused the ire of local Hasidim.[94] In 1869, we find him aligned together with the rest of the local Jewish gentry on the side of Zalkind Minor, the government rabbi of Minsk whose reelection was being hotly contested.[95]

The rise to prominence of such men as Günzberg, Rapoport, Feigin, and Seltzer added a dimension to Jewish political activity that, according to one prorabbinical observer, had its drawbacks. The activity of the new aristocracy, he argued, tended to be detrimental to the efficacy of rabbinic involvement in political affairs.

> In the most recent period, ever since there arose among our people the great ones and the enlightened ones, the people began to say: "Now we have brothers in the palace" . . . so that only they were deemed fit for public activity, and it was to them that the people looked for salvation. And thus, since that time, the power of the rabbis to accomplish anything was diminished.[96]

The writer, Yaakov Halevi Lifschitz, went on to say that the rabbis had done a much better job and kept faith with the people more than the new elite did.[97]

This judgment is surely self-serving in its zeal to promote the primacy of the rabbinic leadership, whose militant partisan Lifschitz was. Nonetheless, it accurately reflects the context of mid-century, in which the rabbinic elite, having inherited the mantle of the va'adim and the discredited kahal, was increasingly faced with a rival, independent lay leadership. There developed a greater plurality—not to say a cacophony—of political voices within the broader Jewish social elite.

Lifschitz himself provides ample evidence that rabbinic initiative was still very much in evidence even as this process gained momentum. Moreover, his account makes clear that the leading rabbinic figures constituted not so much a leadership threatened with extinction as a shadow government that allowed the notables to take the limelight while continuing its own activities behind the scenes.[98]

In 1851, for example, in response to news of the reclassification order that the government was about to announce,[99] a covert gathering of rabbinic leaders and their associates was held during the market of Zelva.[100] Under the threat of a strict (and illegal) herem, to guarantee secrecy, word was to be passed of a special tax (also illegal) based on total family assets, to fund a mission of deputized shtadlanim. The two central figures in this episode were R. Israel Salanter, then living in Kovno, and R. Isaac Elhanan Spector. With the support of the wealthy Elya Levinson Kratinger, who donated 1,100 rubles of his own, they instructed R. Elhanan Cohen to proceed to St. Petersburg and establish himself there as their agent.[101] A second conference was held in Minsk, again led by Salanter and Spector, where a mechanism for collecting the campaign fund was elaborated, involving a group of trustees in Minsk and local rabbis in each area who would act as couriers. The plan, which of necessity involved a large number of people and depended on absolute secrecy, was betrayed and ended in a fiasco.[102]

The same group was behind the Gomel petition of 1852 that asked the tsar to repeal the higher conscription quota imposed on the Jews that summer.[103] Not leaving it at that, they conferred that year, yet again, in Bobruisk. Two wealthy shtadlanim—Meshulam-Faivl Friedland (Fridlianskii) of Dvinsk (Daugavpils; Dünaburg) and Nissen Katzenelson of Bobruisk—were chosen, armed with funds and letters of attorney for the Lithuanian and White Russian communities, and sent off to the capital.[104]

Elya Kratinger continued to maintain Elhanan Cohen in St. Petersburg for many years. He was apparently quite effective in providing advance word of imminent policy changes in the various ministries. Yehuda Leon Rosenthal, a close associate of Baron Horace Günzburg and treasurer of the OPE (Society for Promoting Enlightenment Among

Jews in Russia; see discussion in chap. 5) was to lament, after Cohen's death, the fact that Cohen had not been replaced by anyone as capable as he; else, he argued, the pogroms of 1881 would not have taken the Jews by surprise.[105]

It was, indeed, the illegal apparatus of communal institutions and functionaries that allowed the local communities to maintain a good deal of their activity. The communities raised funds through the meat *korobka* that were far in excess of the official communal budget. These funds were used to pay the salaries of unofficial rabbis (the so-called religious as opposed to government rabbis), to support various unlicensed charitable societies, and to provide the bribes to Russian officials, which bought their silence and insured, among other things, that crown schools for Jews not be opened just yet.[106]

The key to this system was the local (unofficial) rabbi, who was sent by his community to the quadrennial bidding for the meat *korobka* lease. By tacit agreement no one else bid against him, and he was, thus, able to secure the lease for a low price. The excess taxes collected by the community then remained with the local leaders.[107]

When, in 1869, Sh. Y. Abramovich published his play *Di takse* (*The Tax*) on the abuses of the local community system, he included the motif of political subterfuge. In reaction to a rumor that the *korobka* was to be abolished, Spodek, one of the chief villains of the piece, is horrified:

> Yes, that would be a real calamity. My word, it's the cashbox that keeps alive the last bit of Jewishness, isn't it? Where else would we take what we need for this, for that, for the things we can't talk about? . . . And besides, every day there are new persecutions decreeing how we are to walk, to stand, to study. As long as we have the little cashbox, we know we can squirm out of it. . . . If they take our tax away, they take away our power.[108]

The shadow government was based on subterfuge practiced on a routine basis and on a grand scale. Here lay the essential difference in approach to the state taken by the rabbinical leadership, on the one hand, and the notables of the new aristocracy, on the other. We need look no further for evidence on the practical limits of *dina demalkhuta dina* in Russian Jewish society.[109]

The state, which did not lend its support to Jewish autonomy in the traditional manner and to which (as most Jews were bound to see it) Jewish children were surrendered as sacrificial victims for the army or for the government schools, could only be perceived by most Jews as a savage beast. That is precisely the way in which Lifschitz described the state: a zoo filled with wild beasts [the officials] that only qualified handlers [shtadlanim] might approach, appropriate food in their hands, without risk of their lives. In learning to deal with the beasts on their level, however, the handlers themselves were debased: They were brilliant procurers, sly flatterers, operators.[110]

Alienation from the state, then, brought with it a distaste for the shtadlan and his methods. It is significant in this regard that Lifschitz's heroes, R. Salanter and R. Isaac Elhanan, never soiled their hands with shtadlanut, always employing others to do so.

It is fascinating that, despite the differences in their perspectives, the maskilic novelist Abraham Mapu may have shared some of these barely admitted sensitivities of Lifschitz. This is an indication, perhaps, of the changing image of the traditional shtadlan in various sectors of Jewish society. Elya Kratinger, the practitioner of politics in the traditional mode, served as the model for the title character in Mapu's *The Hypocrite* (*'Ayit tsavu'a*).[111] With Mapu, it is not the image of the state as an amoral, destructive force that determines the value judgment he makes of the hypocrite; indeed, his character, R. Zadok, is not cast primarily as a politician. Rather it is his lack of moral scruples and his antipathy to a broader humanistic vision that condemn him to a life of fraud, flattery, and subterfuge—the stock-in-trade of Lifschitz's shtadlan.

Equally important is Mapu's double standard in idealizing Baron Günzburg, who appears in a cameo role in the story as Emanuel the Great and to whom Mapu dedicated the novel. Günzburg the court Jew was as different in Mapu's eyes from the hypocrite R. Zadok as day and night. Mapu gushed in his dedication:

> For who else is Emanuel, the great one of his people, who appears as the dawn on the horizon in the first book [of the novel], shining like the sun's rays in all its glory? . . . [I]n his [Emanuel's] greatness one sees a sign that God will yet shine His countenance upon Jeshurun. For that purpose He has raised up your house, my lord, like one of the great heights, that it may be an ensign across the world and to the end of time.[112]

It is to the maskilic approach to politics that I shall turn next in my analysis. In the evolution of the Russian maskilim as actors in Jewish public life, we shall see the most dramatic aspects of change and realignment in relation to the Jewish political tradition. They replaced neither the existing rabbinic leadership nor the notables who spoke for Russian Jewry. There was, indeed, no question of who spoke for Russian Jewry, for the mechanism of representation was gone. What is more important is the fact that the interaction of rabbis, notables, and maskilim in the political arena was to affect Jewish political development in a crucial way, to the extent that the rabbis themselves had at times to acknowledge the advantages of the maskilim in public life and, eventually, adopted some of the forms of activity (such as journalism) pioneered by the maskilim.

These developments must be seen in context in order to be understood. That context has been sketched in this chapter. The leitmotiv has been that of disorder: the decline of the structure of autonomy and the fragmentation of political representation. The tightening control of the state over Jewish communal life led to a multifaceted response. Tactically, there was a tendency on the part of much of the communal and rabbinic elite to retain quietism while divesting the "royal alliance" of any normative meaning. Structurally, there developed a greater reliance on new informal leadership networks; yet neither these nor the remnants of the kahal structure found any alternative means of resolving issues of power and control within the community. The overwhelming power of the state remained the most decisive fact in Jewish politics.

4

A Dual Role: Maskilim and the Russian State

In assessing the capacity for political leadership in East European Jewry prior to the 1880s, David Vital has argued, "[t]he modernist movement among Jews—the haskala . . . was almost devoid of men capable of thinking in systematic political and economic categories. It was essentially literary in character and expression and, in the broadest sense of the term, philosophical."[1] Systematic they may not have been, but the leading figures of the Russian Haskalah certainly expressed a consistent and abiding concern with the public life of their society and were determined to play a central role in reshaping it. In their literature and philosophy, they espoused a program of change that depended for its fulfillment on a major social and political reorientation in both Jewish and Russian society, and they demonstrated an awareness of the social forces that either impeded or promoted such a reorientation. They emerged as vocal critics, but also articulate defenders, of the Russian Jewish community and found themselves at odds with many influential and active elements in that community. Their changing methods of waging their battle are an indication to us of the transition to a new structure of Jewish politics.

They were affected by the trend in Russian intellectual discourse that, beginning in the reign of Alexander I and reaching its peak in the reign of Alexander II, stressed the need for social consciousness and social utility in all art and all science. One of its earliest formulators, Vasilii Popugaev, wrote in 1801:

> Many people often consider enlightenment to be knowledge of languages, science . . . and . . . knowledge of the ways of the world, the reading, generally, of novels, poetry, and so on. All of these views of enlightenment are, while not false, at the very least partly incorrect. Such understandings give us relative or partial enlightenment. But [true enlightenment necessitates that] a person who lives in society must know his place as a citizen, the aim of the collective community, his relationship with the whole—in a word, he must know private and public political relations. . . . Scientists are useful and even necessary among a people, but as a collective entity it must possess political and philosophical consciousness of its rights and its welfare.[2]

Finally, the maskilim lived in the midst of a decisive period in European industrial and political development, which they witnessed from the relatively backward, if vast, Russian Empire. The unfavorable comparison between Russia and Western Europe in terms of development fueled much of Russian state policy as well as the greater part of Russia's internal social and political debate. The race to catch up was not merely a matter of pride, in the political context of that era. Considering the issue from the perspective of all the less developed European countries at that time, Berend and Ranki explain the drive for more rapid development in terms of stark alternatives:

> The challenge of the West was . . . a challenge to a nation's very survival. . . . By the turn of the nineteenth century . . . nationalism and the romantic movement were putting "the" question of the age in terms quite far from economic: It was a choice between the nation's extinction, or the nation's heroic self-realization—the overcoming of all impediments to its progress.[3]

Were the Russian maskilim also animated by the drive to push forward in order not to be left inexorably and definitively behind? From the urgent and didactic tenor of their writings, one should conclude that they were. This underlying message came through in explicit terms again and again, as we can see in the following fairly typical examples.

An anonymous writer in *Ha-Maggid,* signing himself "a lover of my people," addressed this blizzard of mixed metaphors to the Jews of "Romania" (often a maskilic euphemism for Russia) in 1860:

> The years pass, Time travels onward like rushing wheels. What lies underneath is beaten down, crushed and demolished, while what is uppermost is hurled forward. . . . The wind of time is the breath of God, blowing new life into whatever lies before it, enfolding it in its wings to bear it onward and upward to its destined place. And woe to those who cling to the clods

of soil under them, who with all their might hold fast to their own place lest the wind carry them off, for presently the wheels of time will ride over them and they will be crushed, and they will be left mired and lost.[4]

Eight years later Avraham Ber Gottlober wrote:

> The times have changed, the epochs have turned, and many things which the ancients could not imagine are now necessities of civilized life. All of the nations are moving forward at Time's clarion call of "Onward!" But Israel tarries yet with his ancient rites which have lost their sense. . . . Like the shade of one long buried rising from the earth . . . he stands before us with unrecognizable tatters and alien gestures.[5]

In both cases the predominant images of stasis are those of death and destruction; forward movement is associated with life. Clearly, these were the views of men involved in, and committed to, the destiny of their own society in what they perceived to be a crucial century—even the most decisive—in the history of the Jewish dispersion.

Yet it was to be a matter of decades before they were able to elaborate what Vital would call systematic political ideas and to create the organizational base for their propagation. The beginnings of Russian maskilic politics, in the 1830s to the 1860s, were closely bound up with traditional patterns of Jewish political behavior. A basis for a restructuring of Jewish politics did not develop until after 1868. During the following decade, as we shall see, the preconditions were set for the emergence of political ideologies and parties and the nationalist orientations that came to characterize modern Russian Jewish politics after 1881.

Power, Conflict, and Legitimacy

The maskilim were a tiny minority in Russian Jewry and, strictly speaking, were only part of the sector of Jewish population that exhibited tendencies toward acculturation and partial resocialization into the Russian milieu. The process of acquiring a more modern education, newer occupational skills, a facility with the Russian language, European habits of dress and etiquette, and, often, a lapsed orthodoxy in religious practice began to make itself felt among Russian Jews quite early in the nineteenth century. Its impact remained limited, however, to individuals and pockets of Central European influence at least through the 1840s.[6] Within this context the maskilim per se were isolated and rare in most Jewish communities, and they were under considerable social pressure to conform to more traditional standards.

Avraham Ber Gottlober, living in Chernigov with his young family in 1829, was required to divorce his wife when his traditionalist father-in-law discovered that he was the possessor of "heretical" books.[7] In 1834, in Vilna, which could justifiably claim to be a major locus of maskilic activity, Mordecai Aaron Günzburg wrote, "Among [all other peoples] men of knowledge [i.e., arts and science] are the pride of their people; among us they must conceal themselves like criminals."[8]

Almost ten years later, he was to reiterate the statement, referring to the towns of the Pale where, he asserted, secret scholars existed in significant numbers, "But," he lamented, "let one talmudist so much as raise a threatening finger and they will deny philosophy and say it signifies nothing."[9] In 1840, a young Lithuanian maskil, Shneur Sachs, while traveling through Dubno, was the victim of traditionalist informers who had him arrested on false charges. He was freed owing to the efforts of nearby maskilim. The writer, Isaac Erter, noted in a letter to one of them that, as beleaguered members of a small group, maskilim must always come to one another's defense.[10]

Even in the 1860s, maskilim who found themselves in the smaller towns and townlets of the Pale were subject to feelings of profound alienation and loneliness. In 1866, Moshe Leib Lilienblum, who made his living as a private tutor in the Lithuanian town of Vilkomir, was left without pupils when he was reported to be a heretic. Lilienblum's living depended on yeshiva students and the children of Orthodox families: There was but one tutor in the town who instructed the sons of the wealthy in a more modern spirit. Fortunately for Lilienblum, the other tutor, an older man, was taken ill in 1868 and went to Vilna in search of medical care. Lilienblum then took over his place and was thus able to earn his daily bread.[11]

After the 1868–69 publication of Lilienblum's proposals for religious reform (in *Ha-Melitz*), he reported to Judah Leib Gordon:

> You can imagine what a commotion was aroused in that town of fools, Vilkomir! What can I tell you, honored sir! For six continuous weeks my name was on the lips of everyone in town: fishwives, woodcutters, horse thieves—the very dregs of humanity. On my way through the streets I heard women curse me soundly. . . . For six weeks, wall placards denouncing me were pasted on all the synagogue doors, on streetposts and on the public toilets. On the Shavuot festival the rabbi exhorted a large gathering to boycott me and drive me out of town. The government rabbi told me the next day that it had been decided to send an incriminating letter about me to the governor-general in Vilna unless I agreed to take 50 rubles and leave town, and even he urged me to do so.[12]

Gordon himself, whose correspondence with the miserable Lilien-blum brought the latter such solace, was himself trapped in the prov-inces, living in the town of Telz (prior to moving in 1872 to St. Peters-burg). In June 1870, he wrote to a friend in Kovno of his utter loneliness in the town, where he felt as if he had been "cast into a barren desert." He complained, "There is not one single person to whom I might show my works and from whom I might get an opinion or advice."[13]

If by 1881 men like Gordon, Lilienblum, Leon Pinsker, and their fellow maskilim were playing leadership roles in Russian Jewish politics, it is clear that somehow the maskilim were able, over the course of two generations, to transform a position on the extreme periphery of Jewish life into a beachhead of considerable strategic advantage and even a certain degree of legitimacy. It is also clear that they must have accom-plished this not simply by dint of cultural or literary activity, but through a political struggle. The first steps along this road were taken in the period of 1830–70 and may be understood as the appropriation by the maskilim of two crucial roles in Jewish politics: those of informer and shtadlan. In addition they assumed the role of social critic, formerly associated with the traditional preacher.

The Maskil as Informer

Informing—recourse to the gentile authorities as a means of outflanking Jewish communal authority or as a weapon of social control wielded by the communal leadership itself—was, as we have seen, built into the very fabric of traditional Jewish politics. As long as a quasi-governmental structure existed in Jewish society that (by necessity) derived its power from the state, it was always vulnerable to efforts to go over its head directly to the sources of power. Equally, it was always tempted—and sometimes pressed—to invoke gentile power in its own defense. On the eve of the nineteenth century, this was demonstrated yet again in the Vilna rabbinate controversy and the battles between Hasidim and Mitnag-dim. In the nineteenth century, both smuggling and the various irregulari-ties connected with military registration and conscription afforded ample opportunities for informers to be active on a regular basis.[14]

When we consider the routine subterfuge in the population registry, in tax collection, and in unauthorized communal activity and when we take into account the way in which the state loomed ever-larger in the Jews' daily lives as the kahal progressively lost its function as a buffer, this should come as no surprise.[15] In fact, although certain aspects of local kahal politics gave the impression that real power was being wielded by the few over the many, the kahal structure and its prerogatives were so attenuated and subject to direct state supervision that it might justifiably be said that the appearance of power merely masked an underlying impotence. The rampant growth of informing indicates clearly that there was no real power in the Jewish community other than that of the state.[16] In the best of times, power in the Jewish community was largely derivative, and these were not the best of times.

Thus, if Russian maskilim of the 1830s and 1840s tended to favor state intervention in Jewish affairs—a fact noted by all historians of the Haskalah—we need to recall that this was not simply a function of idiosyncratic factors: their supposed lack of self-confidence and their particular faith in the benevolence of the Russian state (or their particular insensitivity to the Jews' oppression by that state, as some would have it).[17] In their identification of the state (or the tsar) as the decisive locus of political sovereignty and in their perception that a struggle with the kahal establishment necessitated taking its place in communication between the state and the Jews, the maskilim were operating within the assumptions of the Jewish political legacy and according to the terms of reference in both Jewish communal politics and Russian political discourse of the early nineteenth century.[18]

The earliest example we have of a maskilic denunciation to Russian authorities of the traditional social and economic arrangements in the Jewish community is that of Yaakov Hirsh of Mogilev to the provincial administration in 1783. It dealt essentially with school reform; but in arguing that communal taxes already in existence could amply provide for a new school, it noted that two thirds of the funds collected each year "went to waste" on needless communal expenditures.[19] The implication was that the funds might be restored to a useful purpose, for example, the school project, with official insistence.

This example provides the germ of the maskilic genre of informing. Whereas in the rest of Jewish life, informing was a weapon for personal gain, vengeance, extortion, and the redress of a specific grievance, the maskilim generally used it as a weapon of ideological warfare. Government intervention was sought as a means of introducing social change, not merely as a momentary expedient, although there are examples of the latter as well, as we shall see.[20]

For the purposes of our analysis, we should try to distinguish between informing, as such, that is, the tendering of reports or proposals detrimental to specific Jewish activities, and the more general strategy of securing state support for the maskilim and their program. The two were, of course, linked, and in the minds of their traditionalist opponents were indistinguishable aspects of maskilic perfidy.[21] Nevertheless, there was a distinction between the two. One might cite as an act of persuasion aimed at securing a general policy favorable to the Haskalah the letter written by Benjamin Mandelstamm to Bezalel Stern in 1843 in the first days of Uvarov's school-reform conference that Stern was attending. Mandelstamm urged Stern, in no uncertain terms, to make the most of this opportunity: "Now, now is the time in which those who have been chosen for this sacred task [of enlightening the Jews] should fix their eyes and hearts on the source of the corruption out of which has sprung Israel's sickness, and on those degenerate customs which are such a stumbling block."[22] Mandelstamm's letter cannot be defined as informing in the strict sense of the term, although he was clearly making the case for securing officially sanctioned pressure against the obscurantists who stood in the way of Russian Jewry's enlightenment.

Of quite a different order was the unsuccessful attempt by maskilic figures in the Berdichev vicinity to discredit the traditionalist banker and shtadlan Jacob-Joseph Halperin as an opponent of government policy and thus prevent him from taking part in that same conference of 1843.[23] Although unable to disqualify his participation, in the end his maskilic opponents hounded Halperin into financial ruin and debtor's prison.[24]

Stanislawski has argued persuasively that it was the nexus between state policy and the Russian Haskalah that was the decisive factor in the numerical growth and institutional maturation of the maskilic camp.[25] He notes, as well, that the strength of this nexus—in which both maskilim and traditionalists believed—was, at least until the 1840s, a myth. This, however, was less important than the perception that "the power of the maskilim was pervasive."[26] It is here, indeed, where the political role of the maskil-as-informer inhered in its more general sense. As Gideon Katznelson observed concerning this issue, "In the final analysis, the entire struggle of the maskilim was pervaded by the consciousness that the state was on their side, and that the traditionalists' arguments against Haskalah were, by the same token, anti-government propaganda."[27]

Indeed, it was this very argument that the militant traditionalists of Lithuania recognized as their main weak spot and sought to turn to their own account in their counterattack of 1870. The maskilim, they charged, by pouring wrath and scorn on their own people for alleged moral failings and antigentile attitudes, were sowing hatred between Jew and non-Jew. Thus, the maskilim were in direct rebellion against the will of "our gracious and noble king, Alexander II," whose reign had been entirely devoted to bringing about civil peace and harmony.[28] They took care to cite a proclamation of the Holy Synod of the Russian Orthodox Church and the tsar's own declaration (of 13 May 1866) calling religion vital in the preservation of public morality, faithfulness to the state, and obedience to its laws and therefore basic to a sound education.[29] These were clever, if naive, attempts to turn the tables on the maskilim using their own ammunition. Their polemical value outweighed their political usefulness as they were published in Hebrew only.

Related to this issue of the general collaboration (perceived and real) between the state and maskilim is the vexed issue of the official rabbinate. Alexander I had, in 1804, laid the groundwork for the emergence of this office when he required that all rabbis, within eight years, know Russian, German, or Polish and be responsible for keeping the population registry. The police duties of the rabbi were further spelled out in the Jewry law of 1835 and an oath of fidelity to the state was required.[30] The official rabbinate that developed was tarred with the brush of informing—potential and otherwise—and its status in the community became part of the routine subterfuge of Jewish communal life. It was an open secret that the elected government rabbis, usually men of little scholarly or religious standing, were figureheads or front men;[31] the real rabbis were those whose salaries were paid out of the slush fund siphoned from the meat *korobka*. Particularly after the crown rabbinical seminaries were functioning (founded in 1847 in Vilna and Zhitomir) and newly appointed rabbis were required to have a diploma from one of these institutions or another state school (1857), the government rabbinate was generically equated with the Haskalah, and both with state tutelage.[32]

According to one observer, taking a retrospective view of the rabbinate problem in 1869:

> As government rabbis the Jewish communities generally choose people who do not have the most brilliant reputations, because no one of stature in the community would agree to take upon himself this duty; and this was in turn due to the prevailing attitude among the Jews toward anything bearing the name or imprint of the state. . . . [T]he government rabbis . . . were considered to be a burden on the community . . . [and] finally [were] people to be feared.[33]

The government rabbinate was but one state office in which maskilim served an often ambiguous role, partaking of the informer model as well as aspects of the shtadlan model (to be discussed later). The other positions of this sort were those of censor and of "learned Jew" (*uchonyi evrei*) or Jewish affairs adviser.

Jewish Censors
The censorship of Hebrew and Yiddish books and, later, periodicals
necessitated the employment of Jews or former Jews in the capacity of
government censors.[34] The efficiency of the system was vastly increased
in 1836 when the number of Jewish presses permitted to operate in
Russia was reduced to two (see later discussion). The censors of Jewish
books were therefore based in the locations of the two presses: Vilna
and Zhitomir (or Kiev). Later, there was also a Jewish censor in St.
Petersburg.[35] In the early part of Nicholas I's reign, the Vilna censor was
Wolf Tugendhold (whose brother Jacob was the censor in Warsaw).[36]
From the late 1830s to the mid-1850s, Iosif Seiberling, who had earned a
doctorate in Germany, served as the southern censor in Kiev.[37]
    It should be noted that the appointment of western- and Russian-
educated men as censors was not at first considered necessary. In 1836,
when the new censorship law was introduced, the inspection of already-
published works in circulation was to be the responsibility of a rabbinical
commission.[38] The plan was not implemented, however. After the rabbinical seminaries sponsored by the government were opened (1847), it
became part of the duty of the Jewish director of each one (first in
Zhitomir, later in Vilna, too) to serve as censor[39] and the link between
the Haskalah and censorship was sealed (see Table 2).[40]

Jewish Affairs Advisers
The practice of attaching Russian-speaking Jewish advisers to various
offices of the state bureaucracy seems to have grown out of two separate
processes. On the one hand, there was the state's need to impose greater
order and direct supervision on the Jewish population—a significant
proportion of the empire's western provinces and an ethnoreligious minority considered to present special problems. The Jewry-law of 1835
had envisioned a hierarchical structure of official rabbis to answer this
need: The local government rabbi was to be supervised by a provincial
oberrabbiner. There was, however, no implementation of this plan, and
the provincial administration remained in need of a substitute.[41]
    At the same time, Uvarov's plans for the educational reform of Rus-
sia's Jews depended on the advice and cooperation of "enlightened"
members of the Jewish community. Max Lilienthal's appointment and
his three-years' activity in the Ministry of National Enlightenment was
to be followed up on the provincial level through the appointment of
Jewish advisers to the district school superintendents (curators).[42] Leon
(Lev) Mandelstamm took over Lilienthal's position in St. Petersburg in
1846, retaining it until 1857.[43] Shmuel Yosef Fuenn, the Vilna maskil

Table 2. Censors of Hebrew and
Yiddish Books in Vilna, Kiev,
Zhitomir, and St. Petersburg (partial
list)

Vilna

1827–64	Wolf Tugendhold
1855	P. Kukol'nik[a]
1866	Jacob Brafman[b]
1865–1904	Joshua Steinberg
1870s	Asher Wahl

Kiev

1830s–1855	Iosif Seiberling[c,d]
1852–71	Vladimir Feodorov[b,c]
1871–1901	Herman Baratz[c,d]
1897–1904	Aaron Zeitlin[c]

Zhitomir

1850–62	Jacob Eichenbaum
1862–73	Haim Selig Slonimskii

St. Petersburg

(1860s?)	I. Landau[a,b]
1851–55	Daniel Khwolson[b,c]
1862	Iosif Seiberling[c,d]
1869	Jacob Brafman[b]

Sources: EE; Margaliot, *Dubna rabbati;* Zinberg,
History 12; Gottlober, *Zikhronot umasa'ot;* Fuenn,
Kirya neemana; Shochat, "Kovets derushim"; Ginsburg, "A pruv tsu fervehren," in *Historishe verk* 1;
idem, *Meshumodim;* Steinberg, *Mishlei Yehoshu'a.*

[a]Identity untraced

[b]Converted to Christianity

[c]Served also or subsequently as *uchonyi evrei*

[d]Member of a Rabbinical Commission

and later editor of *Ha-Karmel,* was appointed to the Vilna school district's
supervisory staff. In the Kiev school district, Usher Rosenzweig was consultant for the Jewish crown schools and (contrary to the ministerial
guidelines of the time requiring that a non-Jew serve as school inspector)
was made head of the Jewish crown school at Mogilev Podolsk.[44]

The problem of Jewish consultants for the provincial administration,
as such, was solved by attaching a "learned Jew" to each governor-

Table 3. Maskilic Jewish Advisers (*uchonye evreii*) to the Russian Government

Advisers	Place/Ministry	Year
Dr. Bernard Abramson	Kiev	1847
Herman Baratz	Kiev-Podolia-Volhynia	1863[a,b]
Shmuel Yosef Fuenn	Vilna School District	1856[c]
Lev Levanda	Vilna	1861
Usher Rosenzweig	Kiev School District	late 1850s
Marcus Gurovich	New Russia–Bessarabia	1852
Daniel Khwolson	St. Petersburg, Ministry of National Enlightenment	1857
Iosif Seiberling	St. Petersburg, Ministry of National Enlightenment	1857[b,c]
Moisei Berlin	Smolensk–Vitebsk–Mogilev; St. Petersburg, Ministry of Internal Affairs	1853 / 1856[c]
Yaakov Gurland	St. Petersburg, Ministry of National Enlightenment	1859
Vladimir Feodorov	Kiev	1859[d]
A. Ginsburg	Chernigov	1865
Aaron Zeitlin	Kiev	1860s
Aaron Mandelstamm	Mogilev	1860s
Eliezer Genikes	Odessa	1860s[b]
Jonah Gerstein	Vilna	late 1860s
Baron Joseph (Yozel) Günzburg	St. Petersburg	unofficial[e]

Sources: Ha-Ẓefirah, no. 3, 1874; Rosenthal, *Toledot OPE* 2; Greenberg, *Jews in Russia; EE;* Gottlober, *Zikhronot umasa'ot;* Lerner, *Evreii v novorossiiskom krae;* Ginsburg, *Amolike peterburg;* Shochat, *Harabanut mita'am; Ha-Maggid,* nos. 15, 17, 1861.

[a]In 1862 Baratz was attached as Jewish consultant to the Interior Ministry's Department of Foreign Cults. He was a member of the 1861 Rabbinical Commission
[b]Also served as censor, previously or simultaneously
[c]Seconded by the Ministry to the 1861 Rabbinical Commission
[d]Appointed as special assistant to the governor-general of Kiev
[e]Participant in 1861 Rabbinical Commission

general. A Jewish adviser was also appointed to the Ministry of Internal Affairs (see Table 3).[45]

The "learned Jew" for New Russia in the last years of Nicholas I's reign and the early part of Alexander II's was the Odessa maskil, Marcus Gurovich. He undertook two field missions (1854 and 1856) to assess the impact on the Jews of the southern provinces of government policies.[46] Gurovich's report of 1856 must have seemed dismal, indeed, to his superiors. He reported that there were wide discrepancies between "law" and "life": that the Jews continued to "wallow" in ignorance, refused to obey the spirit of the rabbinate regulations, continued to establish and maintain unauthorized synagogues and burial societies, and generally had not yet responded to the government's attempts to instill in them civic values.[47] In short, Gurovich provides us with a clear example of a specific denunciation by a maskil. On the other hand, it was Gurovich's assessment that the rabbinical (*bet din*) arbitration procedure for small civil suits was innocuous that provided the basis for Governor-General Alexander Stroganov's recommendation against its abolition.[48] It was another *uchonyi evrei,* Lev Levanda, who was instrumental in quashing a ritual-murder affair in the Kovno province in 1861.[49]

Whether assigned to the provincial administration or the St. Petersburg chancelleries, the Jewish affairs consultants were visible and undeniable proof of the official nexus between the state and the maskilim. Although government rabbis also served as *uchonye evreii*—apart from Madievskii of Poltava/Kharkov there were also the rabbis of Simferopol, Zhitomir, and Riga[50]—only in the case of the Hasid Madievskii can we speak with any certainty of a nonmaskilic "learned Jew."

Maskilim and Specific Denunciations

In addition to the indelible brand of collaboration that adhered to maskilim involved in public affairs by virtue of their generic association with the state (at least in Jewish eyes), there were, of course, specific instances in which maskilim resorted to explicit denunciation. The case of Jacob-Joseph Halperin is one such example (see earlier). Of far greater significance, however, were condemnations of traditional practices or particular activities that maskilim sought to bring to the state's attention, with recommendations to impose coercive measures. As was the case across the border in Austrian Galicia, this often occurred in Russia within the context of anti-Hasidic campaigns.[51]

In the early to mid-1830s, this coincided with a series of events surrounding the issue of censorship and the Jewish presses. Many of these had been established from the 1780s through the first decades of the nineteenth century, largely in Hasidic-dominated areas, as the literary output of that sector of Russian Jewry expanded rapidly.[52]

The state's interest in Jewish publishing and the Jewish book import trade was aroused between 1831 and 1835 by several disturbing reports. In 1831, Wolf Tugendhold (the Jewish censor of Vilna) reported to the Enlightenment (education) Ministry that many Hasidic books were in circulation that had not been submitted to any censorship committee for approval. The report was passed along to the Ministry of

Internal Affairs, but it was apparently disregarded at that time.[53] In 1834, the issue was raised by the Minister for Internal Affairs, Count Bludov, in a letter to Count Uvarov. Bludov cited a report on illegal importation and publication of uncensored Hebrew books that he received from Professor Savitskii at the University of Kiev and from two Jewish printers, Mekel and Berenstein.[54] Savitskii, in turn, had been in touch with Isaac Ber Levinsohn in 1833, asking the latter to clarify the matter of evasion of censorship by Jewish printers. Levinsohn, fearing a general prohibition of Hebrew publishing, wrote a memorandum that he sent to Savitskii, and it was this plan that Bludov received. In addition to a list containing books that were, in Levinsohn's view, worthy of continued circulation, it urged the strict inspection or proscription of other unworthy books already in use (mostly of Hasidic origin) that had escaped prior control. It suggested, too, that all Jewish presses but three be shut down and that these three be licensed for fifteen-year periods under government supervision.[55]

Bludov commended the plan to Uvarov and though the Minister of National Enlightenment urged moderation and pragmatism—he felt the available censors could not cope with such a task—in the end he agreed that a stricter censorship of Jewish books was required. The responsibility was passed on to a ministerial committee.[56] It is quite possible that the resulting law (1836) that did, in fact, order the closure of all but two Jewish presses was, thus, the result (direct or indirect) of the reports of Tugendhold, Levinsohn, and Savitskii.

There was one other intervening factor that ought to be taken into account however: the battle that raged in 1834 between two major Jewish publishers over the right to publish a new edition of the Talmud. The two rival presses, one Hasidic and one Mitnagdic (actually three, the Slavita press on the one hand and a combination of the Vilna and Grodno presses on the other) canvassed the entire rabbinate of the Pale for support. The split was patched up temporarily by a compromise agreement, but this broke down in 1835 as the first folio volumes came off the presses. The conflict at this stage was taken into Russian courts and in 1836, after a gentile bookbinder employed by the Hasidic Slavita press was found hanged on his employers' premises, the government intervened. The press was closed, its books-in-preparation were burned, and the Shapira family who owned the press was imprisoned.[57]

Lifschitz, who took every available opportunity to blame the maskilim for government persecution of traditional Jewry, did not single out Levinsohn and Tugendhold for blame in the censorship-law affair. Rather, he saw a direct connection between the Vilna–Slavita episode and the closure of the Jewish presses.[58] Although as we have seen, the matter was already under discussion in 1833–34, it is not out of the question that the Vilna–Slavita scandal did its part in creating an impression of a situation dangerously, even violently, out of control.

In 1862, Marcus Gurovich, the *uchonyi evrei* from Odessa, reopened the debate over Hasidic and Yiddish books in general by urging a blanket ban on Yiddish publishing. His proposal to the Minister of Internal Affairs at that time, Pyotr Alexandrovich Valuiev, was enthusiastically passed along to Alexander Golovnin, Minister of National Enlightenment. In addition, the Rabbinical Commission, which was then in session in St. Petersburg, was asked to render its opinion. Gurovich's memorandum was dropped, however, after the Jewish textbook committee under Golovnin's office (Daniel Khwolson, Iosif Seiberling, and Professor A. Mukhlinskii) offered the view that such a ban as Gurovich suggested would be counterproductive. Interestingly, the Rabbinical Commission had been prepared to go along with a partial ban as long as exceptions were made for "useful" books of a religious and moral character.[59]

A second area of programmatic denunciation by maskilim was the question of traditional Jewish clothing (and other aspects of personal appearance) that many maskilim wanted to see exchanged for European-style dress and grooming. A partial ban of the traditional Jewish costume of Polish Jews was included in the Jewry-statute of 1804, which was applicable to Jews traveling to the capitals and in the Russian interior generally and to students at Russian schools. There seems to be little evidence, however, that the travelers' provisions were actually enforced. The same provisions were again incorporated in the revised law of 1835.[60]

In 1840, Wolf Tugendhold offered his view to his fellow maskilim in Vilna that the Jews' habits of dress were a source of needless suspicion and hostility between Christians and Jews, and he urged that Jewish dress be made to conform to the prevailing non-Jewish norms.[61] Shmuel Yosef Fuenn stressed the same point in a letter to Bezalel Stern:

> Anyone with eyes to see knows that the first source of estrangement and hostility between the Jews and the Christians of our land is the difference in dress, in that the Jew is not willing to alter his clothing. Because he is so different-looking wherever he goes, the gap between the Jew and the Christian grows ever wider in the heart of each one. Therefore, before the government takes any [other] step in our favor, it is fitting that we should raise this matter [and suggest] that . . . the government . . . order this barrier removed.[62]

Tugendhold, Fuenn, and their fellow maskilim were stirred into activity by the call earlier that year to the Jewish communities to present their views on changes to be initiated in the government's Jewry policy. Representations by the Jews were to be made to the governors-general and transmitted to the new ministerial committee on the "fundamental transformation of the Jews" under Count Kiselev.[63] At the discussion held in Vilna later that year, involving maskilim from the Lithuanian and White Russian provinces under the Vilna governor-general's jurisdiction, the crusade against "Polish" dress was officially launched.[64]

The ministerial committee adopted a plan in 1842 that envisaged a general tax on all Jews wishing to continue wearing "Jewish" clothing. The plan, not made public at the time, was approved by the tsar early in 1843 and was slated to go into effect after more substantive measures were taken (establishment of the Jewish crown schools and abolition of the kahal). Objections were raised, however, by the Orthodox members of Uvarov's Rabbinical Conference—then beginning its deliberations in St. Petersburg—who were apprised of the state's intent.[65]

Benjamin Mandelstamm—in a letter to Bezalel Stern (a member of the conference) at that time—urged particular vigilance in standing firm against outlandish Jewish customs, dress in particular.[66] A campaign to thwart Orthodox opposition, apparently at the prodding of Uvarov, produced a petition signed by twenty-three prominent Vilna maskilim in mid-1843.[67] According to Fuenn's testimony:

> They composed their words skillfully and sent them to the government, stating that it would be a good thing for the state and would not violate the Jews' religion to roll away this heavy burden of shame. . . . And the benevolent government saw the merit of their words and resolved to abolish all visible differences between the Jews' clothing and their neighbors'.[68]

The traditional majority viewed the matter in a very different light, as Fuenn and his colleagues well knew.[69] Moisei Berlin, the "learned Jew" for the Ministry of Internal Affairs, wrote in 1861 in his ethnographic study of Russian Jewry that older Jews in particular found it wrenching and horrible to contemplate any change in their customary apparel or appearance, though, he claimed, the younger generation found it less difficult.[70] This last was probably Berlin's way of putting a more favorable light on what was well known as the general Jewish attitude to the dress codes. The campaign waged by the maskilim to obtain an official ban against the old-style clothing and traditional headgear—even if much of their effort was made after the ministerial committee had made its own decision and obtained Nicholas's confirmation—was accurately perceived by Russia's Jews as an act of *malshinut.*

A purely maskilic scandal of the time took place at the end of 1867 when Avraham Uri Kovner, reaching desperate limits in his bitter feud with Alexander Zederbaum, the editor of *Ha-Melitz,* submitted a denunciation to the New Russia governor-general that named Zederbaum and his paper as subversive purveyors of disguised obscurantism.[71]

In later years, there was a greater tendency among maskilim to eschew denunciation as an illegitimate and counterproductive weapon. In 1873, for example, Judah Leib Gordon warned the pro-maskilic preacher, Zvi-Hirsh Dainov (see later discussion), not to denounce to the authorities those who harassed and threatened him. "Keep your self-control," he counseled, "and do not take your anger before the high officials, for why should [our opponents] say that Dainov has become an entrapper and an informer!"[72] Still, Gordon had not been quite as fastidious in his own conduct. As late as 1870, when he became the target of criticism in the Orthodox *Ha-Levanon,* Gordon wrote to a friend in St. Petersburg suggesting that the influence of the OPE (headed by Baron Günzberg) be exerted to lobby for a ban on the sale of *Ha-Levanon* in Russia.[73]

Similarly, Ilya G. Orshanskii advocated such methods as closing print shops, administrative pressure, and legislative action to curb the influence of the Hasidic rebbes. He was, however, sharply criticized by the liberal editor of *Evreiskaia biblioteka,* Adolf Landau, who argued the ineffectiveness and illegitimacy of police methods in matters of religious conscience.[74]

Indeed, this was the conviction of certain observers even at a much earlier date. Avraham Yaakov Bruk of Ekaterinoslav (now Dnepropetrovsk) wrote in 1865 that although there were some rabbis who exploited the ignorance of the people, the government ought not to force its will upon these "sowers of folly." Bruk continued, " 'Not by might nor by power' can folly be rooted out from this land, but only by the spirit of wisdom and understanding."[75]

Apart from the new-found freedom that state patronage granted the maskilim in their relations with the traditionalist majority (a point Stanislawski has made so forcefully), recourse to the state's political power placed the maskilim in a strategic intermediary position. In the scheme of the traditional Jewish political order, it was this position, held jointly by the informer, the kahal, and the shtadlan, that conferred power and influence. Although their bid to conquer the communities (through the government rabbis and crown seminaries) was to prove ineffective, the maskilim were more successful at establishing themselves in the role of shtadlan. This is an aspect of the maskilim–state nexus that virtually all historians have largely ignored, preferring to stress the coercive thrust of maskilic politics.

In the past, this was dictated by ideological reasons, with nationalist historians portraying the post-Haskalah era as a rejection of everything the maskilim stood for, which included the virtues of enlightened absolutism and what the nationalists viewed as assimilationism. Today, in laying aside this ideological baggage, the historian is obliged to take a more balanced view.

The Maskil as Shtadlan

Duality was the chief characteristic of the political role played by the maskilim. On the one hand, they openly challenged the hegemony of the traditional communal and rabbinical leadership and hoped for state intervention to tip the scales in their favor. On the other, their knowledge of worldly matters and European languages enabled them to function as apologists for Judaism and Jewish society.

The adoption of the role of shtadlan by intellectual figures involved an important transmutation of the part. The traditional intercessor worked closely with his community. As we have seen, the Russian maskil operated in an altogether different climate: His emergence as a political figure was conditioned by the breakdown of routine mechanisms of policymaking and collective representation. The old-style shtadlan, in addition, specialized in discretion. He submitted petitions and documents, when necessary, for circulation within a particular bureaucratic or judicial apparatus. The maskilic apologist, although he may have sometimes engaged in this sort of activity, was above all a literary polemicist. Moreover, as an apologist who was also a radical critic, he occupied an anomalous position, and it was therefore important for him to address both a Jewish and a gentile audience in carrying out his public relations mission. Here, again, he departed from the older shtadlan prototype that had involved no internal appeal to the community.

This phenomenon of the dual message may be seen in the Hebrew versions of maskilic apologetic literature that, from the beginning, accompanied or preceded their Russian versions. The pamphlet that Lev Nevakhovich wrote in 1803, "The Lament of the Daughter of Judea," is a case in point.

Nevakhovich argues in the standard European Enlightenment fashion for religious tolerance as the only means of transcending medieval barbarism. He chides Christians for being untrue to their own faith when they continue to hate Jews, and he stoutly maintains that any faltering in civic or moral virtue among Jews individually is a relic of the past that can only be overcome by granting to the Jews a dignified place in society.[76] In his effusive expressions of patriotic appreciation of Russia and its benevolent, enlightened rulers, the author clearly wants to be seen by the sophisticated Russian reader as an exemplar of what all Jews might be, once freed from the burden of gentile hostility.[77] Judaism itself, he proclaims, trains the Jew to be a model citizen: "The Israelite law is not opposed to any civil order or form of government. . . . In the book of *Avot* the Jews are enjoined to pray for the welfare of the state. Our rabbis taught: 'the law of the kingdom is law,' and we are forbidden to violate customs regulations and the like. And the adherents of this upright faith are themselves upright."[78]

In republishing "The Lament" in Hebrew, however, Nevakhovich had the chance to turn his message around and, with his face now toward his fellow Jews, to argue that enlightened culture, civic virtue, and love of country are what all Jews should take as their ideals. In Hebrew, the passages about the disastrous effects of religious prejudice and insularity resonate with a double meaning. It is not only the gentile who must learn to overcome the narrowmindedness of the past.

It was in his introduction to the Hebrew reader, finally, that Nevakhovich revealed his sense of mission as his people's champion. "Perhaps," he stated, "it was God, who has ever been my guide, who has brought me here so that I might be a defender of my people."[79] Further, he enunciates the view that this duty is his by virtue of his ability "to speak for the remnant of Israel before kings and princes"—a traditional formula associated with shtadlanut—and that, indeed, such is the obligation of anyone in his position.[80] Here we have, in its simplest form, the credo of the maskil-shtadlan. It is not his position of trust in the community (Nevakhovich had none), but his education alone that makes public service incumbent upon him. It is not a commission, but a calling. Thus, the peripheral and alienated figure, condemned as a rebel by most Jews, could turn a liability into an asset and claim a legitimate place in the Jewish community.[81]

Nevakhovich's position was adopted by the father of Russian Haskalah, Isaac Ber Levinsohn. Unlike Nevakhovich, however, who enjoyed the patronage of the Zeitlin household and of Neta Notkin,[82] Levinsohn was a more backstage figure. Whereas Nevakhovich played in St. Petersburg to Russian bureaucrats and ministers and eventually became a Russian writer, Levinsohn remained in the provinces, did not venture far into Russian culture, and died almost penniless. Nevertheless his correspondence with key figures in Jewish political life and with Russian officials made him one of the most widely acknowledged personalities of the Russian Haskalah.[83]

Levinsohn addressed a Jewish audience primarily, especially in his programmatic *Te'uda beyisrael,* in his larger opus, *Beit yehuda,*[84] and in *Zerubavel* (Odessa: 1863/Warsaw: 1875),[85] but he himself conceived of

the works as serving a dual purpose, and they were written with a view
toward their eventual translation as apologetic works into Polish and
Russian.[86] *Zerubavel* in particular deals extensively with Jewish–gentile
relations and was written primarily as an apologetic tract. *Beit yehuda,*
which is an account of Judaism from the age of the patriarchs down to
Levinsohn's own day, briefly discusses such themes as moral obligations
toward non-Jews and touches on the blood-libel issue,[87] but it is more
concerned with giving a general picture of Judaism from an enlightened
Jew's point of view—a setting straight of the historical record, as it were,
rather than a specific defense or polemic.

In 1852, Lipmann Seltzer wrote to Levinsohn and asked him for a
précis of his major works on Judaism. Seltzer wished to publish, in
Russian, a simplified explanation of the Jewish religion (with the stress
on defending the Jews) but leaving out the historical and scholarly apparatus of Levinsohn's own oeuvre.[88] Similarly, Litman Feigin (one of the
few Jewish grandees to render practical support to Levinsohn's work)
saw him as an important apologist-propagandist and wrote to him in
1834, bringing him up to date on the latest efforts to resolve the Velizh
ritual murder affair.[89] Levinsohn apparently also corresponded with Jacob Tugendhold, the Jewish censor in Warsaw, while the latter was
working on his Polish translation of Menasseh b. Israel's apologetic tract
Vindiciae Judaeorum.[90]

Levinsohn himself wrote to Leon Mandelstamm about the twelve years
of work that he put into *Zerubavel* in order to produce a comprehensive
and definitive defense of Judaism in general and of the Talmud in particular, "I doubt that a single vicious charge against the Talmud and our faith
which our enemies have ever made . . . escaped my notice as I wrote this
book. . . . You know, sir, that the book *Netivot 'olam*[91] . . . contains
every calumny, leaving nothing out. . . . And so I chose to refute it
specifically, working for many years."[92]

That Levinsohn, who died early in 1860, attached to his work as
defender of the Jews an importance equal to that of his labors on behalf
of Jewish Enlightenment is also evident in the epitaph that he composed
for himself:

> With the enemies of God
> Have I engaged in battle,
> With words, not weapons of iron.
> The innocence of Jeshurun
> Have I revealed to the nations,
> Bear witness, *Zerubavel* and *Efes damim.*[93]

In addition to *Beit yehuda* and *Zerubavel,* which actually comprise one extended project, Levinsohn wrote a sharply polemical refutation of an anti-Jewish tract, *Derekh selula* by the Jewish renegade-turned-missionary Asher Temkin (published in Hebrew and Russian in St. Petersburg in 1835); it remained in manuscript until 1881.[94] Levinsohn's *Efes damim,* a refutation of the ritual murder accusation, was written in 1833 and published in 1837.[95]

It is in *Efes damim* that Levinsohn permits us to look more closely at his own view of Jewish politics in his day. We note, first, that the work was commissioned by unnamed rabbis and notables of Lithuania and White Russia, who presumably turned to Levinsohn because of his erudition and polemical skills but who failed in the end to provide the promised financial support.[96] This experience left Levinsohn understandably critical of the prevailing standards of public spiritedness in Russian Jewry—a failing that he attributed to the psychological habits of self-interest inbred by generations of business activity.[97]

The failure of the traditional leadership to take proper responsibility is what prompts Levinsohn to take the lead himself. Adopting as his motto R. Hillel's dictum in *Avot* 2:5, he states, "I have endeavored to be a man in a place where there are no men."[98] Although, as we have seen, Russian Jewry was not quite bereft of spokesmen and leaders at this stage, there was enough disorder and lack of coordination to justify Levinsohn's claims, if only in part.

He takes one step further and lectures to the would-be leaders of the community on the fine points of successful public relations work. Thus, in anticipation of a book in German by Marcus Jost, along similar lines to his own, Levinsohn counsels them on how to proceed with the greatest dispatch in obtaining a copy for translation and for censors' approval. "You should also," he coaches them, "approach our mighty lord, the emperor . . . Nicholas I, and request his permission to dedicate the book to him in Israel's name." In general, he urges that in all manner of activity in defense of the Jewish people it is well worth seeking the advice and support of the government, which wishes the Jews only the best.[99]

Here we see Levinsohn incorporating the internal half of the maskilic dual message in a special address to his Jewish readers and offering the tactical expertise of a "professional," which is clearly the view he took of himself.

Others took a similar view, and he was approached on several occasions with requests for his personal intervention with government authorities. In 1836–37 in the wake of the oppressive censorship law (that he himself had played a role in bringing about), three communities sent urgent messages to Levinsohn asking his help in softening the blow.[100] Common to these appeals was the depiction of Levinsohn as a man of extraordinary ability and influence—this may be partly attributed to flattery, partly to a real perception of the "sage of Kremenets" as a formidable force in public matters (however exaggerated the perception may have been). Two of the letters describe Levinsohn with formulaic attributes reserved for shtadlanim, "[S]peaking before kings and princes . . . an advocate for the good of the Jews . . . [you] have the ability to stand in the palace."[101] The third appeal, from Dubno, offers to supply him with a formal power of attorney if necessary.[102] All three express confidence in his powers of persuasion, his love for his people, and his access to the highest state authorities—and all express willingness to abide by his advice and by the word of the tsar.

In 1840, the rabbi and the kahal of Brest Litovsk sent Levinsohn an urgent message requesting him to draft a petition on their behalf to secure a reprieve from the expulsion order that was to take effect the following year.[103]

R. Yitzhak-Ayzik of Vilna turned to Levinsohn in 1856 as the only one who might help avert a major crisis over the Vilna rabbinical seminary. As a leader of the Vilna community, he had been asked to plead for Levinsohn's intervention with the government: both to defend the community against charges that it was obstinately and unjustifiably seeking to sabotage the seminary and to bring about some radical changes at the school, which in general had a bad reputation from a religious and educational point of view.[104]

Levinsohn's somewhat surprising involvement in public affairs—surprising in view of his backwoods location, lack of financial means, and ill health—is explainable only as a deliberate effort to make the promotion of the modernization and well-being of Russian Jewry the pivot of his life. His philosophical works and literary activity were meant, first and foremost, to serve this purpose. If he did not achieve the establishment of an institutional structure for Russian maskilim, his assertion of the leadership role as the proper function of the maskil was significant in and of itself.

Moreover, Levinsohn's involvement in shtadlanut, unlike that of Nevakhovich, was not an isolated phenomenon. During the period from 1830 to 1860, the same role was undertaken by a variety of other maskilim. For example, while Levinsohn was writing *Yemin tsidkati* in 1836, an otherwise unknown maskil from Pinsk, Reuven Holdhor, composed and published (in Vilna) his own rejoinder to Temkin's *Derekh selula*.

Like Temkin's bilingual tract, Holdhor's *Divrei shalom veemet/Slova mira i pravdy* was issued in a parallel Hebrew and Russian text; thus it was meant to address two audiences. For the Russian reader, Holdhor's quotations from biblical and rabbinic literature affirming the Jews' duty to love their fellowmen, to obey the law of the land, to deal honestly and fairly with Jew and non-Jew alike, and to loyally serve their gentile ruler were meant to demonstrate the misleading character of Temkin's contrary citations. The Jewish reader, reading between the lines of the Hebrew version, was bound to see a sermon on the need for Jews to live up to the ideal image being presented.

More strictly apologetic works in this period were published by the Tugendhold brothers: Jacob's translation of Menasseh b. Israel's *Vindiciae Judaeorum,* 1831, and Wolf's novella *Der Denunziant,* 1833 (see chap. 3, n. 22).

Probably one of the best-known single works of Jewish defense in the period before the 1870s was Daniel Khwolson's refutation of the blood libel.[105] Khwolson converted to Christianity in 1855 in order to become a professor of oriental studies at St. Petersburg University, but he remained actively involved in Jewish affairs.

Another maskil-turned-convert who devoted considerable effort to Jewish defense was the Kiev (later Warsaw) censor, Vladimir Feodorov. Feodorov, born Hirsh Grinboym in a small Volhynian town near Kremenets, had studied in Dubno and in Kiev (at the university), where he converted after being turned down for a post in one of the planned crown schools for Jews.[106] He maintained his links with Russian maskilim however (Gottlober, Levinsohn, Leon Mandelstamm among them), and in 1846 he submitted for publication a Russian translation of the Talmudic tractate *Sanhedrin.* His introduction, entitled "On the Talmud and Its Significance," was a vigorous defense of a much-maligned work. His manuscript was not approved by the censor, however, and the essay was not published until 1871.[107] In 1847, he wrote of his motives for embarking on the project in a letter to I. B. Levinsohn:

> Many [Christians] believe [of the Talmud] that it is the quintessence of wickedness and corruption. . . . [But] in my heart I remember it as the first book of my youth. . . . [So I determined] to refute all the slanders that have been cast upon it and to publish in Russian translation at least one tractate. . . . And I thought it beneficial, as well, to offer some of my thoughts on the Talmud as a whole, in a separate essay . . . [where] I expound on its great value for [understanding] the Torah of Moses. I hope that both Jews and Christians will read it and exclaim: "What a treasure we have discovered!" . . . There are some Jews who do not understand

what I have done for them. The fools believe me to have become one of those who speak ill of them to the authorities, God forbid! I am after all one of them, and if in spirit I am today a Christian, in my flesh I am still a Hebrew, and how can I look upon their pain [indifferently]?[108]

Feodorov also wrote a Hebrew translation of Mendelssohn's *Jerusalem* that was published in 1876.[109]

Another maskilic defense of the Talmud, written in response to an attack that appeared in the Russian newspaper *Den',* was published by Moisei Berlin, the "learned Jew" at the Ministry of Internal Affairs. Berlin's essay is polemical, rich in sarcasm, and focuses on the errors and contradictions in the anti-Talmudic diatribe.[110]

Gottlober used the opportunity of Alexander II's succession to the throne to interweave apologetic passages into the odes he presented to the new tsar in 1856. Of the Jewish people, Gottlober said:

> As faithful as they are to God and their
> fathers' Law, so are they to the king, and
> keep his laws.
> For in going forth into Exile they were commanded
> to seek the peace of the country
> to which they were driven,
> even to shed their blood for it, if required.
>
>   . . . . .
> The heart of this people is faithful
> to God and His annointed one:
> With all their heart and soul
> they love their king.[111]

The poem, a eulogy for Nicholas I, was published along with two others in 1858 in a single volume dedicated to the new tsar. This was a major public relations project whose sponsors (over one hundred locally prominent Jews) were led by Yozel Günzburg. Isaac Ber Levinsohn provided a letter extolling the work (a maskilic version of the traditional rabbinic approbation). The volume of Hebrew verse was accompanied by a section in German and by the letter of appreciation that Gottlober received (in the tsar's name) from the director of the Volhynia schools district.[112]

The occasion of the coronation of a new tsar was a vital opportunity, Eliezer Silbermann (publisher of *Ha-Maggid*) urged in his sixth issue in January 1857. Noting the fine example set by the Jews of Prussia, who recently celebrated their king's brother's jubilee, he proposed that each major community in Russia forward to him a brief but esthetic composition in the tsar's honor. He would print these in book form so that Russian Jewry might present Alexander with an album, to be entitled *Minha tehora* (*Pure*—i.e., perfect—*Offering*), representing the entire community.[113] As was the case with Levinsohn in his preface to *Efes damim*, Silbermann acts here as expert political counselor and would-be national spokesman.

Indeed, one important function of maskilic literature in this period was the promotion of the unique talents of maskilim as shtadlanim and of the need for a new style in defense activity. In 1836, Mordecai Aaron Günzburg translated into Hebrew Philo's *Embassy to Gaius* (from the German version of 1783 [Leipzig]), the Alexandrian sage's account of a classic act of shtadlanut. Günzburg published it, not as an outward-directed effort in apologetics, but out of his desire to acquaint Jewish readers with it and to promote the values that he found it represented:

> The world's great thinkers, always ready to accept what is good [worth learning] from any man, regardless of his nation, have taken this work to heart and translated it into all the languages of Europe. Only we, the people to whom this author [Philo] does such credit and on whose behalf he so concerned himself, only we have failed to immortalize the book. . . . And I, out of love for my people and veneration of great sages, have translated his words into pure Hebrew to the best of my ability.[114]

Günzburg emphasizes Philo's combination of philosophical and religious erudition as the primary factor in his ability as a spokesman and polemicist. He notes that Philo was the first to defend the Jews against the blood libel (a reference to the book's immediate relevance to Russian Jews).[115] Philo wrote his work in Greek, Günzberg declares, because it was the scholarly language of his day, known even among the early rabbis—a broad hint about the advantage and propriety of Jewish education in German in the nineteenth-century context, to which the traditionalists were opposed. Philo, then, is to be taken as the ideal maskil: imbued with love for his people and capable of defending them with reason, worldly knowledge, rhetorical skill, and the personal stature that comes with great wisdom.[116]

The use of well-reasoned argument to defeat the Jews' enemies is a theme to which Günzburg returned in his account of the Damascus blood-libel affair of 1840: "Our foes come against us with force, and we fortify our position with truth. They wage an offensive battle and we, a defensive one."[117]

But Günzburg goes further, mocking Eastern Europe's Jews for their unworldliness and criticizing their criteria for recognizing leadership and bestowing prestige. He compares them unfavorably with the West European Jewish aristocracy, whom he admires as the practitioners of a new political approach.

In responding to the crisis, he writes, the Jews had no weapons to use but their voices, but this resource was put to a very different use in different communities:

> Those who dwell in Poland, unaccustomed to the ways of the world, whose strength lies in the synagogues and who look to God for salvation, proclaimed a fast, a day of wailing and mourning, and left their brothers to heaven's judgment. More than this was done by our brothers in Germany, whose strength is in wise speech. . . . They made a commotion in all the newspapers . . . and [those who had rejoiced at the news from Damascus] were astonished to see that the Jews no longer, as they had of old, took their shame quietly . . . [nor] did they turn the other cheek, but rather took up a pen with an able hand.[118]

The greatest credit, however, belonged to the leaders of French and especially British Jewry, who used their political leverage with their governments, crossed a sea, and negotiated with the sultan.[119] The lessons to be learned from their example, Günzburg states, are that, first, wealth alone is no protection or basis for respect: Only its effective use, as demonstrated by Moses Montefiore in this case, determines its value. Second, wisdom, too, should not be honored for itself alone, automatically conferring status on its possessor, but for how it is put to practical use when the necessity arises (citing here Adlophe Crémieux's role in saving the Jews of Damascus). These two attributes, wealth and learning, the traditional bases for prestige and leadership in Jewish society, are no longer sufficient. Concomitant courage and practical decisive action are needed to make these attributes worthy of admiration.[120]

Günzburg's blast at Russian-Polish Jewry's political impotence and his fairly explicit attack on the nature of the prevailing leadership—the rabbis and notables—of his community is one of the earliest examples of the maskilic critique of traditional Jewish politics.

The idea that a new class of leaders imbued with modern enlightened views ought to take its place at the head of Jewish society also emerges in maskilic Yiddish fiction of the period. Chone Shmeruk has remarked on the penchant of quite a few maskilic writers for introducing a character named Mordecai-Marcus as a positive hero. This character is the embodiment of secular enlightenment, an affluent merchant and man of the world, generally on very good terms with the non-Jewish authorities. As such, he is the source of great benefit to the backward Jews around him. This character represents a maskilic rehabilitation of the buffoon-type Mordecai of eighteenth-century burlesques of the Esther story. The biblical Mordecai, the archetypical court Jew, is the basis for the positive Mordecai-Marcus convention of nineteenth-century Yiddish literature.[121] Thus, Mordecai-Marcus, whose knowledge of gentile languages and entrée to those in power enables him to serve his community, is made a natural and legitimate leader.

That the maskil's aptitudes and worldview were more likely to predispose him, rather than his less enlightened brethren, to play a beneficial public role is also the point of a savagely satirical Yiddish fable, "The Deputies" (*"Di deputatn"*) by Avraham Gottlober. In Aesopian fashion, he pits the clever fox—the maskil—against the uncouth, half-educated, and inept deputies of the kahal (Gottlober's word) of domestic and forest animals, who fail miserably to represent their community in an audience with the imperial lion—the tsar.[122] The clear implication is that the articulate, worldly fox would have been the only logical choice for deputy (shtadlan).

The fable was probably composed in the 1830s or 1840s.[123] It is not clear whether Gottlober had a particular incident in mind or was generally lampooning the traditional shtadlan in a period in which Jewish political activity was at a low ebb. What is certain, however, is that Gottlober was not only suggesting that the maskil was Jewry's ablest mouthpiece but was also asserting that his own role as a writer included the function of political pundit and critic. These roles were later to be institutionalized in the maskilic press.

The emergence of the maskilim as a significant political force in the Jewish community was predicated on, and was a reflection of, the fragmentation of a national community into local units and multiple sociocultural enclaves. Its political potential was similarly fragmented through the diffusion of political roles: rabbis, notables, "learned Jews," and maskilic informers-cum-intercessors. There were many who claimed to speak on behalf of the Jews but there were few, if any, whose word carried universal authority within the community; none enjoyed the exclusive patronage of the state. The need for a national leadership remained acute, even though no formal mechanism existed for the accreditation of such leaders.

The political activities of the maskilim should be seen as one aspect of this general situation. The communities, though powerless to prevent them from sending off memoranda and reform proposals to government ministries, were at times able to regard them as useful and influential propagandists for Israel's good name.

For the maskilim themselves, the defense of the Jews' human dignity was a way in which they could declare their unequivocal affinity to their community while allowing them scope to promote the values of enlightened religious tolerance, the importance of learning the language of the land and earning the trust of the state. In short, these activities gave them an opportunity to air their conviction that both Jews and non-Jews must come to regard Russian Jewry as an integral part of Russian society. Their political activities were the factor that transformed them from literati to public figures.

5

Toward Political Reconstruction: Russian Maskilim and the Modernization of Jewish Politics

Institutional Clusters (1850s–1870s)

Obtaining positions of influence in Jewish affairs through intervening between the state and the Jewish community was only one step along the road to maskilic power. The next step consisted of the establishment of an institutional base; however, because the maskilim were divided among themselves (along lines of generation, education, social position, personal antagonisms, and degree of religious conservatism), no single base could emerge. Instead, we should speak of several institutional clusters that served overlapping parts of the maskilic sector of the population.

The first cluster to be established was that of the crown schools (1844) and rabbinical seminaries (in Vilna and Zhitomir, 1847), whose importance Stanislawski, in particular, has emphasized.[1] Indeed, the argument that the state schools led to the development of a critical mass of maskilim and provided them with a secure source of livelihood (until the 1870s at any rate) lies at the heart of Stanislawski's thesis that, "[T]he most important accomplishment of the new school system . . . was its essential contribution to the institutionalization and consolidation of the Haskalah" and that "we can date the emergence of a coherent Russian-Jewish intelligentsia to the latter part of the rule of Nicholas I."[2]

The school system was a creation of the government, although it was paid for out of the candle tax imposed on the Jewish communities and, strictly speaking, could not have functioned had it not been for the cooperation and willing participation of the maskilim. One may say that is was the latters' greatest (and last) success in using the political techniques, inherited from the Jewish tradition of communal politics, of capitalizing on state tutelage.

By the 1860s, however, maskilim were among the strongest critics of the seminaries and the crown schools, believing them for various reasons to be woefully inadequate for the purpose of what they called "true" Haskalah. The official rabbi of Minsk, Zalkind Minor, to cite but one among many disenchanted maskilim, complained in his 1864 report on the crown school in his city that it could be "seven times" more effective were its Polish headmaster replaced by an educated Jew and some of its undertrained, overzealous, and tactless Jewish teachers replaced as well.[3]

The crown schools and seminaries were admittedly significant in the social and intellectual development of the Russian Haskalah and in the absorption of Jewish students into Russian gymnasia and universities.[4] Their role in the process of political development among the maskilim, however, was very quickly overshadowed by that of two other institutional clusters: the Society for Promoting Enlightenment Among Jews in Russia (OPE), founded in 1863,[5] and the maskilic press, dating from the founding of *Ha-Maggid* in 1856.

The significance of these two institutional bases, from the point of view of political development, lay in the fact that they were autonomous from state tutelage, that is, they played no administrative role in Jewrystate relations (though they were, of course, subject to licensing procedures and, in the case of the press, censorship controls). Indeed, with the partial exception of the Hasidic community's development as a relatively compartmentalized, semiautonomous society involved only minimally with the Russian state, the maskilic institutions of the late 1850s and early 1860s were the first Jewish public bodies to be neither associated with the kahal nor directly under the state's aegis. Although, as we shall see, the press carried on the already-established maskilic attitudes toward the tsar and the government and although the OPE, with Baron Günzburg as its chief patron, was widely perceived as a vehicle for traditional shtadlanut, both the press and the Haskalah lobby represented structural innovations in Jewish politics. In the end, it was the press that pioneered a reorientation toward a new focus of legitimacy and, by implication, authority: public opinion and the people. The OPE, pursuing liberalization through conservative methods and largely ineffective in its forays into political affairs, was nevertheless perceived by many Jews as a new center of gravity in Jewish–state relations. It became a central address in what had been an amorphous system at least since the demise of the deputies at the end of Alexander I's reign, and increasingly so ever since the state began the steps leading to the abolition of the kahal.

These innovations were not attributable solely to Jewish initiative, however. In withdrawing from the support of corporate Jewish communal institutions, the state itself helped to create the structural space in which new forms of Jewish political activity might grow—without the benefits of derivative power, but also without its burdens.

The OPE

The Society for Promoting Enlightenment Among Jews in Russia— whose license was approved by the Internal Affairs Ministry on the Enlightenment Ministry's recommendation on 2 October 1863—was formed by a committee of twenty-one "patrons and dignitaries."[6] The notables predominated on the OPE board that was chosen in December: Joseph (Yozel) Günzburg, chairman; Abraham Brodskii, "elder"; Yehuda Leon Rosenthal, treasurer; Horace Günzburg, first vice-chairman. The list of original "distinguished members," however, was a "who's who" of Russian maskilim: Haim Leib Katzenellenbogen of Vilna; Zalkind Minor of Minsk; Dr. Abraham Neumann, rabbi of St. Petersburg (formerly of Riga); Osip Rabinovich, editor of the short-lived Odessa *Razsvet* (1860–61); Haim Selig Slonimskii, headmaster of the Zhitomir rabbinical seminary, scholar of natural science, and publisher of the then-dormant *Ha-Zefirah;* Shmuel Yosef Fuenn of Vilna, publisher of *Ha-Karmel;* Professor Daniel Khwolson, the orientalist; Alexander Zederbaum, publisher of *Ha-Melitz;* and Dr. Simeon Schwabacher, the German rabbi of Odessa.[7]

By the end of its first year, the OPE had 175 members, but it remained a relatively small organization. From 1865 to 1875, membership oscillated between a low of 226 (in 1869–70) and a high of 294 (in 1875). From 1878 to 1880, membership increased significantly, reaching 349 in 1879 and jumping to 552 in 1880.[8]

The chief task of the society was the material support of worthy projects (books, libraries, schools, scholarships for university and professional education, and stipends for teachers, among others).[9] In twenty years (1864–84), the OPE spent 310,000 rubles: 11.5 percent went for subsidizing the publication and distribution of books, Bibles, and journals; 9.7 percent for "temporary assistance," loans, and teachers' pensions; 18.2 percent for the support of higher education (including rabbinical schools); 2.7 percent for higher and professional education for women; and 38.1 percent in unitemized grants by Horace Günzburg and Leon Rosenthal, representing funds contributed by them.[10]

The function of the society was primarily that of an educational foundation, according to the preamble to its bylaws and judging by its budget. From the very beginning of its career, however, it was understood to serve two other purposes as well: that of maskilic pressure group and that of anti-defamation or defense agency for the Russian Jewish community. Leon Rosenthal stated to the board at its second session, in December 1863, that a two-front battle had to be waged in order to rehabilitate the Jewish community. One campaign was to be an open struggle against external foes, to refute their accusations against Jews. The second was a quieter, gradual struggle of persuasion to be waged within the community in order to win the hearts and minds of the traditionalist opponents of change.[11]

Several months later, Judah Leib Gordon wrote to the board, "Experience has shown that individual persons have no hope of victory in their struggle with the masses of people who cling to prejudice and superstition. It is necessary to join all the individual forces together into one [central force]."[12]

The OPE board, meeting in February 1864, found a direct connection to exist between the internal tasks of Jewish Enlightenment and the external situation of the Jews. Particular note was taken of the legal disabilities and residence restrictions that made Enlightenment an issue in Russia, in contrast to the West where emancipated Jewries took for granted such matters as secular schooling and speaking the language of their country.[13]

However, the OPE said nothing of this in a petition it submitted at that time to the Ministry of National Enlightenment. The petition merely urged the government to continue to support the Jewish crown school system and noted the OPE's opposition to the rumored intention of abolishing the tax on candles imposed twenty years earlier on the Jewish communities. The tax, the OPE argued, remained essential.[14]

A year later, the OPE had still not translated its perception of the link between Enlightenment and emancipation into a political initiative. The sense of the board's discussion in 1864 was that the general legal disabilities—particularly the restriction of Jewish residence to areas where the majority of the non-Jews were themselves not Russian speakers—lay at the heart of Jewish social and linguistic exclusiveness. Yet what the OPE asked for in April 1865 was not the amelioration of these conditions, but a permit to publish a Russian translation of the Bible in order to bring Russian into Jewish homes.[15]

The OPE seemed ill at ease with the idea of fulfilling a broader function as a chief bureau for shtadlanut, yet this is precisely the way in which it was perceived.

In January 1864, Haim Selig Slonimskii wrote to the board asking it to obtain for him a special license to continue publishing *Ha-Ẓefirah.* Having taken up the post of inspector (headmaster) of the Zhitomir rabbinical seminary, where his duties also included the censorship of Jewish books and newspapers, he had had to cease publication of his own newspaper. He hoped, with the OPE's influence, that he might be granted a special dispensation to renew his journalistic activity. The society, after a lengthy correspondence, finally told Slonimskii that such a matter lay outside its proper purview.[16]

Other maskilim who turned to the OPE during its first year of activity with requests for shtadlanut included Ilya G. Orshanskii, who had submitted a Russian translation of the Jewish prayer book to the Kiev censor for approval early in 1863. A year later, the matter was still being held up in the Ministry for Internal Affairs. Orshanskii himself could not manage a trip from his home in Ekaterinoslav to St. Petersburg and asked the OPE to intercede for him. The board proceeded cautiously, demanding to see samples of the work before acting for Orshanskii.[17]

In related matters Joachim Tarnopol' wrote to the board in June of that year asking it to verify the whereabouts of his manuscript of *Opyt sovremennoii osmotritel'noi reformy v oblasti iudaizma v rossii,* sent to the censors two years earlier. He asked the OPE to read the book and approach the censors on his behalf to secure a permit.[18]

Slonimskii, in another letter of that spring, urged the society to do what it could to obtain permission for a second Hebrew printing press in Zhitomir. Additional presses had already been approved for Vilna and Odessa, but in Zhitomir the traditionalist press, which refused to publish maskilic books, had thus far succeeded in thwarting would-be competitors.[19]

A group of Jewish merchants from Ekaterinoslav sent two letters to the OPE board in September 1864 asking it to intercede in their behalf. In their first request, the merchants noted that in New Russia, unlike the traditional areas of Jewish settlement, there was a serious dearth of Jewish domestics. They asked the board of the OPE to do something about their problem inasmuch as Jews were forbidden by law to have non-Jewish live-in domestic help. The Jews in general, and those of New Russia in particular, they claimed, could certainly be trusted not to seduce Christians away from their faith; moreover, the presence of Russian maids and nannies in Jewish homes would do a great deal to speed the process of linguistic Russification among Jews. In their second letter the Ekaterinoslav merchants asked the OPE's help in securing for the Jews the right to be elected mayor. Should not their contribution to commerce and industry go hand in hand with active participation in municipal affairs? The board responded, however, that neither of these matters was within its province.[20]

A plea arrived the next month from a Jew from the neighborhood of the Lithuanian city of Kovno, again approaching the OPE as an address for shtadlanut. It seemed that Jewish farmers in the area, who had been allowed to work parcels of state land for a trial period of ten years, were about to be evicted by the government. The Jews were heavily in debt and, the petitioner claimed, had received no help or supervision from the Jewish community. But now, he warned, the matter involved the good name of the Jewish people, and he asked the OPE to obtain a two- to three-year extension for the farmers.[21]

The following year, members of the OPE from Kishinev wrote to the board asking it to do what it could to obtain a relaxation of the laws barring most Jews from living within 50 versts of the border. The board declined to take any action on this.[22]

In 1866, however, a matter of very grave Jew-baiting in the official journal of the Vilna general-government, *Vilenskii vestnik,* brought tremendous pressure on the society to act. A series of letters written to the OPE board in May 1866, by members and nonmembers of the OPE alike, expressed indignation over the articles that had lately appeared in the *Vestnik*. All of the letters made the point that the case surely merited the attention of the OPE.[23]

A group from Vileike, for example, asked the OPE "to take counsel [on how] to remove this wickedness" and, in addition, enclosed a reply to the *Vestnik* that, they proposed, the OPE board use its influence to place in one of the Russian newspapers.[24]

The maskilim Yehuda Shereshevskii, M. Plungian, and Haim Leib Katzenellenbogen wrote a joint letter, expressing their alarm at the new editorial line of the Vilna paper. There was no telling where the incitement would lead, they warned, and pressed the OPE board "to remove these serpents from us."[25]

A group from Ponivezh urged that legal action be taken to have the editor of the *Vestnik* stopped. It noted that the OPE had been attacked in one of the offending articles, and it concluded: "Who else but the Society for Promoting Enlightenment, which is dedicated to the honor and the future of our people in Russia, can sally forth against these abominations?"[26] The group enclosed a detailed memorandum making its case against the editor of the *Vestnik,* and it asked the OPE to present the memorandum to the Minister of Internal Affairs in St. Petersburg. Similarly, a group representing "every shade of opinion in the Jewish community of Vilna" sent a brief against the *Vilenskii vestnik*—addressed to the Vilna governor-general—to the OPE.[27]

Shlomo Zalkind of Vilna, having written a long rebuttal of the *Vestnik*'s anti-Jewish incitement, sent it to Horace Günzburg, asking his advice on which Russian newspaper would be likely to accept the article for publication. "The eyes of all Vilna's Jews," he wrote, "are raised in hope to the board [of the OPE] and are desperately awaiting its help."[28]

In June, the OPE sent a letter of protest to the censorship authority at the Ministry of Internal Affairs, with a copy to the Vilna governor-general, Konstantin Petrovich von Kaufmann. The letter contended that the editor of the *Vilenskii vestnik* had violated the recently enacted law against inciting religious hatred and asked for an official disclaimer of government responsibility for the views expressed in the *Vestnik.* The OPE's standing in the case was explained by the fact that it stood for bringing Jews and non-Jews closer together—a desire shared by the government—and that the OPE's work of three years was being nullified by the hate-mongering editor of the Vilna newspaper.[29]

The OPE's status in the matter was rejected by the ministry, however. In its reply to the board of September 1866, the ministry contended that the OPE must limit itself to "promoting enlightenment among Jews," as stated in the society's bylaws. It further contended that: (a) anyone who was injured by slander in the press always had recourse, as individual Jews and individual members of the OPE, to the law courts; and that (b) the OPE had not presented convincing evidence to support its request for limiting the criticism of Jewish society in the press.[30]

The climate of hostility was underscored when von Kaufmann appointed Jacob Brafman, author of the *Vestnik* articles, to the post of censor (1866) and appointed a special commission to investigate Brafman's charges regarding the subversive character of the kahal and its secret existence. The battle against Brafman would be led by individual maskilim and, in 1869, by a coalition of maskilic and traditional leaders (see later discussion).[31]

The Jewish public continued, nonetheless, to approach the OPE as a national political body. In 1868, it was asked by a Jewish land surveyor to press the government to employ Jews in the capacity of state-appointed surveyors (i.e., as state officials). The OPE agreed to petition the government in this regard, but it was again rebuffed. A group of Jews in Minsk also asked the OPE to intervene in this matter, and the board agreed to "look into it."[32]

In 1872, the OPE issued a public appeal to "the people" and to the rabbis urging greater cooperation in the work of Enlightenment that was bound to lead to emancipation when the Jews were ready for it.[33] In response a number of moderate modernizers among the rabbinate urged the OPE to make respect for religious sensibilities an explicit part of its program and to seek permission for a rabbinical conference. Only in the latter framework, they argued, could a consensus be worked out for cooperation with the OPE.[34] This, however, the OPE was unwilling to support:

> The truth is that we do not see [such a conference] as the great hidden solution, nor do we foresee its successful conclusion. We know very well that many rabbis are not in agreement with these [rabbis who propose the conference]. . . . By convening such an assembly now, when the time is not ripe, a complete split and irreparable damage could result. . . . But even were we [to believe that a conference would be beneficial], we still would not be prepared to go before the tsar's officials with such a request, knowing in advance that there was not the slightest chance that the request would be granted.[35]

Later in 1873, however, Baron Günzburg allowed himself to be persuaded to engage in an effort to forestall the dismissal of all uncertified traditional *melamdim* (grade-school teachers) that was due to take effect in 1875. The campaign for a reprieve was originally set in motion by R. Isaac Elhanan Spector of Kovno and traditionalist figures in his circle. The Kovno group dispatched an emissary to canvass the major communities and elicit further rabbinical support. In Warsaw the emissary (Moshe Kaminetskii) met with R. Eliezer Simha Rabinowitz, rabbi of Suwałki, and R. Shmuel Mohilever of Radom. The latter effected a contact with Baron Wilhelm von Rothschild in Frankfurt am Main, who agreed to recommend to Baron Günzburg (then in Paris) that some intercession be carried out.[36]

Günzburg consented to return to St. Petersburg and to receive a delegation. Mohilever and Rabinowitz were sent to the capital, along with R. Yaakov Barit of Vilna, to meet him. Mohilever, however, seemed intent on a renewed effort to merge the efforts of the moderate rabbis and the moderate maskilim. He proposed a general school reform for the Jewish community that would reflect Jewish tradition and would place the entire effort in the hands of Jewish educators. At this point

Günzburg proposed that the whole matter be put into the hands of a subcommittee of the OPE that would include Drs. Abraham Neumann, Iosif Seiberling, and Abraham Harkavy.[37]

The traditionalists of Kovno, on the advice of R. Israel Salanter (then in Berlin), quickly moved to suspend any dealings with Günzburg and the OPE and wired to their three representatives to return at once to Kovno. (Mohilever, however, remained in the capital for some time.)[38] The involvement of the OPE in running the traditional religious schools was not what they had had in mind; they had hoped for a personal intercession by Günzburg. They apparently sought a loophole in the law whereby the schools would stay open and the *melamdim* employed, possibly by reconstituting all the schools as charity (*talmud tora*) schools.[39] However, this sleight-of-hand approach did not work with Günzburg, who may have seen in Mohilever's reform plan an opening through which the OPE might finally make a substantial impact on the majority of the Jewish population.

That the OPE was less than successful during the late 1860s and early 1870s is reflected in its stagnant membership roster, which declined from 277 in 1865 to 226 in 1870, reaching its 1865 level again only in 1872. Expenditures also remained modest in these years, reflecting a slow pace of activity. By 1873, the society had amassed a total of 120,182 rubles, but had spent only 95,535.[40] In its report for 1873, reflecting ten years of activity, the OPE was forced to admit that it had experienced some setbacks. Though funding was not a problem, the report explained, public indifference to the society and resistance to its aims were preventing the implementation of its program.[41]

Given its disappointing record, it was only natural that by the 1870s it became the object of criticism in liberal maskilic circles. Judah Leib Gordon, who was soon to accept the post of OPE secretary, wrote privately to Zvi-Hirsh Dainov in 1870 that he had "lost all confidence in the capabilities of the committee [the OPE board] and all its endeavors; experience has taught me two or three times already that we should not entertain very great expectations of it."[42] Public criticism of the notables was a late stage in the development of the Haskalah. When it did come, it was expressed in the maskilic press.

The Maskilic Press: Social Function and Political Process

The roles of informer and shtadlan that the Russian maskilim adopted and transformed were played by those who stood on the outer margins of Jewish society. Their contact with gentile authority gave them the leverage that made them the political equals of the kahal and rabbinic elite.

There was a third element in Jewish society that stood in a secondary position vis-à-vis the highest communal leadership but whose role was entirely internal: the preachers and writers of ethical (*musar*) literature. It was to them that ordinary Jews looked for instruction, criticism, and entertainment. They functioned not only as educators but as social critics and interpreters of the Jewish ethical tradition. Whether itinerant or salaried, their position in the community was sometimes precarious.[43]

In considering how nineteenth-century maskilim adapted traditional roles to new sociopolitical conditions, it is worth noting that the art of preaching—particularly in the literary mode—was added to the repertoire of Russian Haskalah in its earliest formative stages. In the field of musar literature, there were several authors of the late eighteenth century who, as transitional figures, incorporated maskilic messages into their works.

Judah b. Mordecai Hurwitz of Vilna, for example, author of the musar book *Tsel ma'alot* (1764–65), was a Western-educated doctor, a correspondent of Moses Mendelssohn's, and an admirer of the Berlin maskil, Naftali Hirsch (Herz) Wessely.[44]

Another native of Vilna, Pinehas-Elijah b. Meir Hurwitz, was the author of a unique compendium, *Sefer haberit* (Brünn: 1807), combining kabbalist philosophy, popular science, and ethical preaching.[45] Apart from the scientific sections of what was intended as an encyclopedic work, this book had several other protomaskilic features. Hurwitz included, for example, the following notice (on the verso of his title page):

> Every reference in this book to idolaters, to foreigners or to the gentile nations is meant to apply only to actual idolaters, worshipping the stars, fire, water or the moon, and the like (such as the people of India, China and Japan). Very different are the peoples among whom we dwell . . . who believe in divine providence and God's revelation, even if they do not observe all its laws, because they are not commanded [by God] to do so. . . . We are obligated to pray for their welfare, as it is written . . . in Jeremiah 29, and thus have we been adjured by the sages of the Talmud (*Avot* 3): "Pray for the peace of the kingdom."[46]

Although this may have typified the approach of certain traditional scholars of the early modern period,[47] Hurwitz elaborated on the theme of tolerance ("love of fellow men") in a less traditional, rather humanist, fashion, and also interspersed arguments drawing on a utilitarian/social-contract perspective rather than on rabbinic dicta. It was this introduction of authoritative argumentation from nonrabbinic discourse in addition to his tone of liberal optimism about social progress that stamps the work as protomaskilic:

> All of Creation was meant for the sake of the entire human species and for its benefit. . . . Therefore [we] and all men should love one another in the common bond of humankind, all of society [*hakahal*] living under one law—for foreigner and citizen alike—and strive to benefit one another through our labor and commerce. . . . All nations have given their bond, and the kings have together determined to keep the covenant of peace and brotherhood of all mankind . . . and they will create one unity, one society, and in it we too will be rehabilitated.[48]

These were themes that Russia maskilim incorporated in their writings. Indeed, they sometimes preserved some of the forms and conventions of the ethical guide and infused it with modern content. The most famous and an early example was Mendl Lefin Satanower's *Ḥeshbon hanefesh*. A popular work, it was later to become influential even outside maskilic circles, and it had its imitators.[49] Menahem Bendetsohn, a Vilna maskil (who translated Wolf Tugendhold's *Der Denunziant* into Hebrew), was the author of a maskilic musar book, *Higayon la'itim* (*Timely Thoughts*). He discusses all aspects of social ethics from the Jewish point of view, not forgetting to instruct his readers on "the duties of the man of Israel toward his ruler."[50]

A similar book—in the form of chapters on philosophical and ethical precepts—was written by Joshua Steinberg, who served as government rabbi in Vilna in the early 1860s and taught Hebrew and Aramaic in the rabbinical seminary in the latter part of the decade in addition to serving as censor.[51] His section on the Jews' civic duties, entitled "Love of Motherland," includes the following typically maskilic statements:

> It is the sacred duty of each member of society to freely and sincerely fulfill his obligations to the civil order, to obey the law of the king and his officials without any subterfuge or deception, for an oath to God is witness between [the citizen and the state]. This is a universally ordained order, established upon the holy mountain. . . . Hear me, my brothers, pay heed to the voice of the father of our country who calls to you with love and the compassion of a true father for his children. What does he ask of you but to learn to do the right thing, and to turn your faces, not your backs, to science and manufacture? . . . Your king, the annointed of God [*meshiaḥ elohim*] assures you of [your right to] your faith and the law and the just precepts of the Torah. Only be strong and become civilized people: Love your country with a pure heart, for you are its children equally with the other inhabitants.[52]

In this context, it is also of interest that Eliezer Zweifel, instructor in rabbinics at the Zhitomir rabbinical seminary, began his career as a tutor and a preacher.[53]

Finally, there is the case of the maverick preacher of Slutsk, Zvi-Hirsh Dainov, who in 1867 began to make Haskalah the central theme of his preaching. Dainov traveled up and down the Jewish Pale, from Vilna to Odessa, incurring the wrath of traditionalist audiences and winning the approval (and financial support) of maskilim and the OPE. He hoped for a special government appointment, with suitable emolument and immunity from popular hostility. Sometime after 1873, he left Russia and continued to preach in London until his death in 1877. His traditionalist origins, appearance, and preaching technique were judged by maskilim (Judah Leib Gordon in particular) as enormously effective with the Jewish masses.[54]

This perception should be taken with a certain skepticism, given Dainov's own testimony of his hostile reception by most nonmaskilic audiences. The true success of maskilic preaching was to come in a wholly new form: journalism. The emergence of the maskilic press would regularize and institutionalize the role of the maskil-as-preacher.

In the early summer of 1856, following the conclusion of the Crimean War, a rabbi and former *shohet* (kosher slaughterer) from White Russia, Eliezer Lipmann Silbermann, established Russia's first Jewish weekly newspaper, *Ha-Maggid*, on the Prussian side of the Lithuanian border. On its masthead, *Ha-Maggid* announced that it would "tell [the House of] Jacob of everything occurring in the world that touches them and that they need to know, for their benefit and for the benefit of the beautiful Hebrew tongue." *Ha-Maggid* (literally, the teller) was also the word commonly used for *preacher*.[55] *Ha-Maggid* was, therefore, not merely to speak but to teach and preach. In his third issue, Silbermann intoned the following prayer, worthy of any traditional preacher, "Look down from Your holy dwelling-place upon Your servant as he goes forth to serve Your people, the seed of Jacob . . . to show them the path [*derekh*]—the path of civilization [*derekh erets*]—on which they should walk . . . in humble awe of You and of their king, seeking the welfare of their country and its inhabitants."[56]

Indeed, not only *Ha-Maggid* but the rest of the maskilic press as well (in Hebrew, Yiddish, and Russian) was to see one of its main functions as that of didactic mission. Eleven years after the founding of *Ha-Maggid* and seven years after the establishment of *Ha-Melitz* and *Ha-Karmel* (and the short-lived *Razsvet* [1860–61]), Haim Jonah Gurland still used explicit references to education and to the terms *metif* and *mokhiah* (preacher), to refer to the work done by the three Hebrew weeklies.[57] Alexander Zederbaum, publisher of the Hebrew *Ha-Melitz,* the Yiddish *Kol mevasser,* and the Russian *Vestnik russkikh evreev,* explained that in publishing his journals he had "shouldered the burden of being a preacher [*metif*]" to the Jewish people.[58]

Within their overall commitment to the propagation of Enlightenment values, each journal pursued its own characteristic course, often disagreeing violently with the policies of its rivals. *Ha-Maggid* was moderate in tone, muting its criticism of Jewish social and religious life (until 1868), whereas *Ha-Melitz* (and the Odessa *Razsvet*) tended to be more militant.

Adherence to a policy of discretion earned Silbermann some enemies in the maskilic camp as early as 1859, before competitors had begun to publish. These "jealous people," in the time-honored fashion, had complained to the Ministry of National Enlightenment that *Ha-Maggid* was ineffectual and bland and thus unlikely to justify the ministry's support.[59] Silbermann, in equally traditional fashion, asked Yaakov Gurland, the ministry's *uchonyi evrei,* to act as his shtadlan. The latter, indeed, succeeded in retrieving *Ha-Maggid's* good name. In thanking Gurland for his efforts, Silbermann explained his editorial strategy of avoiding the use of fiery polemics and satire in terms of a calculated method of gradually persuading the majority of the readership to accept the value of secular knowledge alongside religious education and piety:

> [I]f it [*Ha-Maggid*] doesn't trumpet the Haskalah with every breath, if it doesn't mock and poke fun at the things it doesn't agree with, if it doesn't smash and destroy in the heat of anger—then that is to its credit. . . . [It] speaks to its brothers as one of them . . . opening the hearts of young and old alike to love of Torah and [worldly] wisdom together, and to love of king and country.[60]

Silbermann was astute enough to know that newspapers could be a force for social dislocation, even if they also brought a great many benefits to modern society. He was uncommonly aware of his awesome responsibilty as a willing tool of the knowledge revolution, an idea he expressed in an editorial in February 1860:

> The growth of publications and the number of writers has become limitless, and has turned man into a new creature. This revolution in man's intellectual horizons is, on the one hand, very good. . . . [B]ut good also has by-products that are not good. Today we learn and teach only by the written word. . . . [W]e amuse ourselves [with literature]. . . . [W]e make speeches [from written texts]. In all of this, there is little living spirit, no

true dialogue, only lifeless letters. . . . The old, with their knowledge
gained by experience, are no longer respected by the young, whose reading has allowed them to surpass their elders. . . . They have all the phrases
at their fingertips when they speak in public, regardless of how profoundly
they understand what they say. . . . We have literally become "men of
letters" ["*Buchstabmenschen*"].[61]

His perception of the popularity of the press and of the fairly traditional bent of many in the public whom he addressed in his journal is
borne out by the recollections of Yaakov Halevi Lifschitz, who was to
become one of the more militant Orthodox activists, secretary to R.
Isaac Elhanan Spector, and advocate of Orthodox journalism. In 1856,
Lifschitz lived in the Lithuanian town of Vilkomir, where groups of four
persons would chip in and buy a joint subscription to *Ha-Maggid*. There
were about thirty such groups in the town, and he was one of the most
enthusiastic readers of the paper.[62] Later, in a different town, he himself
had to organize a group to buy a subscription, and special arrangements
were made with a carter (there being no regular mail service in the town)
to deliver *Ha-Maggid*. After the opening of a post office in 1860, he also
became a subscriber to Shmuel Yosef Fuenn's *Ha-Karmel*.[63]

Lifschitz testifies that, after the Crimean War, people became accus-
tomed to the idea of reading the news, and it became a social need. He
attributed the successful growth in the maskilim's prestige and influence
to the press, a tool that they seemed best able to exploit. "The power of
the expanding journals literature enabled the freethinking maskilim . . .
to implant the seed of their ideas, to stand before the young generation
and present themselves as Israel's wise men, heroes of the spirit and
leaders of the nation."[64] Lifschitz clearly perceived the link between the
didactic character of the press—preaching a new Torah—and the leadership role in the community to which the maskilim aspired.

It was in pursuit of national leadership that the publishers and writers of the maskilic press combined the didactic function of their work
with the externally oriented function of shtadlan-apologist. The Odessa
newspapers in particular were very conscious of this aspect of their
work, having been founded in 1860 on the heels of a pogrom in that
city.[65] *Razsvet,* the first Russian-language maskilic newspaper, was established by Joachim Tarnopol' and Osip Rabinovich with the active
help of Lev Levanda. Tarnopol', in a letter to the Paris *Archives israélites,* explained the motives behind seeking to publish a Jewish periodi-
cal in Russian. Alongside factors related to Jewish social, cultural, and
educational development, Tarnopol' spoke of the external factor:
Those in Russian society who generally favored Jewish rehabilitation

and emancipation would welcome the chance to learn something of Judaism and Jewish history and literature. Those others who still unjustly accused the Jews as a group would have to be combated "with sober logic and the facts."[66]

Odessa's Hebrew newspaper, *Ha-Melitz,* established in 1860 by Alexander Zederbaum, was similarly intended as the Jewish community's spokesman. On its masthead *Ha-Melitz* (*The Mediator*) announced its purpose as mediating "between the Jewish people and the government, between religion and enlightenment."

But whereas *Ha-Melitz* could transmit to the Hebrew reader information and opinion regarding government policy and about Jewish communal, philanthropic, and educational activity, it could not truly speak for the Jews in the general Russian context, for the obvious reason. When the Hebrew *Ma-Melitz* responded to anti-Jewish claims with apologetics and refutations (see Table 4), the editor's righteous indignation or sermonic references to civic virtue and patriotism contained a hidden agenda: The maskilic claim for full-participant status in Russian society was being advanced in Hebrew in order to convince the Jewish reader, not the Russian.

Logic dictated that the shtadlan role be emphasized to a greater extent in *Razsvet* than in the Hebrew journals. A division-of-labor concept was indeed proposed in *Ha-Maggid* in the early spring of 1860 when *Razsvet*'s establishment was announced:

> There is no end to the benefit this will bring to all Israel. Israel now has a voice with which it can answer its slanderers, to show the inhabitants of this land [our] innocence and righteousness, and [our] true service to God, king and native land. And if the purpose of the Jewish journal . . . in Hebrew, apart from promoting the holy tongue, is to rouse [the Jews] to every good and useful social purpose, a journal in the language of the country should pave for the Jews a high road into the hearts of their countrymen.[67]

Table 4. Frequency of Articles Referring to Benevolent Tsar, Jewish Loyalty, Defensive Response, 1868–69 (100 issues)[a]

Journal	Tsar	Loyalty	Defense	Total
Ha-Maggid	12%	8%	4%	24%
Ha-Karmel[b]	10	6	12	28
Ha-Melitz	24	14	15	53

[a]Calculated by the author.

[b]Not including Russian supplement, for the sake of comparability.

In fact, however, Rabinovich's view of *Razsvet* was quite different. Although the battle for Jewish dignity and civic status was part of the paper's program, so was forthright self-criticism. After the paper's first issue, in which Lev Levanda made the backwardness of Russian Jewry the theme of a major article, a storm of protest broke over Rabinovich's head.[68] Leybush Glozberg, in *Ha-Maggid* of 11 July 1860, argued that the license to publish imposed certain obligations. The long period of Jewish silence preceding the emergence of *Razsvet* dictated that a set of priority issues should be addressed first, and foremost among these was the duty to give the lie to all the contempt that Russian writers had poured on the Jews. It was time to show the Jews' good points and argue for raising their civil status, not to speak sarcastically and critically of Jewish faults.[69]

Others noted that *Razsvet*'s tone seemed grating, even hostile, and lacking in sincere love and empathy for the Jews.[70] One writer criticized the extremists of both the traditionalist and modernist varieties, pleading (in vain) for a truce in the internecine struggle, "Let us fight under the banner of truth and peace for the sake of Torah and wisdom and the honor of the Jews: let not Jew strike his fellow Jew." He further proposed a national conference of rabbis and maskilim to work out a compromise policy.[71]

Joachim Tarnopol', Rabinovich's initial partner in publishing *Razsvet,* withdrew from the venture at the end of September 1860. In his letter explaining his own position, Tarnopol' stressed the duty of a Russian-language Jewish journal to defend the Jews and, when proposing reforms in Jewish life, to do so with care, forethought, and due regard for the principles of rabbinic Judaism.[72] Moshe Shvarts seemed to sum up the debate in a poem printed in the winter of 1860–61:

> How will the nations' kings look on us with grace
> If our own people's benefactors put us in disgrace?[73]

Razsvet managed to last a few months longer and then was forced to cease publication one year after it had begun.[74] The editorial policy of its successor, *Sion,* was oriented more toward defense, but *Sion* lasted only until 1862. Not until 1869 did Russian Jewry once again have a Russian-language newspaper (apart from the small Russian supplement to *Ha-Karmel*). During the years 1856–69, then, with the brief interlude of 1860–62, Jewish defense per se was undertaken mainly by maskilim writing in the general Russian journals and seconded in the Hebrew press.[75]

The need for a Jewish organ in Russian, primarily to answer anti-

Jewish polemics in the Russian press, was emphasized by H. J. Gurland in 1869, with the inauguration of the Odessa *Den':*

> A [Jewish] journal in the language of the country is required, not for us, but for our brothers the Christians and for the government. . . . Such a [Russian] newspaper must shoulder the responsibility of being a courageous spokesman and mediator between us and the king. It must show to one and all [the character of] our spirit and our abilities. Through it we must protest vehemently against those who make us appear hateful and contemptible. There we can fight our battles for our Torah and our religion.[76]

Similarly, when Zederbaum and Aaron Goldenblum (Zederbaum's son-in-law and colleague at *Ha-Melitz*) were about to establish their Russian newspaper, *Vestnik russkikh evreev,* Zederbaum described it as "a defender against all who speak ill of us."[77] "Most of all," he wrote, it would "give our brothers the Russians . . . a true and faithful conception of the nature of Russian Jewry, the spirit of Judaism and the root-principles of Jewish nationhood, so that they may understand and make a correct evaluation of us."[78]

Zederbaum, of all the Jewish publicists, was considered by many—himself first of all—to be the shtadlan par excellence in the maskilic community. While en route to St. Petersburg in 1869 to seek a license for *Vestnik russkikh evreev,* Zederbaum stopped in Kovno for a month-long visit. Yaakov Lifschitz described his reception by the Lithuanian maskilim as being worthy of Montefiore himself.[79] His conduct, indeed, seemed like that of a national dignitary, and even R. Isaac Elhanan Spector was "obliged" (Lifschitz's word) to pay court to the Odessa publisher. Spector and his Orthodox entourage asked him to discontinue publishing articles on matters of religious reform; he, in turn, posed a series of questions about the rabbis' authority and conduct, in the manner of an inquisitor. According to Lifschitz's account, Zederbaum then said to them:

> Know this! I go "to stand before kings" [a formula for *shtadlanut*], and when I enter the ministries and offices of high officials and priests of the churches, they invariably debate with me on matters of religion. That is why I raise these questions in [my] newspaper, so that these matters will be clarified and I will know how to give proper replies to the officials.[80]

Added credence for this account of Zederbaum's posture comes from a letter he wrote to R. Isaac Elhanan in 1870. Zederbaum was reacting to a critical and (Zederbaum believed) derogatory article that Judah Halevi Lifschitz, one of the participants in a debate with Zederbaum in Kovno, had published.[81] Zederbaum's response shows us that he took his role as publisher-spokesman-leader very seriously indeed. He did not, he told Spector, wish to add further fuel to the fire by continuing the polemic. But, on the other hand:

> I have a duty to protect my honor [just as a king is not free in Jewish law to allow his honor to be impugned, and rabbis are comparable to kings], for although I am neither king nor rabbi, I am in a way a bit of both. The king has devolved some of his authority upon me in making me a publisher in Israel, and many rabbis have put their trust in me and found me worthy [*samkhu beyadai,* literally, laid their hands upon mine, the terminology of ordination] . . . and I therefore find reason to doubt that I am at liberty to forgive the violation of my honor. . . . [It being before Yom Kippur, he is willing to allow Lifschitz to make an apology.] It is a sacred obligation [in this season] to make peace even with private individuals whom one has wronged, and this applies all the more to the reconciliation of the congregation of Israel with its spokesman [*melits*].[82]

Turning to the actual record of the maskilic journals in the area of public relations, we note again that between 1856 and 1869 this task was mainly in the hands of the Hebrew press, with the obvious limitations entailed for its effectiveness. The *Razsvet* episode of 1860–61 was generally considered to be a failure. After 1869, with the publication of the Odessa *Den'* (1869–71) and Zederbaum's *Vestnik* in St. Petersburg (1871–73), a more vigorous defense was waged.

The entire approach was a modern one, in both style and substance, in that it was based on the assumption that defense was a matter of rational argumentation and on the axiom that an appeal to justice was its own justification. Moreover, as we saw in the case of Zederbaum, the role of public defender was presumed to confer leadership status.

The stark contrast between this approach and the more traditional one is brought out in the introduction to the Orthodox pamphlet, *Milḥama beshalom*. The author of this antimaskilic broadside considered the question of whether a defense of Judaism ought to be written in Hebrew or Russian. Although the goal of self-defense would seem to dictate writing in Russian, nevertheless, he chooses to do so in Hebrew for various reasons. Most important for our discussion are the following points:

> I know that I go forth for the sake of the sons of Jacob, this small and unfortunate people. I do not go out as a warrior who tries to provoke his enemies on the day of battle. For who would presume to challenge—even if only with words—those who are stronger than himself? And how should those who [like ourselves] are "strangers and sojourners" in the land of a strange people presume to show arrogance [by criticizing] the lords and

inhabitants of the country? . . . Perhaps there is a [good] reason that lies deep in the hearts of our people's sages, that prompts them to keep their tongues still rather than answer all those who attack us . . . just as Moses said to the children of Israel when Pharoah pursued them: "The Lord will battle for you—you hold your peace." And if so, why should anyone say of me: See the boor play leader! Who appointed him to do battle for us? . . . Perhaps, too, my abilities as advocate will be inadequate and instead of defending my people I will inadvertently provide more weapons to our foes.[83]

The maskilim acted in each case precisely on the opposite assumption of every caveat expressed here. This was certainly so with regard to the Russian-language papers, whose entire logic was diametrically opposed to the thinking of *Milḥama beshalom*. It was equally true of the Hebrew press, where the question of Russian language did not apply, but the other issues did: the Jews' native status in Russia, the value of defensive polemic, and the legitimacy—even preeminence—of the self-appointed spokesman. In each case, the maskilim resolved the issue with a positive answer.

As we have seen, the assumption of the role of guide, pundit, and teacher was characteristic of the maskilic writers. "Who would raise himself up to be a teacher to the general public?" Fuenn asked rhetorically, "[A]nd who would presume to offer [advice] that has not been required of him? . . . [But] we have been *summoned* to make our best endeavor, to honor our obligation as far as we are able, and we are 'not free to desist' from [this labor]."[84] Surveying the two themes of "the maskil-as-leader" and "the press-as-teacher or guide" in *Ha-Maggid, Ha-Karmel,* and *Ha-Melitz* (for 1868–69), we find that they appeared in 10 to 18 percent of the issues published (Table 5).

Explicit or implicit apologetics–polemics were incorporated under three headings or themes: praise or appreciation of Alexander II as a benevolent, enlightened ruler; the Jews' loyalty to the state and obedience to its laws; and refutations of specific charges leveled against Jews.

Table 5. Frequency of Appearance of Articles Referring to Maskil-Leader or Press-Guide, 1868–69 (100 issues)[a]

Ha-Maggid	18%
Ha-Karmel	10
Ha-Melitz	15

[a]Calculated by the author.

Table 6. Varying Frequencies in *Ha-Maggid* for Themes of Benevolent Tsar, Jewish Loyalty, Defensive Response, 1856–60 and 1863–67

	Tsar	Loyalty	Defense	Total
1856–60[a]	22.0%	12.4%	13.3%	48%
	(n = 50)	(n = 28)	(n = 30)	
1863–67[b]	24.0%[c]	11.6%	8.0%	43.6%
	(n = 60)	(n = 29)	(n = 20)	

[a]Total number of issues surveyed, 225.

[b]Total number 250.

[c]This theme was emphasized especially in the wake of the attempt on Alexander II's life in April 1866.

Taking the period of 1868–69, the pattern emerging in the three journals can be seen in Table 4. Finally, surveying *Ha-Maggid*'s development over a longer course of time, we observe the trends shown in Table 6. With the exception of the outpouring of pro-Alexander sentiment in 1866, the emphasis on these themes in the early years of *Ha-Maggid* declined in later years (taking the figure for 1868–69 into account as well). By contrast, in *Ha-Melitz* these themes were still very prominent in the late 1860s.

The Press as an Arena of Conflict

Even more than in its function of apologist, or shtadlan, the role of the press in reformulating the parameters of internal conflict demonstrates its innovative impact on Jewish politics. As we noted at the outset, the maskilic press was primarily conceived as a didactic tool. Fuenn put it succinctly in his first issue for 1868, "It is not a matter of reporting what has occurred, but of teaching what must be done."[85] Transmitting information was always a secondary purpose, if that. The central purpose was persuasion and, in the nature of that kind of endeavor, those in need of persuasion were those who took a different view.

Moreover, the persuaders themselves differed with each other over tactics, pace, the limits of what was desirable or practical, and so on. Although one may say that it was the editor–publisher who sat as supreme judge, selecting certain pieces for publication and adding editorial comment to articles or correspondents' reports, in truth, he was only an intermediary. Once the type was set, the arguments for or against had to stand on their own merits in the eyes of the final arbiter: the reader. The opinion of the editor was important; the verdict of the reading public, however, was the *raison d'être* of the entire journalistic enterprise. This remained essentially true even when true debate gave way to authoritative pronouncements by editor–preachers.

The assumption that underlay the maskilic commitment to rational debate was that the result of the debate could not be predetermined. A political arena for conflict was thus created in which different parties might form, but in which recourse to any authority outside the circle of writers-editors-readers was strictly against the rules. Avraham Uri Kovner's denunciation to the authorities of Zederbaum and *Ha-Melitz* was an aberration in this respect, and one that had no serious consequences.[86] Much more indicative was the case of the Odessa *Razsvet,* which staked out a position that proved untenable within the liberal Jewish public's bounds of tolerance and, thus, failed politically even before it ceased publication. Similarly indicative was the feud between *Ha-Maggid* and *Ha-Karmel* that, despite Silbermann's fears, never went beyond polemics.[87]

Formal recognition of the sovereignty of public opinion was expressed by Silbermann in his first issue for 1863, in which he introduced the term *da'at hakahal* (literally, the public's opinion). Public opinion, he asserts, was the main force shaping modern, enlightened civilization.[88] Just as he had earlier pointed to the groundswell of public protest over the forced baptism of a Jewish child in Italy (the Mortara affair) as ultimately signifying more than the act of intolerance itself, so now he asserted that the power of the collective consciousness was greater than that of armies or fortifications.[89] "[T]he rulers [of nations] say: The voice of the people is the voice of God in our time [i.e., *vox populi vox Dei*]. . . . This public opinion is always in favor of the weak and the victim. . . . [A]ll eyes look to it in hope. . . . Not only nations, but also kings strive to win the people's favor if they want their policies to succeed.[90]

Silbermann heeded his own principles. In 1869, he ran a series of major opinion pieces (February to May) that offered various analyses of the crisis affecting Russian Jewry along with various (sometimes conflicting) proposals for action.[91] After presenting these to his readers, Silbermann contributed his own analysis of the situation and asked the readers to consider all opinions and to choose what seemed best: "Perhaps together we can succeed in carrying something out."[92]

The moderate modernist (and future nationalist) R. Yehiel Mikhl Pines wrote to the Vilna *Ha-Karmel* about the principle of public debate: "I have seen how necessary *Ha-Karmel* is, for in truth, without it we in Lithuania would have no vehicle for expressing the public opinion [*da'at hakahal*] through which we must discuss and weigh honestly, forthrightly and without partiality, civic and political questions."[93]

Debate implied conflict, and *Ha-Karmel* expressly approved of it: Although distressing to the desire for unity, it was also a sign of health and growth. Conflict indicated that leaders and scholars were aware that there were problems requiring solutions—challenges to be met. On the whole this was better than apathy, smugness, and paralysis. "These battles . . . for the sake of principle testify to the spirit of life that animates both parties to the controversy . . . and this is the sign that they also grasp the essence of life . . . that, after all, lies in change and motion, the replacement of one outward form by another."[94]

Zederbaum struck a remarkably similar note (adding Darwinian overtones): Controversy was a sign of health, as all nature and society required conflict and motion to reinforce their better qualities. Inertia and suppressing conflict through cultural isolation meant extinguishing the spark of life:

> As long as [two sides] confront each other out of their natural and inner points of view, attempting to prove the truth of their position through the evidence of reason, and do not pervert [the terms of conflict] by abusing their power and dictating [to the other], then this is beneficial to the group, reviving and revitalizing its health and strength so that it may go on living forever. . . . This battle is what helped the nation of Israel to survive to this very day. . . . [W]e see today that in the enlightened countries . . . the spirit of battle has been revived among our brothers who are of differing opinions . . . , the two camps having chosen equal weapons— words and the pen—to wage the war of change with each other. We who watch from afar . . . see in this only the life-spirit in the heart of the community.[95]

The political reorientation implicit in this notion of conflict—one in which no final authority is vested in either the state or the rabbis— cannot be overstated. It was not missed by Yaakov Lifschitz, who gives us the view from the traditionalist standpoint, recalling the period before the 1860s:

> In those days the Torah alone was still the only nationality we had. . . . The rabbis wore the crown of Torah and spoke to the people through the communal leaders who were at one with [the rabbis'] thoughts, so that Torah [learning] and distinction [social status] went hand in hand . . . , leading the people according to the national spirit, the Torah. The people at large were disciplined, pious and humble . . . and did not presume to speak their minds in public, questioning the thoughts of the leaders. . . . Then it was as yet unheard of to pay heed to the opinion of the crowd in the name of "public opinion" and internal disputes were brought before God, through those who were great in Torah, the sages, who were the ones to pronounce judgment.[96]

The revolutionary character of what the press had wrought lay precisely in the authority now vested in the "voice of the people." In analyzing the differences between the Jewish political tradition and modern democracy, Bernard Susser has explained that

> [i]ndispensable for the genuine sovereignty of popular will is its ability to be critical of the present, to consider alternatives. . . . To this end the protection of free speech, thought, communication . . . —those prerogatives that prevent the experience of the past, the weight of precedent and tradition, the authority of founders and lawgivers from congealing into a reified state and crushing the sovereign popular will—is a *conditio sine qua non.* . . . Those rights preserving a substantial "public space" for the sovereignty of human will over the force of law and institutions are therefore preconditions for the open-mindedness of the democratic life.[97]

In Russian Jewish political development, it is precisely the "public space" for conflict without coercion and for open-ended debate that was achieved through the maskilic press of the 1860s and 1870s.

In Search of Political Community

By the 1870s the maskilim had begun to alter the basic forms of Jewish politics. They had established institutions that were autonomous of state tutelage and had introduced a new point of orientation—"the voice of the people." In consequence, the forms of internal conflict that in the state-oriented kahal system had gravitated toward state intervention were beginning to lose importance and were being replaced by a wholly internal form of competition and conflict based on weapons of persuasion. By this time, as well, the maskilim were emerging from their deep alienation and isolation and, at least in their own self-perception, asserted a leadership role in the national community. In 1872, Lev Levanda wrote:

> Twenty, thirty years ago it was the rabbis, the scholars, the "clergy," who stood at the head of our nation, watching over our national interests to the extent of their capability and understanding. Now these leaders are departing the stage. The new age, with its new demands, is passing the reins of leadership to us, the younger generation. . . . A great and sacred mission has been given to us: to transform, reeducate our coreligionists, to set them on the high road to walk hand in hand with all humanity. We must be the rabbis, teachers, writers and intellectuals.[98]

This consciousness of leadership, however much it might have been challenged by the traditionalists, rested partly on the public activity of maskilim ever since the 1840s and partly on the development of their institutional base since the early 1860s. But it also rested on their accurate perception of the diffuse and *ad hoc* character of Jewish communal leadership in Russia that they saw as a manifestation of chaos and apathy and to which, they came to believe, they possessed the solution. From Levinsohn to Levanda, they looked at Russian Jewry and said: Here there are no men; therefore we must strive to be men.

Although Levanda stressed the intellectual leadership of the younger generation (i.e., the maskilim), his reference to safeguarding Jewish national interests made political and intellectual leadership virtually synonymous. The identification of the maskil with national leadership is certainly at the heart of Judah Leib Gordon's 1879 poem, "Tsidkiyahu beveit hapekudot" ("King Zedekiah Imprisoned"). Gordon here portrays the last biblical king of Judea as a religious skeptic, a patriot, a pragmatist, and a rationalist—in other words, a maskil—and contrasts him with Jeremiah.[99] In this biblicized reworking of the contemporary struggle for hegemony between the maskilim and the rabbis, Gordon states:

> For from the very first day of this nation's life
> and ever after, a battle has raged
> between men of government and men of Torah.[100]

Indeed, Gordon's depiction of an ongoing debate between the various types of leaders—notables, maskilim, and rabbis—is closer to the truth than Levanda's bold assertion of national responsibility, for the rabbinical and lay leadership of the communities still exerted a wider authority in the 1870s than did the maskilim. It was out of their own frustration as would-be leaders that they simultaneously condemned the existing non-maskilic elites, exhorted them to action, and castigated the disunity of the Jews in the face of pressing social and economic problems. Out of these theme of Israel as a captainless ship, some of the maskilim developed a modern ideology of national politics.

The Communal Crisis

In 1842, Max Lilienthal issued his call to Russian Jewry, *Maggid yeshu'a,* in which he put the case for voluntary Jewish cooperation with Uvarov's education policy.[101] Lilienthal's argument in favor of a conference of rabbis that would meet with Uvarov and second his plans with proper enthusiasm, ran as follows:

> And if you say . . . [,] "We remain in all things faithful to God, even when we are sorely pressed . . . [because] we know the day of final judgment is coming and life eternal, we fear God and avoid sin"—well and good, my

brothers, but who else knows this? Who speaks for us and who takes up our cause? Where are the men who can stop the mouths of our adversaries? . . . Yes, we live in love and humility, charity and compassion, but who brings our case before the powerful ones [i.e., the government]? . . . There is not one person to speak for his people, and we hear only accusations, degrading our honor and soiling our dignity in the eyes of the peoples. . . . How, then, shall you not rejoice at the chance to stand before the king and the princes to speak for the sake of your people . . . to sit in council with the high officials . . . ?[102]

Whereas Lilienthal couched the renewal of Jewish representation in terms of the rise of spokesmen out of the community itself, Avraham Gottlober saw Lilienthal himself as the people's "shepherd" and "father":

May you be the father to the children of Israel until they have grown to manhood. . . . [F]or if you leave these sheep . . . who will care for [them] after you? . . . Oh God! Do not remove from us the crown of our glory! May Menahem [the comforter, i.e., Lilienthal's Hebrew name], restorer of our soul, grow old in peace [among us] and be our comforter! In his light we will walk confidently and never falter, he will lead us unerringly to life.[103]

If Mordecai Aaron Günzburg looked on Lilienthal with a more jaundiced eye, it was the lack of true leadership even among the maskilim themselves that formed the context of his complaint. His anger at Lilienthal was rooted in his belief that Lilienthal was, in fact, incapable of properly representing the maskilim, despite the efforts to prop him up as the savior of his people. In Günzburg's view the attributes of true leadership must include a deep understanding of the "needs of the people" and impeccable scholarly credentials as well as the ability to speak directly to the ministers of government. This combination of desiderata was still missing, and Lilienthal was certainly not the one to fulfill it.[104]

Abraham Mapu urged Joseph Günzburg to be the leader of his people and pointed to the distressing chaos and disunity in the community at the time of the Rabbinical Commission of 1857:

What sort of generation is it? It is a scourged generation upon which "God will not turn His countenance" [Lam. 4:16], both the older and the younger generations. That which one calls good, to the other is worse than bad. Now Jacob has been told: Choose yourselves people who will mediate between the nation and the government [i.e., the Rabbinical Commission]. But the man who is acceptable to one side is unacceptable to the other. Strife and contention prevail. The adversary, hatred, walks between them and cuts them in two. And where there are wounds there is spilled blood, for there are those who find a quiet way to defame their opponents in the ears of the powerful [i.e., the government]. . . . The breach grows ever wider.[105]

It is in this situation that Baron Günzburg is described by Mapu as the "staff of Judah" (the Jews' leader) whom "God has called in this generation."[106]

Eliezer Silbermann urged the rabbis in 1857 to take up the slack reins of political initiative, arguing that the laity was incapable of it: "The one is occupied all the time with his business, the other pays lip service and nods his head."[107]

Avraham Gottlober returned to the theme of the shepherdless flock in the wake of the Lilienthal fiasco.[108] In early 1860 he wrote that the root cause of the Jews' degradation and low esteem in the government's eyes was their lack to true leaders. This, he argued, was the result of the decline of the rabbinate: "In the course of time the crown of Israel [the rabbis] fell and their wisdom was lost, they forgot that the rabbi's function is not merely to teach the people what to do but also to stand at their side and defend them, be their voice to the government. . . . Who will now demand justice [from those who do us evil], who will fight our cause and deliver judgment for us? There is no one to answer."[109] Therefore, Gottlober concluded, the Jews must rejoice at the government's policy of training rabbis who would speak Russian (i.e., in the Vilna and Zhitomir seminaries) and, in addition to their learning, would "be the voice of their flock and [would] raise their people's honor."[110]

As we saw in his satire of the "Deputies," Gottlober had no time for the traditional lay leadership of the communities and considered it inept and hopeless. He reiterated that idea in two other satiric poems, "Der seym" ("The Assembly") and "Di asifeh" ("The Meeting"). In "Der seym" Gottlober derides the kahal:

> Each one says he is the most able,
> and each wants to be in charge.
> But when it comes to trouble and to lean times,
> all of them are worthless.
> Each wants to be the *rosh* kahal [kahal chairman].
> Well and good, it's a fine title. . . .
> But what happens if an official should come to town?
> What does he do then, my fine *rosh* kahal?
> Woe to the community, he stands like a mute. . . .
> All he can do is bow and scrape. . . .
> And what good are conferences, what possible worth,
> when the conferees are like dumb brutes?[111]

In "Di asifeh," in a similar vein, he mocks the local town dignitaries for their ineptitude at organizing meetings.[112] It is against this background that his promotion of the maskilic government rabbis as spokesmen ought to be understood.

The community's lack of leadership and organization was implicitly laid at the door of the government's policy of restricting the kahal by Osip Rabinovich (editor of *Razsvet*) in 1860:

> In all the countries of Europe the Jewish communities have their own representation. In Germany it is called the *Vorstand,* in England it is the Board of Deputies, in France—the *consistoires* . . . in Italy, the presidents of the congregations and their deputies. . . . The absence of such institutions among us gives rise to disorder. If a question arises regarding the establishment of a philanthropic institution, who is to take the initiative? Not the town authorities responsible for taxes and conscription; not the synagogue board, limited to supervision of the synagogues . . . ; not the hospital supervisors, who are charged with the administration of existing institutions; and not the deputies chosen to oversee the meat tax. . . . These may turn to the authorities in matters of their specific jurisdiction, but are not empowered to speak for the community [*obshchestvo*] in any other matter. . . . [R]epresenting the entire Jewish community before the government in seeking some alleviation . . . or responding to official queries . . . on the basis of accurate knowledge, or reporting on the state of the community and its needs—this, too, is prevented for the same reason.[113]

As against this picture of a rudderless, helpless society, the depiction of the leadership role of maskilim took on quasimessianic proportions, as in the words of "P. L." of Warsaw in an article entitled "A Word for Our Time: Footsteps of the Messiah."[114] The messianic salvation promised by Scripture, he argued, was not a matter of restoring the nation to the Land of Israel but of its elevation to high station; and the saviors of the nation are those "within the congregation of Jacob" who act to achieve this. Among the "saviors" of the new age he lists the *Alliance israélite universelle* and "all the Jewish newspapers and their writers and supporters, who work in Hebrew among the Jews, and in the various languages of the other nations." To these he adds "the men of wise heart and courage who fight God's battles in debating their enemies" and the "protectors, those in high positions and wise in matters of state . . . such as that wise and just man among men, Dr. Khwolson of St. Petersburg."[115]

It was in 1868–69 that a major crisis provoked a new look at the arrangements for communal activity and leadership and a new wave of criticism that was to engulf even the hitherto universally admired notables.[116] In those two years famine struck Russia's northwestern provinces, the heart of the Jewish Pale of Settlement, and the number of

Jews who became poverty-stricken and dependent on communal charity increased out of all proportion to existing philanthropic arrangements.

Many maskilim saw the situation as a vindication of what they had been saying all along about the bankruptcy of traditional Jewish education, one that produced an overabundance of pious scholars and a dearth of marketable and productive skills.[117] Others, however, either combined this critique or replaced it with a sociopolitical analysis registering dissatisfaction over the state of Jewish civic consciousness and suggesting the establishment of more organized forms of collective activity for the public welfare. We may say, therefore, that 1868–69 was a landmark period in maskilic political development—a first crisis, with respect to the second, more dramatic crisis that would come in 1881.

The abysmal state of Jewish civic affairs was noted in the maskilic press in early 1868, even before the worst of the famine became apparent.

In February 1868 Fuenn wrote of his concern over the dwindling membership of the OPE. He attributed this to the lack of "public spirit" and concern for the general good among the Jews of Russia, "who have not yet learned what can be accomplished by joining forces." He noted with approval that in Odessa the leaders of the community were establishing new charitable societies. But he also lamented the unfortunate experience of Sh. Y. Abramovich and his colleagues in Berdichev, whose attempt to centralize all of the philanthropic work of their city under one roof body fell victim to what he saw as the community's lack of civic consciousness.[118]

He went on to locate the source of this failure. On the one hand, he found, the rabbis, "out of their love of Torah," limited themselves to a narrow range of religious instruction and supervision of ritual minutiae when, in fact, they had "a sacred obligation to watch over public affairs and to unite the hearts of the communal leaders."[119] On the other hand, it was not only the rabbis who were at fault but also "the highest leadership of the people." If the rabbis had in their favor the argument that their scholarship came first, "it is difficult to defend the leaders of the people, the communal chiefs, who are fully aware of the requirements of our time and the people's needs." The terrible silence of the communities in all matters of civil improvement and common efforts to adapt to modern times was merely "the calm before the storm." Yet instead of taking action in these pressing matters before the storm broke, the communal establishment was caught up in meaningless squabbles over personal prestige, the appointment of ritual slaughterers and the like.[120]

A far more scathing attack on the state of Jewish affairs in Fuenn's own city of Vilna was published at the same time by an anonymous correspondent in *Ha-Melitz*. The communal leadership of the city, he charged, was completely at the mercy of circumstance and whim. Those who wished to call themselves leaders did so uncontested. Changes in all sectors of communal activity were required, but the community was incapable of coordinating such an initiative. If pushed into action, the leadership might finally call a conference. This, however, invariably turned into a farce and nothing was accomplished. In reality one or two people continued to determine how things would be decided. Public charity was not properly organized at a time when Vilna was being overrun by the poor flocking in from surrounding areas.[121]

A second writer from Vilna continued in the same vein:

> Any honest person at all familiar with the affairs of the city, its leaders and its customs . . . knows that it is far indeed from either spiritual or material well-being . . . and no one has entered the breach to support the masses and restore the souls of the unfortunate. . . . Many of the city's dignitaries stop their ears to the cry of the daughter of Jerusalem. . . . All the charitable work they do is a facade, meant mainly to benefit their vanity. . . . [I]t is their fault that the recent call-up for military service turned into a fiasco . . . and that the deputation [to the Vilna investigatory commission under Governor-General von Kaufmann and his successor] is made up of only middle-level figures whose strength lies only in words . . . and have not the power to help the people.[122]

As the dimensions of the famine pushed most other issues to one side, both *Ha-Karmel* and *Ha-Maggid* stepped in to assert the power of the press. *Ha-Maggid* called for the establishment of local committees in each town, headed by trustworthy lay leaders and the rabbi, to transmit to *Ha-Maggid* the names of those requiring aid. Silbermann would then act, through a central committee for famine relief that he established, to funnel to the local leaders funds contributed by Jews from Western Europe.[123] This committee indeed disbursed funds throughout the period of the famine, but very few communities responded to Silbermann's effort to centralize all planning down to the grass roots level.[124]

Ha-Karmel, for its part, spearheaded the drive to convince the rabbis of Lithuania to ease certain food restrictions over Passover so that inflated wheat costs might be avoided.[125] Fuenn's efforts in this regard were partly rewarded in Vilna itself, though not in other towns.[126] He was embroiled in a controversy over the proper role of maskilim in rabbinic concerns. To his traditionalist critics Fuenn replied with a blanket justification for maskilic involvement in all aspects of Jewish life, including communal and religious affairs.[127]

Fuenn also proposed organizational steps to alleviate what he saw as the root causes of the spiraling poverty problem: overcrowding and a surplus of petty merchants, innkeepers, and small craftsmen. Resettlement of Jews on farmland offered by the government within the Pale and of artisans in the Russian interior (also as proposed by the government) could solve many problems over the long term, but this would require prodigious sums of money. He, therefore, called on the "leaders of the nation" to set up two public committess (under government license, of course) to take charge of these resettlement projects.[128]

The theme of uniting for effective action was echoed by many other writers. Long-term solutions, said Joshua Levinsohn of Jelgava (Mitau), for example, depended on rousing the community from its inexplicable torpor and turning it "into one united force."[129] The solution of organizing a coordinating body in each town or city in order to transcend the ineffectual local charity system was offered by Elijah Pollack of Minsk.[130] Yehiel Mikhl Pines, seconding Fuenn's proposals of the previous year, wrote in 1869 that it seemed "no surprise" that nothing had been done about them, "owing to the fact that Jews were typically difficult to rouse to do anything on a national scale [although] they willingly give money [individually] when asked to help the poor." He called on the Jewish leaders of Western Europe and on the rabbis to prod the Russian Jewish community into action.[131] Yaakov Halevi Lifschitz entered the fray, denying that the rabbis had any influence at all in public matters and arguing that the sole responsibility rested with the wealthy lay leaders.[132]

Ha-Maggid became an open forum during 1869 for proposals on improving the condition of Russian Jewry in which the respective obligations of the rabbis and the notables remained the focus of maskilic attention. One analyst ("M.B.I.A.") reiterated the idea that charitable feelings were not lacking, but that "a general inertia in all practical matters related to the national welfare exists among us." Most people were too involved in their own affairs to be able to consider the needs of their society, and they were lacking in the training and talent required for public activity. When there were people with such abilities, they often lacked wealth or status and were, therefore, disregarded. The rabbis wielded great authority in religious matters, but the lay leaders believed the rabbis had nothing to contribute when it came to social and practical affairs.[133]

The government, M.B.I.A. went on to say, had been ready to help in setting up Jewish farm colonies, but it had not been successful. Such an undertaking must be shouldered by the Jews themselves. "Who else could initiate this but the great ones of Israel whom the government respects?" The eyes of the community were on the "princes" of wealth and learning: Let them take an example from the French Jewish *Alliance* and the British Board of Deputies and petition the government for a license for such an organization for Russian Jews. The organization must be located in St. Petersburg, with branches throughout the country. Funds should be collected both in Russia and abroad. Once that would be done and a central, policy-making organization established, the solutions and their implementation would surely follow. The public would be able to air its views in the press and the machinery would be in place to make a reality out of serious proposals.[134]

The writer had confidence, then, that a restored political community—a centralized leadership, a supporting local structure and the organs of public debate—would do away with the root causes of public inertia and helplessness in the face of deep crises.

His position was given qualified support by Silbermann. He, indeed, asked the notables of the OPE why they had not yet applied for permission to constitute a public Jewish body to organize projects for social and economic rehabilitation and to take counsel together on the pressing problems of the day. They were obligated to speak for the Jews and secure for them the right to migrate to the interior of Russia.[135] But, he believed, M.B.I.A. was letting the rabbis off too easily and underestimating the importance of their cooperation:

All of our labors to improve the conditions of our brothers there [in Russia], and all the money that will be devoted to that purpose, will be in vain unless people arise from among them to take the first step toward necessary and beneficial reforms. . . . The rabbis must be the first to speak out, to carry along the rest of the community. . . . The rabbis must . . . gather in one place, such as Vilna, to confer . . . Like a pillar of fire they will go before the nation to light the path ahead.[136]

Not St. Petersburg, but Vilna, should be the cornerstone; and it was R. Israel Salanter, not Baron Günzburg, whom Silbermann singled out as the one man capable of leading the rabbis, and through them, the nation.[137] Silbermann thus remained true to his conviction that the social and political condition of Russian Jewry was primarily amenable to internal change through educational and religious reforms—the spiritual aspects of the crisis—where others had gone over to the view that political organization, a centralized leadership and planning, and the material aspect of the crisis were of prime importance.[138]

Isaac Margolies, then living in Kovno, wrote in the fall of 1869 to take issue with Silbermann on the question of the rabbinate's responsibility, but arrived at proposals fairly similar to those of Silbermann. He maintained that the rabbis had not the time, the influence, nor the resources to do anything for the public welfare at the national level. Indeed, the same applied to the local communities, sunk as they were in petty squabbles and acting as islands unto themselves. What was necessary were two things: a consistory or *sanhedrin* to shape the rabbinate into a force for leadership, both internally and in relations with the government; and the organized support of the Jewish notables through an instrument like the French *Alliance*.[139]

This opinion contrasted sharply with that expressed in *Ha-Melitz* by "Y.O.E.L.," in a report from Poland, in which the author contended that neither the rabbis nor the present communal establishment had any proper leadership potential. Salvation could come only if Western Jewry—the French *Alliance* in particular—helped a new, better-educated generation to arise among Russian Jews.[140]

Adolf Landau, soon to become the founding editor of the St. Petersburg *Evreiskaia biblioteka,* was also critical of the inactivity and timidity of the lay *Prominenz*—the OPE board in particular.[141] He was eager to promote, instead, a politically active communal organization for the Jews of St. Petersburg that might serve as a quasi-representative communal center for Russian Jewry as a whole.[142] In this he was joined by another St. Petersburg maskil, David Feinberg, a key figure in establishing the capital's synagogue and its congregational board in 1870 and a man who believed that the local communities could be modernized and made politically effective.[143]

What made this entire trend of advocating stronger central leadership and organization (and/or cooperation with the French *Alliance*) so remarkable was that it developed in the shadow of a new political assault on the kahal. Between 1866 and 1869, Jacob Brafman was the prime figure in the Vilna commission investigating the entire problem of Jewish "exclusiveness" and the Jewish communal apparatus. His charges of a secret Jewish brotherhood were aimed specifically at the OPE and the *Alliance*.[144] The debate in maskilic circles over forms of Jewish communal leadership was thus not only significant for the internal discussion itself but also as a statement of resolve with respect to the Russian authorities and Russian public opinion.

In 1868 when the governor-generalship of Vilna passed to Alexander Potapov, the Jewish communities of the provinces under Vilna's jurisdiction were authorized to delegate representatives to discuss the recommendations of the inquiry commission. The delegates and other invited participants came from both maskilic and traditionalist sectors. Lev

Levanda and Jonah Gerstein, "learned Jews" under the provincial administration; Emanuel Levin of the OPE; Hirsh Shapira, a prominent Kovno maskil; and Zalkind Minor of Minsk constituted the maskilic contingent. R. Yaakov Barit of Vilna and the veteran shtadlan of Vitebsk, Lipmann Seltzer, were among the more traditional of the delegates.[145] The delegation met with the governor-general and with the commission's chairman, Spasskii, in October 1869.

Even in the preliminary phases of the Vilna commission's deliberations (its ideas were known to the Jewish public through the Jewish representatives who sat in on the discussions), Zederbaum had expressed guarded alarm at the Brafman proposals to do away entirely with the Jewish communal apparatus (population registry, *korobka* and separate taxation, recruitment officials, school system).[146] When the final recommendations were submitted by the commission, their truly draconian character became apparent.

Among the chief provisions (that ran to several "chapters"), were: Jews were to be entirely integrated individually into town and village administrative units, ending anomalous collective, administrative vestiges of the kahal, although their rights to representation on local councils were to continue to be restricted so as to prevent Jewish supremacy in the many towns where they constituted a majority of the population. The registry of Jewish population records was to be handled by a municipal official. Jewish divorce law was to be liberalized. Jewish elementary schools and yeshivas were to be shut down and Russian schools established in their place. Doctors were to take over supervision of Jewish ritual baths. Small prayer quorums were to be banned and worship centralized in large synagogues where the rabbis or appointed wardens would keep a register of those attending. The selection of rabbis and synagogue officials was to be placed under closer supervision and the number of voluntary societies (*hevrot*) reduced.[147]

In short, this was to be an all-out campaign to uproot Jewish separateness to an extent of which even Uvarov in his day had not dreamed. The proposals were accompanied by such explanatory passages as:

> Attention has been drawn already to the fact that the Jews in Russia constitute an exclusive society, divided from Russian society as a state within a state, governing itself silently with the help of great but concealed power, invisible but spreading evil in its wake. This is the power known by the name of *kahal*. Jews, it has long been acknowledged, are a painful thorn in the side of this country. . . . However, the Israelite nation is also blessed with talent and cleverness, capable of greatly benefitting society at large, which is more in need of [these entrepreneurial capacities] than of

more physical labor. And yet, events and circumstances have caused the Jews to remain a contemptible and abominable nation. As members of civil society, they are like a diseased limb in the body politic, infecting all that it touches.[148]

The pressure on the Jewish delegates was, therefore, considerable. The strained relations of that time between the modernist and traditionalist factions in Russian Jewry could only have magnified the potential in this highly charged situation for a split among the Jewish spokesmen. In fact, however, no such split occurred. The delegation, led by R. Yaakov Barit, unanimously refused to discuss what they considered a proposed invasion of religious freedom and rejected the claim that the Jewish communities constituted a state within a state. In the end Potapov accepted their arguments and the entire project was shelved.[149]

The victory for the Jewish community was a significant one. Its importance in our context lies first in the fact that maskilim came to the defense of the community as an organized sociopolitical phenomenon; second, in the visible role maskilim played as political spokesmen; and third, in the cooperation between the maskilim and Yaakov Barit, a man they respected for his open-mindedness on educational matters, indicating a possible common ground between moderates from both traditionalist and modernist camps.

This cooperation was expressed in the refusal of the maskilim to play along with the Vilna commission's religious and educational proposals. Waging war on the traditionalists through the medium of state power was not a legitimate option: Maskilic politics had come full circle since the 1830s and 1840s.

Israel Bartal has demonstrated how this transition was reflected in the writings of major literary figures of the Russian Haskalah. Prior to 1869 a standard convention of these writings was the alliance between Russian officials and maskilim against the obscurantist rabbis and kahal committeemen.[150] Whereas even in the 1870s the older maskilic ideas sometimes reappeared in the essays and literary work of these writers, for one group in particular (the "radical maskilim" in Bartal's study) the new decade of the 1870s saw a reassessment and an abandonment of this idea. Examining the 1873 work, *Di kliatshe* (*The Nag*), by Sh. Y. Abramovich, Bartal finds that the officials of the regime are now portrayed as corrupt petty bureaucrats who hinder rather than help the young maskil in his attempt to break out of the traditional Jewish mold. The regime itself, with the tsar at its head, is allegorically depicted as sadistic, capricious, and anti-Jewish. Russian liberals are ineffectual and hypocritical, whereas the Jewish maskil, when used for the state's purposes, becomes guilty of exploiting and oppressing the Jewish people.[151]

In *Di kliatshe* (as well as in his 1869 play, *Di takse* [*The Tax*]), Abramovich is savagely critical of the local kahal boards and their hangers-on, not only for exploiting the poor—a theme with a long pedigree in maskilic social criticism—but also for their political failings. The communal council meeting is depicted as sheer bedlam.[152] The town notables are surrounded by obsequious busybodies and parasites, overly eager to curry favor with the authorities.[153] The overwhelming impression is one of a rudderless ship, adrift on an unnaturally calm sea: "My blood boils looking at it, the way we—for our many sins—have no one to deal with, no one to take action. Nobody is serious! . . . The society is asleep, off in dreamland. It doesn't consider, isn't aware, does not even know its true situation."[154]

The Jews are cursed with men of wealth who give money to all but the right social causes; with a sense of compassion that is exercised only at the last minute, when those in need of it are already at death's door; and with a perversity that makes successes of Hebrew and Yiddish newspapers, whereas no support goes to newspapers in Russian that could actually fight for the Jews in the arena of public opinion.[155]

But unlike his position in *Di takse,* in *Di kliatshe* Abramovich no longer calls on the government to "liberate us from the yoke of Jewish [i.e., local communal officials'] oppression [*golus*]."[156] Instead, he demands unequivocal and unconditional recognition of the Jews' human dignity.[157]

Abramovich's position enabled him not only to point to the results of inner political paralysis on Jewish society but to effect a direct identification with "the people," over the heads of the established Jewish leadership and in the face of Russian intellectual animosity. Lilienblum struck a similar position in responding to Orthodox polemics: "Do they really wish that we honor the rabbis more than the good of the people, or that in order to protect their dignity we refrain from speaking of the people's sufferings, of the great disaster which they are going through because of the negligence of their leaders?"[158]

Indeed, the entire thrust of the famine-related polemics in the press and the critique of the existing educational, social, and political mechanism of Jewish society was informed by this turning to "the people" with a new empathy. The existing leadership was addressed in an accusatory mode that was both reminiscent of traditional preachers and similar to contemporary radical social criticism.

The consequences in terms of the maskilic self-image as well as for the

future development of Jewish politics were crucial. We may take the
feelings expressed in 1866 by Avraham Gottlober as representing one
pole of maskilic self-perception: "Let's not fool ourselves and claim to
be 'the people.' We are the exceptions. Only as teachers and writers . . .
can we hope to change the people's minds."[159] Ten years later, however,
Reuven Asher Braudes began to publish his novel *Hadat vehahaim* (*Religion and Life*).[160] In it the wealthy maskil, Shraga, bursts into a meeting
of the town rabbi and leading citizens and defends his right to be present: The only valid criterion for participation in public affairs should be
the possession of a social conscience:

> (Shraga): I haven't come in my own behalf. Thank God I have been
> blessed and my trade has prospered. . . . It is for the poor that I wish to
> speak, for the starving!
> (R. Eliakim): Who are you to preach at us?! Who gave you the authority
> to speak such words in my house?!
> (Shraga): Who? The afflicted and downtrodden people! The hungry, the
> thirsty! Our brother Jews who are in distress![161]

Radicalization and the Early Growth of Political Ideology

It was during the crucial years from 1869 through the late 1870s, too,
that the basic elements of radical new ideologies—nationalist, "Hebrew
socialist," and populist—were articulated. In the case of Jewish nationalism, this trend was reflected in a new Russian-language journal, the St.
Petersburg *Razsvet* (founded in 1879).[162] And David Gordon, coeditor
of *Ha-Maggid,* became in this period one of the principle propagators of
the idea of Jewish colonization of Palestine.[163] But a more explicit nationalist theory, based on a critique of both liberal Haskalah and Orthodoxy
as having failed to grasp the nature of Jewish national distinctiveness,
was articulated by Peretz Smolenskin, who in 1869 began to publish a
new monthly, *Ha-Shahar,* in Vienna.

The radical nationalist idea first took root during a major controversy
over religious reform that began just prior to the famine of 1868–69 and
lasted well into the 1870s. During those years leading Russian maskilim
asserted their leadership in the Jewish communal affairs and already
enjoyed a certain status in public life. This had been reinforced by their
role in the Vilna Commission of 1869. It was at this juncture that they
embarked on a renewed campaign for educational reforms that would
permit a radical transformation of the ailing Jewish economy; a liberalization or rationalization of ritual life that they hoped would win back
.the allegiance of the growing number of disaffected young Jews who

were receiving Russian educations; and an overhaul of the rabbinate through the adoption of Western rabbinical training methods.[164]

The most vociferous of the polemicists in favor of religious reform, Moshe Leib Lilienblum, demanded that the entire corpus of rabbinic law be reexamined and modernized. Most important in our context, Lilienblum and his fellow critics insisted on the equal participation of maskilim in the rabbis' deliberations.[165] Thus, although maskilic representatives declined to have anything to do with officially coerced religious reforms, as demonstrated at the Vilna Commission, they tended to view internal reform as a necessary step and their own leadership in the process as essential. In taking this latter position, they had recourse to arguments that tended to emphasize the national character of the problem—the poverty of the masses on the one hand, the russification of Jewish students on the other, and the need for united, concerted action for the good of the whole community—over purely rabbinic or religious concerns.[166]

Taking these points to their logical conclusion, Peretz Smolenskin argued that the rabbis could play only a subordinate role in the determination of religious practice: The deciding factor was "the will of the people."

> [F]or in the House of Israel the Law is not the possession of a clergy; rather, it is the inheritance of the entire Congregation of Jacob, and it may do with this inheritance what it wishes. The rabbis are simply chosen from among the people and they must do all that is asked of them. Therefore, if the entire nation wishes to alter or to abolish [laws], it is within its rights and no one may rightfully oppose it.[167]

Customary Jewish practice, as determined by the masses, dictated the evolution of Judaism. The rabbis had to yield their claims of leadership to those who spoke for the people. Judaism, Smolenskin declared, was not a religion in the narrow sense of the term, but an evolving national culture whose spirit reflected the will of the people and its historical destiny.

Most of the rabbis remained unconvinced of the merits of this argument. Although the question of the rabbinate was to agitate Russian Jewish intellectual life for some time, it became a side issue in the context of the crisis of the 1880s and 1890s. Nevertheless, the commitment of many intellectuals and students in the last two decades of the century to secular political solutions owed something to the debate of the 1870s over national priorities and national leadership. Smolenskin's critique of both liberal Haskalah and religious traditionalism and his assertion that the Jews were a nation—albeit not a political entity—formed the bridge between maskilic claims to leadership of "the people" and more articulate nationalist ideas.[168]

It was in the 1870s, too, that the debate over the failure of the established communal and national leadership to alleviate the plight of the "masses" provided the background for political radicalization among maskilim. Just as this problem spurred some of them to call for a thorough reorganization of Jewish communal leadership, it prompted others to see the issue in a wider perspective—in accordance with Marxian or Russian radical theories—that allowed the social and economic problems of Jewish society to be understood as aspects of the social and political problems of Russia as a whole. The negative depictions of the state and the bureaucracy that began to appear in the works of such writers as Abramovich in the 1870s were an expression of this development. Populist or socialist points of view within maskilic circles were also expressed in the existing periodicals, within small networks of like-minded radical maskilim and finally in a short-lived Hebrew socialist paper, *Ha-Emet,* published by Aron Liberman in London in 1877.[169]

The development of Jewish socialism in Russia owes much to the emergence of an indigenous strike movement and worker organizations among Jewish workers and to the involvement of Jewish students in radical groups in Russian schools and universities, some of whom later helped organize socialist activity among Jews. The trend within the Haskalah, as such, toward socialist ideas—not a predominant trend at that—was thus only one element in a larger process. Moreover, as subsequent developments were to show, the line between socialism and nationalism was one that proved flexible and permeable in the Jewish context, even if opposing tendencies between the two ideas never ceased to trouble those searching for a synthesis. Thus, the organization of Jewish unions and Jewish radical circles had implications for Jewish cultural and national ideology, whereas the growth of nationalist and Zionist groups was in some cases predicated on the adoption of agrarian, populist, and socialist principles. Such groups sought to play a role in both the nationalist and the socialist movements. It is, therefore, difficult to trace the lineage of Jewish socialism in Russia in a direct line.

Nevertheless, we can say that the emergence of a radical school of social critics among the maskilim of the 1870s, who first articulated their ideas in the Jewish rather than the Russian context (or in a Jewish context that they identified with the larger political context), is consistent with the process of Jewish political development that we have been discussing.

The perception of a fundamental crisis in Jewish society, the drive to play an active role in leading "the people" out of that crisis, access to the press in three languages, the social responsibility attached to intellectual endeavor, and the emancipation from a statist orientation—all these were elements that could and did lead some maskilim to a program of radical social reform or political and social revolution, just as they led others to ideas that were quite different in ideological content.

The Eve of 1881

At the end of the 1870s, several important elements were in place that were to figure in the crystallization of new political forms in the 1880s and 1890s. The maskilim had maneuvered themselves into the position of political critics and spokesmen for the community. The press and the OPE had given the maskilim tools for public activity and at the same time served as an informal grid for conflict and consensus. What was said in St. Petersburg was criticized in Odessa and debated in Vilna. It was here that the scaffolding of a national politics might be discerned in what was otherwise a fragmented modernist camp.

The "voice of the people" had been enshrined in a place of honor.[170] "The people" themselves had become a rallying cry and a legitimizing principle, simultaneously serving to bring the diffusion of political responsibility in the community to its logical extreme and to pose a radical alternative to the rabbis and notables. In the name of the people, the present "order" was criticized as disorder and a solution in the form of new organizational and leadership mechanisms was demanded. Conflict was domesticated as part of the process by which "the people" would determine its course.

Many of these themes were touched upon by Sh. Y. Abramovich in an essay published in 1878, "What Is to Be Done?"[171] The point of his essay was to argue that the proper role of literature was the advancement of national affairs—a role he felt Russian Jewish literature had not yet fulfilled. Along the way, however, he reiterated his critique of the political disorder at the local communal level. There was, he stated, an absence of rational, planned action geared to achieving identifiable goals. Instead, social and political action was taken without proper forethought or—worse yet—had no rationale even after the fact. He found that what passed for political and social activity were inertial, reflex, unreflecting measures taken by "benefactors" who had not the slightest notion of direction and purpose but were fixed in their paternalistic resolve to be the leaders:

> All manner of strange people . . . claim the right to intervene in matters
> related to our people and its requirements . . . , as if the community is a
> society composed of orphans who would be lost without their "benefac-
> tors." They hold themselves to be the very foundation of Jewry, experts at
> the well-placed whisper in the right ears about the right matters, and all
> done with such discretion. They are the cedars of Lebanon, the mighty
> ones of the congregation who know best . . . , our Wall of China, shield-
> ing the people from the winds of civilization.[172]

The function of the writer was to introduce thought and, therefore,
order and planning into the national life of his society. "What I demand," Abramovich summed up, "is a literature for the sake of the
people, not a literature for literature's sake."[173]

This critique of Jewish politics as irrational and out of touch with
reality found parallel expression in Abramovich's novel of the same
year, *Masoes Binyomin hashlishi* (*Travels of Benjamin the Third*). Here,
as Miron and Norich have shown, the imaginary self-perception of the
Jew as a political actor is held up to ridicule against the real-world
standards of political power and initiative.[174] In the novel as in "What Is
to Be Done?," the point is that, properly speaking, the Jew had no
politics. This argument, which was not original with Abramovich,[175]
anticipated subsequent nationalist idealogues—Leon Pinsker, among
the best examples.[176]

Ironically, the year 1878 witnessed a new climax in Jewish political
activity in Russia: a new round in the struggle for hegemony between the
maskilim and the rabbis that culminated in a decisive victory for the
maskilim. It was the year in which, as it seemed to many Jews, the tsar
was going to announce their full civic emancipation.

These hopes were stirred by a series of events beginning with the
Russo-Turkish War of 1877–78. The opinion gained widespread currency
that after the war Jewish patriotism and sacrifice on the battlefield would
be rewarded and Jewish claims finally honored. The subsequent Congress
of Berlin (summer of 1878) seemed another momentous augury; after the
guarantees of equality obtained there for the Jews of Romania, Bulgaria,
and Serbia, surely the Jews of Russia would be next.[177]

The announcement by the Ministry of Internal Affairs that a Rabbinical Commission was to be convened early in 1879, for the first time in
seventeen years, seemed to many Jews a confirmation of these hopes.
To the maskilim the election of commission delegates represented a
crucial test of their political strength and another opportunity to play the
role of national leaders. The sense that the Rabbinical Commission was
being convened in order to set the emancipation process in motion led

Lilienblum, for example, to argue the case for a maskilic rather than rabbinic delegation to the commission:

> Anyone acquainted with the spirit of our rabbis knows how ill-equipped they are to comprehend what is in the Jews' best interest. . . . I have no doubt whatsoever that the rabbis would be satisfied if the Jews did not win equal rights, just as long as every single iota of the prayers inherited from our ancestors could be preserved. . . . The word "exile" [*galut*] is for them like a toy in the hands of a child: They do not want it to be taken away from them. For the real truth is that the Jews without their *galut* are like a body without a soul.[178]

The Jewish communities were divided over whether to elect effective shtadlanim (maskilim) or leading rabbis; many, in fact, chose both: a team composed of both a rabbi and a maskil.[179] The final choice, made by the Minister for Internal Affairs, resulted in a panel that contained only nontraditionalist notables and maskilim. The chairman, the sole rabbi, was the government rabbi of the Kherson Jewish agricultural colonies, G. Blumenfeld, but the dominant personality on the commission was Baron Günzburg.[180]

As the delegates gathered in St. Petersburg, Lev Levanda, invited by the Ministry of Internal Affairs to attend, told the correspondent of *Ha-Maggid* that he had spoken with the director of the ministry's Department for Foreign Cults (under whose auspices the commission was convened). In the course of their discussion, the director told Levanda that he "sincerely wished to see the Jews made equal under the law with all other citizens of our country." *Ha-Maggid* commented, "Thus we are full of hope that the words of this high official reflect the thoughts of [the tsar]. May God grant that the tsar, who is a just ruler, fairness and equity are his staff, . . . remember us for this good [purpose]. And we, on our part, will strive with every fiber of our being to show how much we deserve this favor."[181] On the eve of the commission's opening, *Ha-Maggid*'s correspondent again held out this hope, but cautioned against speaking prematurely about a firm decision in favor of emancipation, such as Zederbaum's *Ha-Melitz* had already in fact announced.[182]

At the very least it was expected that the commission would not deal only with petty specifics, such as marriage and divorce law, but would be given the opportunity for a wide-ranging review of Russian Jewry's social and religious life and would become the basis for a central permanent Jewish consistory. If emancipation were waiting in the wings, the normalization of the Jewish community as a "church" could be expected to enhance and hasten the process.[183]

The victory of the maskilim was hollow and short-lived however. Neither emancipation nor the formation of a maskilic-dominated consistory was on the agenda of the commission. Moreover, in view of the lack of rabbis to deal with the queries raised by the government, the sessions were adjourned within a month.[184] It was, indeed, a bitter defeat, and one that, Mordecai Hacohen argued, might have been foreseen:

> If only the Jews had paid attention to their position in Russian society; if only they had taken note of the contempt and shame spilled on them daily in the Russian press throughout the year of the war. . . . [E]ven while the opinion of Europe as a whole was pro-Jewish, as expressed at the Congress of Berlin, the Russian press ignored this and continued to pour contempt on us as if it were water.[185]

In light of the experience of 1879, the rapid capitulation of many maskilim—students in particular—to profound disillusionment during 1881–82 becomes more understandable. The year of the pogroms and the May Laws was indeed a shock; but it is likely that the definitive and final abandonment of emancipatory rhetoric by many thoughtful Russian Jews in that year was conditioned by their prior letdown in connection with the Rabbinical Commission. The Odessa pogrom of 1871, for example, had not led directly to a permanent shift in Jewish ideological development. Among the factors that made 1881 different was the fact that a crescendo of disillusionment had been building since 1879.

We can point to one other anticipation of post-1881 developments, in which it was not the collapse of emancipation that played the major role, however, but rather the rejection of emancipation as an inadequate solution for Jewish society. This first explicit statement that the Jews' problems went deeper than civic equality could possibly solve and that organized self-help was required was enunciated by Menashe Morgulis in mid-1878.[186]

His argument, based on the already familiar critique of the lack of proper leadership and national organization in Russian Jewry, urged the Jews of Russia to look to Western Jewry for models of what could be done with dedication, unity, and willpower. In effect, he was saying, the desired fruits of emancipation could be attained only if the Jews themselves took concerted coordinated action to lead their own society into the modern age:

> Those who live in a world of illusion believe that with the stroke of a pen the lawgiver can put an end to the misery of the Jews' condition. . . .
> What good will civic equality do for this mass of suffering humanity that

does not know if the next day will be worse than or only as awful as today? What will [the Jew] do with political rights if he does not have his daily bread? What benefit will he derive from the right to resettle anywhere he likes if he hasn't a livelihood or the means to pay for travel? What good did the law do that permitted artisans to live in the interior of Russia? Not a bit! . . . What we need are fundamental social reforms. We need to disperse the Jews from overpopulated areas into other areas of the western provinces, and to help them find a decent livelihood. But who among us is capable of thinking on a national scale of the basic welfare of our people? . . . What we need is to take counsel together and learn from the ways of our brothers from abroad . . . who have devoted their entire lives, their minds and their hearts to the affairs of the nation in all their ramifications.[187]

The answer Morgulis offered was not autoemancipation in the Zionist sense of the term in which Pinsker was to use it four years later. But his solution was something closely akin to autoemancipation, which he identified as a restoration of coordinated leadership on a national level, a rebuilding of political community. Only this—not temporary local philanthropy nor even civic equality—had any hope of actually changing the circumstances of Russian Jewish life.[188]

Conclusion

Jewish communities in the diaspora have always engaged in political activity and have always sought substitutes for sovereign power in order to guarantee their continued welfare and existence. The protection of overlords, the kahal regime, and a traditional legal and social system provided those substitutes during the medieval era. In the Polish Commonwealth Jewish communities struggled, survived, and flourished under those conditions for the greater part of five hundred years, until the end of the eighteenth century. To say that this system was an imperfect one, given the frequency with which it was challenged by external threat and internal division, is merely to point out the obvious. The history of human society consists entirely of such imperfection. On the whole medieval Jewry fared worse than some other small populations but better than many others.

A more serious and pervasive challenge awaited the Jews of the nineteenth century. The old substitutes they had found for sovereign power were rendered obsolete by the processes that led to the emergence of the modern state. The communal life of the Jews that had seemed so self-sufficient from within was now exposed as a delicate construct that had in reality depended to a large extent on external support factors. The changing social, economic, and political environment spelled the end of the traditional diaspora system of self-government. That became apparent through state action to limit the political prerogatives of Jewish communal officers and institutions as well as through an internal crisis of legitimacy and authority.

This breach in the continuity of traditional forms should not, however, be taken for a break in the continuity of Jewish political development. The diffusion of communal responsibility spawned new leadership groups; challenges to the existing communal institutions stimulated the search for new forms of activity; and the loss of the state as guarantor of the community's structural integrity facilitated the discovery of the "people's will" as the foundation for a new type of political community. The call for Jewish autoemancipation grew out of the political crisis of Russian Jewry before 1881.

The politics of self-liberation was a radical ideological reconstruction in Jewish life. What allowed this to take place was the structural emancipation of Jewish politics from state tutelage over the course of thirty to forty years, at least, and in terms of longer trends, ever since the end of the eighteenth century. The attempt to restore political community to Jewish life was related to prior sociopolitical changes: changes that had left Russian Jewry bereft of routinized political mechanisms, authority, and representation. It is these elements that allow us to account for the modernization of Jewish political life in Russia at the end of the nineteenth century.

The crisis of 1881 prompted further programmatic elaboration; but one of the most important aspects of the new politics was a structural innovation that cut across ideological lines: Jewish political activity was now not only autonomous of the state but also autonomous of and, indeed, consciously opposed to, the leadership of the notables who had controlled the Jewish community for decades.[1]

The ideological solutions proposed by Jewish political thinkers in late nineteenth-century Russia varied in content, in their respective constituencies, in popularity, and in political orientation. Most of them were embodied in party programs—adopted at conferences, congresses, and the like—that brought local elements together into national units. Whether nationalist, socialist, or autonomist[2] (none of which were mutually exclusive), the import of the new movements of the end of the century was, at a basic level, the re-creation of a national political community. This was a goal pursued within each movement and also the effect of the political debate among the various movements.

The search for a new politics ultimately meant a search for a recovery of access to power on behalf of the newly reconstituted political community. The radical solution was either social revolution—reordering the political environment to seize power "for the people"; or national self-determination—creation of an environment in which Jews might constitute the majority and, eventually, the state itself. Liberal constitutionalists sought a way to share power once again with the state through an electoral and parliamentary system. Autonomists—whether of the radical socialist, nationalist, or liberal variety—sought a situation in which the state would once again give sanction to a Jewish semi-sovereign body for internal jurisdiction and external representation.

All of the new movements based themselves to a greater or lesser extent (depending on tactical considerations)[3] on the democratic principle that sovereignty was vested in "the people." The political forms adopted—mass parties, press, congresses, elections, debates—were all legitimized by this principle. This was one of the aspects of the new politics that struck traditionalists as wholly new and, thus, wrong. As one Orthodox anti-Zionist tract put it:

> Labor on behalf of the community's welfare has always been a sacred trust among our people . . . and Israel has never lacked for shtadlanim to work for the good of the people and to alleviate persecution. . . . But those involved always kept certain rules inviolate . . . , that the [public's] affairs be conducted privately, without fanfare, concealed from prying, hostile eyes and from the cheap talk of the common crowd. Public affairs must never be the subject of idle chatter of the crowd or of women. There is no greater disaster for the nation than the transfer of its business from the private domain of individual leaders to the public domain, where youngsters and even girls are free to meddle.[4]

The discreet and paternalistic politics of the shtadlan was, of course, pilloried as the symbol of national shame by modernists of all stripes, and seen as an evocation of a political "exile" now superseded by the era of national politics. It was in this sense that the Yiddish writer Y. L. Peretz wrote in 1895:

> Purim is no holiday. . . . It is to Esther that we owe the first victory we ever gained neither against nor over . . . foreign kings. Purim is the birthday of the first "protected Jew," the first court Jew . . . , the first informer and the first royal errand-boy. . . . Purim is a holiday for beggars, fiddlers, masqueraders . . . and for a nation that is like them! Dance away on strangers' beds . . . and on the grave of your pride—drink and forget, if you can.[5]

The hallmark of traditional Jewish politics—its dependence on the state and its consequent articulation through intermediaries possessing access to state officials—was now absolutely rejected. Now Jewish politics were meant to take place at the national level, subject to public discussion and led by representatives of the people. Yet the abiding lack of permanent political institutions embracing the people as a whole meant that political leadership remained fragmented, divided by ideology as well as geography. Moreover, the lack of representative institutions meant that leaders continued to be either self-selected or appointed by committee. Indeed, it was often the leaders who called the constituency organizations into being, rather than the reverse, as was the case with Theodor Herzl and the Zionist Congress. Nevertheless, for all the similarity between the individual diplomacy of a figure such as Herzl and older forms of Jewish diplomacy, no traditional shtadlan ever sought a popular mandate by convening a congress, putting before it a program for its endorsement, and establishing the machinery, in full public view, for the mobilization of a mass membership.

In terms of concrete results over the short term, one may question whether the new politics were any more effective than traditional shtadlanut. Until the State of Israel was established in 1948, none of the new political movements succeeded in their quest for power—with the partial and temporary exception of Jewish Communists in the Soviet Union during the first decade after the Revolution and, to an even more limited extent, the parties that won internal control of local Jewish kehillot in elections in interwar East Central Europe.[6] In that sense the rise of the new movements did not immediately solve the crisis that had plagued Jewish politics since the demise of the autonomous kahal system. Though they pointed the way to different avenues to political power, the movements proved unable to realize this goal before the Second World War.

This, however, could not have been foreseen by those who founded the movements and strove to win political recognition and support for their programs. In conditions of emancipation from state tutelage, this required the mobilization of the people as a political community. Dependence on the old methods of individual intercession would have been misdirected. In the new politics it was axiomatic that the political reconstruction of the Jewish people was a worthy goal in and of itself as well as a means toward achieving power and security.

Glossary

b. (ben) son of

bet din rabbinical court

dina demalkhuta dina the law of the kingdom is law [for the Jews]: a principle of rabbinic jurisprudence

galut (golus) exile, dispersion

halakha (adj.: halakhic) rabbinic law, based on the Talmud

Haskalah (*see* maskil) the Englightenment movement

ḥerem ban

jurydyki urban domains of Polish nobles located in royal cities

kehilla (also kahal) (pl.: kehillot; kehalim) the Jewish community of a given locale or the executive board of the community

malshin; malshinut informer, informing

maskil (pl.: maskilim) (adj.: maskilic) adherent of the Haskalah

melamed (pl.: *melamdim*) grade-school teacher

mitsvot commandments; religious obligations

musar ethics (Musar was also the name of a nineteenth-century movement based on a system of ethical training.)

parnas chairman of a kehilla board

pinkas protocols

R. rabbi

rekrutchina the conscription regime used to induct Jews into the Russian army under Nicholas I.

shtadlan (pl.: shtadlanim); shtadlanut intercessor or lobbyist; lobbying

158

takanah (pl. *takanot*)   communal regulation or bylaw
tsaddik (pl.: *tsaddikim*)   lit., a righteous man; leader of a Hasidic community
va'ad (pl.: va'adim)   council
wojewoda   palatine; district governor

Notes

Abbreviations

APH	*Acta Polonia Historia*
AVK	*Akty izdavaemye vilenskoiu komissieiu dlia razbora drevnykh aktov*
BZIH	*Biuletyn Żydowskiego Instytutu Historycznego*
EB	*Evreiskaia biblioteka*
EE	*Evreiskaia entsiklopedia*
ES	*Evreiskaia starina*
HUCA	*Hebrew Union College Annual*
HVH	*Hagut vehanhaga: hashkefoteihem haḥevratiot shel yehudei polin beshalhei yemei habeinayim*
IESS	*International Encyclopedia of the Social Sciences*
JQR	*Jewish Quarterly Review*
JSS	*Jewish Social Studies*
Levitats	*The Jewish Community in Russia*, 2 vols.: Levitats 1 (1772–1844); Levitats 2 (1844–1917)
MGWJ	*Monatsschrift für Geschichte und Wissenschaft des Judentums*
PAAJR	*Proceedings of the American Academy for Jewish Research*
PML	*Pinkas medinat lita*
PSZ	*Polnoe sobranie zakonov rossiiskoi imperii (Complete Compendium of the Laws)*, ser. 1 and ser. 2: *PSZ*[1]; *PSZ*[2]
PVAA	*Pinkas va'ad arb'a aratsot*

PWCJS	*Proceedings of the World Congress of Jewish Studies*
REJ	*Revue des études juives*
RIN	*Regesty i nadpisi: svod materialov dlia istorii evreev v rossii*
SRH	*A Social and Religious History of the Jews*
Toledot OPE	*Ḥevrat marbei haskala beyisrael,* 2 vols.: *Toledot OPE* 1; *Toledot OPE* 2
Wilensky	*Ḥasidim umitnagdim,* 2 vols.: Wilensky 1; Wilensky 2
ZY	*Zikhron Ya'akov,* 2 vols: *ZY* 1; *ZY* 2

Introduction

1. Jacob Katz, *Tradition and Crisis: Jewish Society at the End of the Middle Ages* (New York: 1961), p. 274.

2. David Biale, *Power and Powerlessness in Jewish History* (New York: 1986). Biale's book and my study agree in certain basic questions. His work appeared after my doctoral dissertation was completed. Thus, my thesis is not, strictly speaking, a response to his invitation to scholars to take up these issues, but it certainly develops some of the points Biale has raised.

3. Hannah Arendt, *The Origins of Totalitarianism* (New York: 1973), pp. 23–24, 54.

4. David Vital, *The Origins of Zionism* (Oxford/New York: 1980), pp. 87, 154.

5. Raul Hilberg, *The Destruction of the European Jews* (Chicago: 1967), pp. 14–17.

6. See, for example, the discussion of these trends in the article on "State" by Frederick Watkins in *International Encyclopedia of the Social Sciences* (hereafter *IESS*) 15, pp. 155–56.

7. Salo W. Baron, *A Social and Religious History of the Jews* (hereafter *SRH*), originally published in 3 vols. (Philadelphia: 1937); the multivolume 2d ed. was published 1952–84 (New York/Philadelphia). Unless otherwise stated, references are to the 2d ed.

8. Salo W. Baron, *The Jewish Community* (Philadelphia: 1942) 1, p. 28.

9. Simon Dubnow, *Nationalism and History,* ed. K. Pinson (New York: 1970), esp. pp. 76–115.

10. Baron, *SRH* 1, pp. 16–18.

11. A more political approach than that of Baron is applied by Yitzhak Baer in his essay "Hayesodot vehahathalot shel irgun hakehilla hayehudit biyemei habeinayim," *Zion* 15 (1950), 1.

12. See Daniel J. Elazar, ed., *Kinship and Consent: The Jewish Political Tradition and Its Contemporary Uses* (Ramat-Gan, Isr.: 1981); Sam Lehman-Wilzig and Bernard Susser, eds., *Comparative Jewish Politics (1): Public Life in Israel and the Diaspora* (Ramat-Gan, Isr.: 1981).

13. Daniel J. Elazar and Stuart A. Cohen, *The Jewish Polity: Jewish Political Organization from Biblical Times to the Present* (Bloomington, Ind.: 1984).

14. Stuart Cohen and Eliezer Don-Yehiya, eds., *Comparative Jewish Politics (2): Conflict and Consensus in Jewish Political Life* (Ramat-Gan, Isr.: 1986), offers case histories, mainly from the twentieth century, but no theoretical framework.

15. Such examples abound. To name but a few: Dubnow, in his *History of the Jews in Russia and Poland,* vol. 2 (Philadelphia: 1916); and in the First Letter, *idem, Letters on Old and New Judaism* (see the edition edited by K. Pinson, *Nationalism and History* [New York: 1970]); Louis Greenberg, *The Jews in Russia: The Struggle for Emancipation* vol. 1 (New Haven Conn.: 1944); Raphael Mahler, in all his work on East European Jewish history; Yitzhak Maor, *Hatenu'a hatsiyonit berusia* (Jerusalem: 1986); Azriel Shochat's *Mossad harabanut mita'am berusia* (Haifa: 1975–76); E. Tcherikover, "Hehamon hayehudi, hamaskilim, vehamemshala biyemei Nikolai I," *Zion* 4 (1939), pp. 150–69.

16. The organization's acronym, OPE, is sometimes rendered as ORPME. In Russian it is *Obshchestvo dlia rasprostranenia prosveshchenia mezhdu evreiami v rossii.*

Chapter 1

1. This is a point stressed by Biale, *Power and Powerlessness,* p. 64.

2. See Baron, *SRH* 4, pp. 50, 53–55, 57, 64–65, 68–69, 72–75, 87. On cooperation between the Jews and the urban patriciate, see *SRH* 9, pp. 215, 221–22, 227–32; *SRH* 14, pp. 197–98, 254–56. On the nobility, see *SRH* 9, pp. 159, 168, 220–21. Eric Zimmer cites incidents from Nuremburg, Ratisbon (now Regensburg), and Frankfurt am Main of successful Jewish alliances with municipal authorities against the crown in the fifteenth century; see *Harmony and Discord: An Analysis of the Decline of Jewish Self-government in Fifteenth-Century Central Europe* (New York: 1970), pp. 152–55. The first articulation in Jewish sources of the idea that the existence of rival empires was providential for Jewish survival occurs in *Seder Eliyahu rabba,* whose date is a matter of some dispute, but whose origin is no later than the ninth century. See Salo W. Baron, *Ancient and Medieval Jewish History* (New Brunswick, N.J.: 1972), p. 82; idem, *SRH* 4, p. 401 n. 7. An early medieval example of Jewish political activity based on this perception is the letter of Hisdai ibn Shaprut (ca. 950) from the court of Cordova to Empress Helena of Byzantium (in Jacob Mann, *Texts and Studies in Jewish History and Literature* [Cincinnati: 1931] 1, pp. 5, 22).

3. See Baron, *SRH* 5, pp. 71, 78; *SRH* 11, p. 20.

4. On the fine line distinguishing ritual coercion from political coercion, see Jacob Neusner, *There We Sat Down: Talmudic Judaism in the Making* (Nashville, Tenn./New York: 1972), pp. 54–66, 81–86, 98–102, 108–14; *IESS* 15, pp. 157–58. On the limitations of the ḥerem and its linkage to political sanctions, see

S.A. Horodetzky, *Lekorot harabanut* (Warsaw: 1911), p. 39; James Parkes, *The Jew in the Medieval Community* (London: 1938), p. 253; Zimmer, *Harmony and Discord,* pp. 94–95, citing the Responsa of R. Israel Isserlein (*Terumat hadeshen: pesakim ukhtuvim* [Venice: 1516]).

5. Neusner in *There We Sat Down* (pp. 46, 100) uses the term *derivative power* in reference to power in the Babylonian Jewish community. Baron states, "There is little doubt that much of Jewish communal evolution can be explained . . . by the state's own self-interest in the effective fiscal and ecclesiastical organization of Jewish subjects" (*Jewish Community* 1, p. 22). Jacob Katz in *Tradition and Crisis* also maintains that "the delegation of a limited amount of enforcement power to the kehilla was the basis for the much-publicized Jewish autonomy" (p. 92). Leo Landman makes a similar point, noting the role played by the dictim *dina demalkhuta dina* in the Jewish power structure, "The Jewish community . . . derived its power from the secular authorities. Its edicts were authorized by the government, and it was by 'the law of the kingdom' that they derived their power. Individual rabbis could not oppose their edict. . . . [I]t was considered rebellion against the crown" (*Jewish Law in the Diaspora: Confrontation and Accommodation* [Philadelphia: 1968], p. 67). Cf. Yitzhak Baer, *A History of the Jews in Christian Spain* (Philadelphia: 1966) 1, pp. 225–26; 2, pp. 77–78.

6. Baer, "Hayesodot," 33.

7. Moshe Frank, *Kehillot ashkenaz uvatei dineihen* (Tel-Aviv: 1937), p. 117.

8. Louis Finkelstein, ed., *Jewish Self-Government in the Middle Ages,* 2d ed. (New York: 1964), pp. 42–43, 152–55.

9. Ibid. Baron refers to this type of recourse to gentile authority as

> the general exception confirming the rule: the leaders alone were allowed for the common good to employ governmental coercion against members abusing governmental support for their private benefit. Perfectly realistic, this practice often placed the burden of decision on the governmental authorities which, when guided by enlightened self-interest, tried to strengthen the communal bonds among their Jewish subjects. (*SRH* 5, pp. 70–71)

10. See Maimonides, *Mishneh Torah: hilkhot ḥovel umazik* 8: 10–11; Responsa of R. Asher b. Jehiel (early fourteenth-century Toledo), R. Isaac b. Sheshet Perfet (fourteenth to early fifteenth-century Spain and North Africa), Simon b. Zemah Duran (first half of fifteenth-century Algiers), and others cited in Simha Assaf, *Ha'onshin aḥarei ḥatimat hatalmud* (Jerusalem: 1922), pp. 63–67, 73–74, 79–80, 83–91, 106. See also *takanot* of the Aragonese communities adopted in 1354 and those of Castile adopted in 1432 (Finkelstein, *Self-Government,* pp. 331–32, 361–65); measures adopted by the communities of North Africa in the wake of the persecutions in Spain in 1391 (Assaf, *Ha'onshin,* p. 80); and the statutes of the communities of Tudela in 1305 and Navarre in 1363 (D. Kaufman, "Jewish Informers in the Middle Ages," *Jewish Quarterly Review* (hereafter *JQR*), o.s., 8 [1896], 217–20). Provisions for the punishment of informers were included in privileges granted to the Spanish communities of

Barbastro (1273), Barcelona (1342 and 1383), Majorca (1347), and Huesca (1390). On the jurisdiciton of the community in the punishment of informers in Spain, see Baer, *Christian Spain* 1, pp. 11, 161–62, 168–70, 221, 231–34, 284–86, 315, 324–25; ibid., 2, pp. 2, 27, 41, 53–54, 67–70, 79–82, 84–85, 91, 263–67, 449–53; Ben-Zion Dinur, *Yisrael bagola: mekorot ute'udot* (Tel-Aviv and Jerusalem: 1965) 2, bk. 2 pp. 48 (no. 14), 66 (no. 117), 47, 173 n. 56, 402–9, 432 n. 73. On informers in medieval northern and Central Europe, see Assaf, *Ha'onshin,* pp. 107–8; Kaufmann, "Informers," 226–27; Irving Agus, *Urban Civilization in Pre-Crusade Europe* (New York: 1965) 1, pp. 172–73, 232–33; ibid., 2, pp. 513, 515, 565, 752–53, 755–56; Dinur, *Yisrael bagola* 2, bk. 1 pp. 81 (no. 8), 223 (no. 8); ibid., bk. 2 pp. 409, 422; ibid., bk. 3 p. 245; James Parkes, *The Jew in the Medieval Community,* p. 250; Frank, *Kehillot ashkenaz,* p. 117.

11. For a case study of the prevalence of resort to gentile courts in a medieval Jewish community, see Yosef Shatzmiller, "Halikhatam shel yehudim le'arkhaot shel goyim beprovans biyemei habeinayim," in *Proceedings of the World Congress of Jewish Studies* (hereafter *PWCJS*)5 (1972) (2), pp. 375–81.

12. Invariably this involved the appointment of a chief rabbi of a given political jurisdiction. See Shmuel Shilo, *Dina demalkhuta dina* (Jerusalem: 1975), pp. 422–30; S. Zeitlin, "Opposition to the Spiritual Leaders Appointed by the Government," *JQR* n.s., 31 (1940–41), 287–300; Mordecai Breuer, "Ma'amad harabanut behanhagatan shel kehillot ashkenaz bamea ha-15," *PWCJS* (1975), pt. 2, p. 146; Frank, *Kehillot ashkenaz,* pp. 14–15.

13. Baer provides examples of such conflicts in the Spanish communities: *Christian Spain* 1, pp. 105, 253; 2, chap. 9.

14. See, for example, Gerson D. Cohen, *Sefer Haqabbalah (The Book of Tradition) by Abraham Ibn Daud* (Philadelphia: 1967), pp. xlviii, 289; Baer, *Christian Spain* 1, pp. 65, 77, 95, 104; S.D. Goitein, *A Mediterranean Society* (Berkeley, Calif.: 1971) 2, pp. 7, 23, 27, 405; Mann, *Texts and Studies* 2, pp. 62–63; Zvi Ankori, *Karaites in Byzantium* (New York: 1959), pp. 37–38, 55–56, 287, 329, 334–36; Baron, *SRH* 5, pp. 223, 271, 284.

15. Recent historians who support this view include Baron *SRH* 9, p. 63; *SRH* (1937) 3, p. 110 n. 23; Moshe Carmilly-Weinberger, *Censorship and Freedom of Expression in Jewish History* (New York: 1977), p. 36; Louis I. Newman, *Jewish Influence on Christian Reform Movements* (New York: 1925), pp. 317–18; Dinur, *Yisrael bagola* 2, bk. 4 p. 141; cf. Yosef Shatzmiller, "Litemunat hamaḥloket harishona 'al kitvei haRambam," *Zion* 34 (1969), 126–38. Baer, on the other hand, states that "the information that has reached us is full of contradictions and of partisan prejudice" (*Christian Spain* 1, pp. 109–10). Even he, however, admits that "Neither side . . . had any scruples about turning to the Church for aid in suppressing the ideas which it regarded as heretical" (p. 110). Cf. Yosef Shatzmiller, "Igrato shel R. Asher b.r. Gershom lerabbanei tsarfat mizeman hamaḥloket 'al kitvei haRambam," *Meḥkarim betoledot 'am yisrael veeretz yisrael* 1 (1970), 137. Azriel Shochat, "Berurim befarashat hapulmus harishon 'al sifrei haRambam," *Zion* 36 (1971), 27–60, writes, "It would appear

that Nachmanides knew of the threat by the rabbis of Orléans that 'it is in their power' to hand over to the authorities anyone not adhering to the ban." See also D.J. Silver, *Maimonidean Criticism and the Maimonidean Controversy 1180–1240* (Leiden, Neth.: 1965), pp. 152–54, 179; H.H. Ben-Sasson, *Toledot yisrael beyemei habeinayim* (Tel-Aviv: 1969), p. 156; Bernard Septimus, *Hispano-Jewish Culture in Transition: The Career and Controversies of Ramah* (Cambridge, Mass.: 1982), pp. 65–66. For the letters containing the original charges, see Baer, *Christian Spain* 1, pp. 400–402 n. 60.

16. Jean Juster, *Les Juifs dans l'empire romain* (Paris: 1914) 2, p. 182 (as per Josephus, *The Jewish War* [London/Cambridge, Mass.: 1927] 7:421; cf. *Against Apion* 2:68). Baron notes that "Palestinian Jewry revealed a considerable irredentist strength to the days of Heraclius and beyond" (*SRH* 2, pp. 213–14).

17. Isaac Abravanel, *Ma'ayanei hayeshu'a* (*ma'ayan* 8: *tamar* 9), p. 506 (Amsterdam, 1661 ed.); p. 349, *Perush 'al neviim ukhtuvim* (Jerusalem/Tel-Aviv: 1960).

18. Ismar Schorsch, "On the History of the Political Judgment of the Jew," *Leo Baeck Memorial Lecture* 20 (New York: 1977), pp. 3–7, 20; Biale, *Power and Powerlessness,* pp. 112–17.

19. See Introduction, p. 6; Schorsch, "Political Judgment," pp. 3, 7; Arendt, *Totalitarianism,* pp. 8, 23; Hilberg, *Destruction,* p. 669.

20. Schorsch, "Political Judgment," pp. 8–9.

21. Biale, *Power and Powerlessness,* p. 6. Cf. Dan Segre, "Colonization and Decolonization: The Case of Zionist and African Elites," *Comparative Studies in Society and History* 20, no. 1 (1980), 28.

22. Ismar Elbogen, *Der jüdische Gottesdienst in seiner geschichtlichen Entwicklung* (Frankfurt am main: 1931), p. 203.

23. Philo Judaeus, *Flaccus* 7:49–50 (Colon trans., Loeb Library ed., Cambridge, Mass.: 1941); Babylonian Talmud, *Yoma* 69a. The tenth-century author of *Yosippon* assumed that prayers for Seleucus were offered in the Temple in Jerusalem (an element that he adds to the account of 2 Macc. 3:12), see David Flusser, *Sefer Yosippon* (Jerusalem: 1978), chap. 11:18–19. Richard A. Freund, "*Principia Politica:* The Political Dimensions of Jewish and Christian Self-definition in the Greco-Roman Period" (Ph.D. diss., Jewish Theological Seminary of America, 1982, pp. 34–36) discusses emperor-worship in the ancient world and its ramifications for Jewish cultic practice. Cf. Asher Aaron Landau, *Sefer ahavat hamelekh* (Breslau: 1832), pp. 2b–3a. On the origins of Catholic practice, see Walter Ullmann, *The Growth of Papal Government in the Middle Ages: A Study in the Relation of Clerical to Lay Power* (London: 1970), pp. 89–90; idem, *The Church and the Law in the Early Middle Ages* (London: 1975); pp. 85–91; cf. Rom. 13:1–4.

24. Shilo, *Dina,* pp. 2, 58, 433–34; on the background see Jacob Neusner, *A History of the Jews in Babylonia* (Leiden, Neth.: 1966) 2, pp. 16, 27, 30, 45, 69, 71, 95, 134–44).

25. Gerald Blidstein, "A Note on the Function of 'The Law of the Kingdom

Is Law' in the Medieval Jewish Community," *Jewish Journal of Sociology* 15, no. 2 (1973), 213–19; cf. Shilo, *Dina,* pp. 9–10, 45–48, 88–89, 96–97, 109–10, 434.

26. Shilo, *Dina,* pp. 45–64, 68–82; cf. Menahem Elon, *Hamishpat ha'ivri* (Jerusalem: 1973), pt. 1, pp. 51–59. On rule by common consent in medieval political theory, see Frances Oakley, "Legitimation by Consent," *Viator* 14 (1983), 303–35, esp. 312–13, 335.

27. Salo W. Baron, "Some Medieval Jewish Attitudes to the Muslim State," in Baron, *Ancient and Medieval Jewish History,* pp. 84, 87.

28. The internal function of *dina demalkhuta* is stressed by Blidstein (see n. 25). Shilo finds that the minimal state interference in Jewish juridical matters kept *dina demalkhuta* a marginal issue in Jewish law (*Dina,* pp. 110, 441).

29. Baron, *SRH* 5, p. 71.

30. Erwin Goodenough offers a brilliant and closely detailed analysis of this camouflage of submission in the works of Philo, a submission that, nonetheless, conveyed in "code" and "innuendo" the philosopher's "resentment at being ruled by Roman conquerors," his belief in absolute divine sovereignty, and his faith in a messiah-king who would embody "true government" (*The Politics of Philo Judaeus: Practice and Theory* [New Haven, Conn./London: 1938], pp. 1, 4–7, 18–19, 24–32, 38–42, 110–19).

Neusner dates camouflage strategy among the rabbis as coming in the wake of the defeat of the military-messianist uprising of Bar Kokhba (132–135 C.E.). The "military program for subversion of Roman rule" was transformed into a spiritualized "passive expectation." But at the same time, he argues, the rabbis offered a program of "extraordinary theurgic activity which was merely masked by political quietism." Prayer for national salvation was nonviolent, but it was considered by the rabbis to be even more effective than violence, and it expressed the inner conviction that foreign rule was temporary and illegitimate (Neusner, *There We Sat Down,* pp. 38, 40–42; idem, *The Jews in Babylonia* 2, pp. 167–68).

A Talmudic example of the distinction between deference to power and acknowledgement of authority occurs in a story of a rabbi's encounter with a state official. The rabbi affirms to the official that God "has made earthly royalty on the model of heavenly royalty and has invested you with dominion." But at the same time, the rabbi intones to himself the biblical verse, 1 Chron. 29:11, affirming God's absolute and unshared sovereignty (Babylonian Talmud, *Berakhot* 58a, quoted in Neusner, *The Jews in Babylonia* 2, pp. 32–33; the passage also contains what may be the earliest reference to an informer and to the right to kill an informer in self-defense).

Yosippon, the tenth-century Hebrew paraphrase of *The Jewish War* by Josephus, reiterated and passed on to medieval Jews the idea of deference to power as the natural political order. In the twelfth-century amplification of the original text, Josephus is made to say:

Understand, then, that with all the earth's offspring, be they man or beast . . . fish or fowl, the greater rules over the lesser [younger], and in this there is no shame to the lesser. . . . In all the world, one part rules another part, and one part submits to another. Do not be stiffnecked and go against the nature of the world. . . . Do not think that this will be considered to your detriment or shame, for your time too will come, and you will return unto the Lord, and then you too will be rulers of the nations. (Flusser, *Sefer Yosippon,* chap. 78:97–106)

A later version is quoted in the Sedilikow ed., p. 124, and in Y. Baer, "Sefer Yosippon ha'ivri," in *Sefer Dinaburg,* ed. Yitzhak Baer (Jerusalem: 1949), p. 185. The original, unembellished version appears in Josephus, *The Jewish War* 5:367. The rule of the powerful is endowed here with a certain legitimacy of its own, but it is a legitimacy contingent on the fortunes of history as decreed in heaven. There is a concession to mastery, not to sovereignty.

Added evidence that Jewish views of gentile government legitimacy were politically determined and contingent on local circumstances is provided in rabbinic Responsa examined by Shilo. He finds that rabbis in the Rhineland were more prone to take a restrictive, antistate position in matters of *dina demalkhuta* than their Spanish contemporaries, who lived under more favorable conditions (Shilo, *Dina,* pp. 70–71, 434).

31. On Jewish serfdom, see Baron's chapters on the subject in his *Ancient and Medieval Jewish History,* pp. 284–322; idem, *SRH* 9, 135–92.

32. See, for example, the charters of Bishop Rudeger to the Jews of Spires (Speyer) (ca. 1084) and of Frederick I to the Jews of Worms (1157, confirming a charter of 1090) in O.J. Thatcher and E.H. McNeal, *Source Book for Medieval History* (New York: 1905), pp. 574–78; cf. Baron, *SRH* 4, p. 74.

33. Baron, *SRH* 4, pp. 70–72. The charter of 1182 was granted by Frederick I to the Jews of Ratisbon (now Regensburg).

34. Adolf Neubauer and Moritz Stern, *Hebräische Berichte über die Judenverfolgungen wahrend der Kreuzzüge* (Berlin: 1892), p. 78; Abraham Habermann, ed., *Sefer gezerot ashkenaz vetsarfat* (Jerusalem: 1945), pp. 163–64; Robert Chazan, "Emperor Frederick I, the Third Crusade, and the Jews," *Viator* 8 (1977), 83–93; E. Synan, *The Popes and the Jews in the Middle Ages* (New York: 1965), pp. 43–49; Kenneth Stow, "Gishat hayehudim laapifiorut vehadoktrina shel haganat hayehudim bashanim 1063–1147," *Mehkarim betoledot 'am yisrael veeretz yisrael* 5 (1980), 175–90; Baron, *SRH* 4, pp. 5–27; *SRH,* 9, pp. 8–10, 82, 137, 139, 145; Dinur, *Yisrael bagola* 2, bk. 1 docs. 1–7 (pp. 117–19); bk. 2 docs. 1, 3–5, 10 (pp. 554–60). Cf. *Yisrael bagola* 1, bk. 1 pp. 168–69, on the mission to Rome (ca. 1012) of Jacob b. Yekutiel; on the same, see Robert Chazan, *Medieval Jewry in Northern France* (Baltimore, Md.: 1973), pp. 13–14.

35. Arendt, *Totalitarianism,* p. 23. Emphasis added.

36. To give but a few examples: A.A. Neuman, *The Jews in Spain* (Philadelphia: 1942), chaps. 1–2; Baron, "Medieval Nationalism and Jewish Serfdom," in *Ancient and Medieval Jewish History,* pp. 312–14; *idem, SRH* 4, pp. 36–53; *SRH* 9, p. 119; Yosef Haim Yerushalmi, "The Lisbon Massacre of 1506 and the Royal Image in the Shebet Yehudah," *Hebrew Union College Annual* (hereafter *HUCA*), suppl. 1 (1976).

37. Commentary on Deut. 28, in Isaac Abravanel *Perush 'al hatorah* (Jerusalem: 1964), p. 270 (originally published Venice 1579).

38. David Kaufmann, "The Prayer Book According to the Ritual of England Before 1290," *JQR,* o.s., 4 (1892), 20–63. Emphasis added.

39. The prayer begins with the wish that God protect and exalt the ruler, then expresses the hope that he and his advisors would be moved to deal kindly with the Jews, and ends with the prayer for Israel's speedy redemption.

40. See the discussion in Eli Lederhendler, "From Autonomy to Auto-Emancipation: Historical Continuity, Political Development, and the Preconditions for the Emergence of Jewish National Politics in Nineteenth-Century Russia," Ph.D. diss., The Jewish Theological Seminary of America, 1987, pp. 64–101.

41. See n. 2 and Baron, *SRH* 9, p. 11, on a similar alliance between a Jewish community in Béziers and the local bishop, which was broken up by the king in 1278. For antimonarchical opinion, see, for example, Isaiah Tishby, "Dapei geniza miḥibur meshiḥi-misti 'al gerushei sefarad uportugal," *Zion* 48 (1983), 55–102, 347–85; Yosef Hacker, "Khronikot ḥadashot 'al geirush hayehudim misefarad, sibotav vetotsaotav," *Zion* 44 (1980), 201–28; idem, "Yisrael bagoyim betiuro shel R. Shlomo leveit Halevi misaloniki," *Zion* 34 (1969), 72–73); H. Berger, "Der commentar des R. Benjamin b. Jehuda zu den Sprüchen," *Monatsschrift für Geschichte und Wissenschaft des Judentums* (hereafter *MGWJ*) 45 (1901), 138, 394; Dinur, *Yisrael bagola* 2, bk. 5 p. 313; Baer, "Don Yitzḥak Abravanel veyaḥaso el be'ayot hahistoria vehamedina," *Tarbitz* 8 (1936–39), 242, 248, 257; Ben-Zion Netanyahu, *Don Isaac Abravanel* (Philadelphia: 1972), pp. 158–86.

42. Baron, *SRH* 9, p. 135. On the role of the lesser princes in establishing Jewish communities near provincial centers after their expulsion from royal cities, see Selma Stern, *The Court Jew* (Philadelphia: 1950), p. 208.

43. Finkelstein, *Self-Government,* p. 331.

44. "Journal de Joselmann," introduced by J. Kracauer in *Revue des études juives* (hereafter *REJ*) 16 (1888), 89–90; Selma Stern, *Josel of Rosheim* (Philadelphia: 1965), p. 83.

45. Kracauer, "Journal," 87–92; Selma Stern, *Josel of Rosheim,* pp. 62–64, 80–81, 90–102, 116–19, 192–204, 224–25.

46. Kracauer, "Journal," 90–91.

47. Baron, *SRH* 16, pp. 23–25, 27–40, 140ff., 158–60; Bernard Weinryb, *The Jews in Poland: A Social and Economic History* (Philadelphia: 1973), pp. 33–37, 48–51, 123–26; Raphael Mahler, *Toledot hayehudim befolin ('ad hamea hatesh'a 'esreh)* (Merhavia, Israel: 1946), pp. 137–42. Baron cites, as an example, the basic charter granted to the Jews by Sigismund I in 1539. Unlike in the West, however, the term *servi camerae* was not applied here to the Jews.

48. Baron, *SRH* 16, pp. 154–60, 187; Binyamin Cohen, "Havoievoda betorat shofet hayehudim befolin hayeshana," *Gal-'Ed* 1 (1973), 1–12; idem, "Hareshut havoievodit vehakehilla hayehudit bemeiot ha-16–18," *Gal-'Ed* 3 (1976), 9–32; Shmuel Ettinger, "Ma'amadam hamishpati vehaḥevrati shel yehudei ukraina bemeiot ha-15–17," *Zion* 20 (1955), 130–31, 135.

49. Weinryb, *Poland,* pp. 112, 119ff.; Baron, *SRH* 16, pp. 28, 107ff., 120ff.; Mahler, *Toledot,* pp. 152–53; Jacob Goldberg, "Bein ḥofesh lenetinut: sugei hatelut hafeiudalit shel hayehudim befolin," in *PWCJS* 1969 (1972), pt. 2, pp. 107–8; idem, *"De non tolerandis iudaeis:* On the Introduction of the Anti-Jewish Laws into Polish Towns and the Struggle Against Them," in S. Yeivin, ed., *Sefer Raphael Mahler* (Tel-Aviv/Merhavia, Is: 1974), pp. 39–52; Murray Jay Rosman, "The Polish Magnates and the Jews: Jews in the Sieniawski-Czartoryski Territories, 1686–1731," Ph.D. diss., The Jewish Theological Seminary of America: 1982, pp. 74–75, 91, 93.

50. Haim Hillel Ben-Sasson in *Hagut vehanhaga: hashkefoteihem haḥevratiot shel yehudei polin beshalhei yemei habeinayim* (hereafter *HVH*) (Jersualem: 1959), pp. 142–43, cites the opinions of R. Benjamin Aaron Slonik (Responsa, *Masat Binyamin* [Cracow: 1633], no. 33) and R. Yehoshua of Cracow (*Penei Yehoshua* [Amsterdam: 1715], "Oraḥ ḥaim," no. 7).

51. Simon Dubnow, "Istoricheskii soobshcheniia: podgotovitel'nyia raboty dlia istorii russkikh evreev: oblastnye kagal'nye seimy v voevodstve volynskom i v belorussii (1666–1764)," *Voskhod,* nos. 4, 12 (1894), 25–44, 139–50; idem, *History* 1, pp. 103–13, 188–98. Cf. Jacob Katz, *Tradition and Crisis,* pp. 112–34; Baron, *Jewish Community* 1, pp. 323–37; idem, *SRH* 16, pp. 27, 109, 133, 157, 163, 237, 291; Israel Halperin, *Yehudim veyahadut bemizraḥ eiropa* (Jerusalem: 1968), pp. 39–107; Mahler, *Toledot,* pp. 157–58, 188, 190, 207–15; Weinryb, *Poland,* pp. 72–78, 169; A. Tsigelman, " 'Iskei ḥakhirot shel yehudei polin ukesharam lehitehavut va'ad arb'a aratsot," *Zion* 47 (1982), 112–44. Records of the Polish Council were reconstructed and edited by Israel Halperin, *Pinkas va'ad arb'a aratsot* (hereafter *PVAA*) (Jerusalem: 1945–46); those of the Lithuanian Council were published by Dubnow, *Pinkas medinat lita* (hereafter *PML*) (Berlin: 1925).

52. Mahler, *Toledot,* pp. 141, 148; Gershon Hundert, "Security and Dependence: Perspectives on Seventeenth-Century Polish Jewish Society Gained Through a Study of Jewish Merchants in Little Poland," Ph.D. diss., Columbia University, 1979, p. 203. The charters granted to Jewish communities have been collected by several historians and most recently made available in a scholarly edition by Jacob Goldberg, *Jewish Privileges in the Polish Commonwealth* (Jerusalem: 1985). Privileges and their confirmations are also found in Maurycy Horn, "Regesty dokumentów z metryki koronnej do historii żydów w Polsce," *Biuletyn Żydowskiego Instytutu Historycznego* (hereafter *BZIH*), nos. 116–24 (1980–82). Cf. M. Balaban, "Pravovoi stroi evreev v pol'she," *Evreiskaia starina* (hereafter *ES*) 3 (1910), 39–60, 161–91 (on general privileges, pp. 161–70; on special privileges, pp. 170–91). Special privileges for the Jews of Cracow are found in M. Shorr, "Materialy, dokumenty i soobshcheniia: (2) spetsial'nyie privilegii krakovskikh evreev (1549–1678)," *ES* 2 (1909), 223–45.

53. One of the Jewish demands in this period was that the Jews' judge *(judex judaeorum)* of the wojewoda's court be selected only from among the land-owning nobility rather than from the burgher class. Such a proviso was obtained for royal privileges granted to the Jews of Lwów (1569), Przemyśl (1576),

Cracow, Poznań, and Lublin (1591) and extended to all of Poland-Lithuania in 1633. See Binyamin Cohen, "Hareshut havoievodit," 12.

54. For example, Rosman, "Magnates," pp. 1–2, 4, 11, 393–94. On the vagaries of gentry support for Jewish privileges and interests, see Mahler, *Toledot,* pp. 168–75; Baron, *SRH* 16, pp. 131–32.

55. Yitzhak Schiper, *Toledot hakalkala hayehudit* (Tel-Aviv: 1935–36) 2, pp. 517–19; Weinryb, *Poland,* p. 138; Mahler, *Toledot,* pp. 142, 148, 150; *PVAA,* no. 993 [1757].

56. Weinryb, *Poland,* p. 136; *PVAA,* no. 993 [1757].

57. Bernard Weinryb, *Texts and Studies in the Communal History of Polish Jewry, Proceedings of the American Academy of Jewish Research* (hereafter *PAAJR*) 19 (1950), pp. 24–25, 36–37; Baron, *SRH* 16, pp. 106–20, 194. On the earlier (1521) abortive alliance among Lwów, Poznań, and Cracow to secure anti-Jewish privileges, see Baron, *SRH,* p. 10.

58. Hundert, "Security and Dependence," pp. 196–203; Weinryb, *Poland,* pp. 353–54 n. 23; Baron, *SRH* 16, pp. 13–14, 194; Mahler, *Toledot,* pp. 290–92.

59. *Akty izdavaemye vilenskoiu komissieiu dlia razbora drevnykh aktov* (hereafter *AVK*), vol. 29, *Akty o evreiakh* (Vilna: 1902), idem, nos. 14–18.

60. Israel Klausner, *Toledot hakehilla ha'ivrit bevilna* (Vilna: 1938), pt. 2, pp. 25–42; Baron, *SRH* 16, pp. 13–15; *AVK* 29, nos. 23 [6 November 1669], 29 [22 April 1673], 31 [4 March 1673], 119, 120 [29 August 1687], 222, 223 [10 August and 10 October 1750].

61. Weinryb, *Poland,* pp. 135, 163, 353; Hundert, "Security and Dependence," pp. 8–9, 195–206, 210–12; idem, "Jewish Urban Residence in the Polish Commonwealth in the Early Modern Period," *Jewish Journal of Sociology* 26, no. 1 (1984), 25–34; Baron, *SRH* 16, p. 151; see, for example, the writ of John III Sobieski in favor of the Jews of Brest Litovsk in *AVK* 29, no. 127 (30 December 1688). On the problems of residential and occupational rights in general, see Azriel Frenk, *Ha'ironim vehayehudim befolin* (Warsaw: 1921/ Jerusalem: 1969); Baron, *SRH* 16, pp. 10–15, 106–20, 194–95; Dubnow, *History* 1, pp. 74–79, 93–95. On Warsaw, see Jacob Shatzky, *Geshikhte fun yidn in varshe* (New York: 1947) 1, pp. 25–28, 45–62; Frenk, *Ha'ironim,* pp. 62–67; Goldberg, *"De non tolerandis iudaeis,"* pp. 43, 48–49. On Przemyśl, Cracow, Warsaw, Kamenets-Podolsk, Vilna, and smaller towns, see Mahler, *Toledot,* pp. 147–50, 292ff., 297ff.; Halperin, *Yehudim,* pp. 148–50. On Mogilev, see Baron, *SRH* 16, pp. 179–80. On the role of Christian artisan guilds, see Mahler, *Toledot,* pp. 299–309; Baron, *SRH* 16, pp. 253–65. On the political struggle between Polish towns and the landowning nobility, see Maria Bogucka, "Towns in Poland and the Reformation," *Acta Polonia Historia* (hereafter *APH*) 40 (1979), 61–62.

62. The Kovno "Purim" letter was found by Shmuel Yosef Fuenn in the course of his research on the history of the Jews of Vilna and is quoted here from Fuenn's work, *Kirya neemana: korot 'adat yisrael be'ir vilna,* rev. ed. (Vilna: 1915), pp. 199–200.

63. The Jewish side of the story was recorded at the time of the events and later copied into the record book of the Mstislav burial society. Dubnow published it in *He-'Avar* 1 (1918), 63–65. Material relating to the uprising appears in *Regesty i nadpisi: svod materialov dlia istorii evreev v rossii* (hereafter *RIN*) 3 (St. Petersburg: 1913), nos. 1916, 1919, 1920; cf. Halperin, *Yehudim,* pp. 277–88 ("Gezerat Voshchila"). A somewhat analogous 1775 case in Bohemia elicited a similar response from Abraham Trebitsch b. Reuben Hayyat of Mikulov (Nikolsburg) in his history of Europe in the eighteenth century, *Korot ha'itim,* with "Korot nosafot" by Jacob Blodek, 2d ed. (Lemberg: 1851), par. 42. Weinryb, too, notes that the Jews' political attitudes underwent no fundamental change in the wake of the "deluge" of the mid-seventeenth century in *Poland,* pp. 200, 205.

64. See Mahler, *Toledot,* p. 139; Baron, *SRH* 16, pp. 154–57, 184–85; Dubnow, *History* 1, pp. 45–46, 52, 59–62, 83–84, 103–06.

65. Dubnow, in *History* 1, p. 73, cites the writ obtained by R. Mendel Frank of Brest Litovsk from Sigismund I in 1531. R. Yehoshua b. Shaul of Vilna obtained a letter of protection from the king in 1714 in order to shore up his authority in the face of an attempt by local Jews to unseat him. See S.A. Bershadskii, *Litovskie evreii* (St. Petersburg: 1883), pp. 21–22. For examples of coercive state authority invoked by the Jewish communities in matters of taxation, see *PVAA,* nos. 231 [1657]; 234 [1658]; 236, 237 [1659]; 253, 256 [1665]; 257 [1666]. *PML,* nos. 517, 518 [1658].

66. Rosman, "Magnates," pp. 97–99, 109, 413, 429–33; Binyamin Cohen, "Hareshut havoievodit," 23–25. R. Avraham b. Asher paid 8,000 zlotys in 1765 for the office of rabbi, of which part went to the wojewoda and part to the Vilna kahal, see Israel Klausner, *Vilna bitekufat hagaon* (Jerusalem: 1942), pp. 9–10.

67. Published in Salomon Buber, *Anshei shem* (Cracow: 1895), app., pp. 236–38.

68. Entry in *pinkas* of Dubno (p. 51a) in H.W. Margaliot, *Dubna rabbati* (Warsaw: 1910), p. 50.

69. Instances of permission granted to seek redress against recalcitrants in non-Jewish courts appear in *PML,* no. 17 [1623]. and in *PVAA,* nos. 126 [1623]; 241 [1661]; 265 [1667]; 289 [1671]; 465, 468 [1691]; 568, 570, 574, 578 [1718–19]; 594, 595 [1724].

70. Halperin, *Yehudim,* pp. 146–48; and in *PVAA,* nos. 21 [1595]; 220 [1658]; 253 [1665]; 268 [1668]; 399 [1672]; 401 [1683]; 438 [1687]; 465, 468 [1691]; 527, 528 [1700]; 570 [1718]; 662 [1747]; 664 [1751]; 774 [1757]; 807 [1762]; 978 [1725]; 987 [1750]; 919 [ca. 1759]; and pp. 74, no. 77, 81, nn. 1, 2. And in *PML,* pp. xvi, xxv; nos. 829 [1691]; 904 [1698]; 952, 956 [1761]; and p. 294 (court decision of 1683). And in *AVK* 13, *Akty glavnago litovskago tribunala* (Vilna: 1886), no. 73 (18 August 1766); *AVK* 29; *Akty o evreiakh* (Vilna: 1902), nos. 75 (23 December 1681), 79 (10 February 1682); *RIN* 2, no. 1581; *RIN* 3, nos. 1872 (3 March 1741), 2272 (4 January 1781), 2297 (21 April 1783); cf. Katz, *Tradition and Crisis,* pp. 113–14; Baron, *SRH* 16, pp. 16–17; Mahler, *Toledot,* pp. 391–

95; Dubnow, *History* 1, pp. 108, 193; idem, "Podgotovitel'niya raboty dlia istorii russkikh evreev," pp. 30–31, 34–35, 39–39; idem, "Va'ad arb'a aratsot befolin veyaḥso el hakehillot," in *Sefer hayovel leNaḥum Sokolov* (Warsaw: 1904), pp. 252–61; Dinur, *Bemifneh hadorot: meḥkarim ve'iyunim bereishitam shel hazemanim haḥadashim betoledot yisrael* (Jerusalem: 1971) 1, p. 120; E. Tcherikover, "Der arkhiv fun Shimon Dubnov," in YIVO *Historishe shriftn* 2 (Vilna: 1937), doc. 4, pp. 572–73.

71. *PML,* app. 2, pp. 294–99 (verdict of 1682); *AVK* 29, nos. 75 (23 December 1681) and 79 (10 February 1682); *PVAA,* no. 401 [1683].

72. *PML,* p. 297:

> And with regard to the great humiliation which each of the four kehillot has caused to the other and those things which were done in the course of the dispute, by which they [the communities] transgressed and quite overstepped the bounds of what is proper, by going to gentile courts to seek to confirm their case and each has had the effrontery to justify its action. . . . It would be fitting to punish both sides by imposing fines and causing their pride to diminish but we have refrained from this, so that contention might finally be stilled.

73. *PVAA,* no. 157 [1628]; first published by Dubnow in "Va'ad arb'a aratsot befolin," pp. 252–53. The reference to the king's command is apparently not to any specific order regarding this case but only to the general jurisdictional agreements between the Polish crown and the Lithuanian grand duchy, following the Union of Lublin. On this dispute and its further development, see Halperin, *Yehudim,* pp. 143–45, 150–51.

74. R. Ephraim of Luntshitz (Lentshütz-Lęczyca), *'Ir giborim* (Basle: 1580), Koraḥ, p. 104b.

75. *PVAA,* no. 178 [1640] reproduces a public pronouncement of the council, issued at Jaroslaw (Yaroslav), citing previous regulations condemning rabbinate purchasing (1587, 1590, and 1597). These were confirmed by the Lithuanian Council, *PML,* no. 207 [1628]. Cf. *PVAA,* no. 297 [1671], no. 734 [1754]. R. Yom-tov Lipman Heller waged a vigorous campaign against such appointments in Volhynia in the 1630s and 1640s; see his *Megilat eiva* (Breslau: 1836), pp. 29–35; and his exchange of letters with major Volhynian kehalim, in M. Brann, "Additions à l'autobiographie de Lipman Heller," *REJ* 21 (1890), 272–77. On the persistence of the practice in the second half of the seventeenth century and in the eighteenth century, see Berakhia Beirakh b. Isaac, *Zer'a Beirakh,* pt. 2 (Amsterdam: 1662), Introduction (first page); Margaliot, *Dubna rabbati,* p. 47 (entry on p. 64b of Dubno *pinkas* for 1734 regarding the rabbinical appointment of R. Joseph of Ostroha); Ben-Sasson, *HVH,* p. 217; Rosman, "Magnates," pp. 429–39; Israel Klausner, "Hamaavak hapenimi bekehillot rusia velita vehatsa'at R. Shimon b. Volf letikunim," *He-'Avar* 19 (1972), 57.

76. *PVAA,* no. 352 [1676]; cf. *PML,* no. 690 [1673]; Dubnow, "Fun mayn arkhiv," *Yivo bletter* 1, no. 5 (1931), 406; the Polish Council in 1671 condemned those who avoided paying taxes by cloaking themselves in the protection of noblemen. Cf. *PML,* no. 942 [1740] and *RIN* 2, nos. 1377, 1404; Yoel Rava,

"Protokol shel kinus va'ad gelil volin bishnat 1700 (ḥalukat mas hagulgolet),"
Gal-'Ed 6 (1982), 219. The granting of individual tax exemptions by Polish
magnates to their wealthy Jewish agents, Rosman argues, was a tactic in the
effort to maintain the superiority of the magnates' authority vis-à-vis the kahal,
see "Magnates," pp. 126, 405–9; cf. Hundert, "Security and Dependence," pp.
36–39.

77. *PVAA*, no. 530 [1700]. The kahal justified its action against the shtadlan,
one Baruch Levi, on the grounds that his own actions in exploiting his connections with the nobility to tyrannize the community left them no choice but to
fight fire with fire. They felt that their course of action was questionable enough,
however, to warrant taking a collective unanimous oath and obtaining the endorsement of the Polish Council.

78. *PML*, no. 908 [1700].

79. Judah b. Mordecai Hurwitz, *Tsel ma'alot* (Königsberg: 1764–65), p. 14b.

80. *PML*, nos. 129, 150 [1628]; 219, 220 [1631]; 747 [1679]; 793 [1684]; 830
[1691]. Assaf, *Ha'onshin*, citing the *pinkas* of Cracow, pp. 129–30. In 1628 the
community of Pinsk expelled a known informer and warned other communities
to take adequate precautions against him. The kahal of Brest Litovsk dealt
similarly with a man from Kobrin and his family. The two men were declared to
be outside the law, and the Lithuanian Council indicated that "their blood is
forfeit" (*PML*, no. 144 [1628]).

81. Weinryb, *Texts and Studies*, doc. 130 [1653], pp. 53–54; Binyamin Cohen,
"Hareshut havoievodit," 32. In some cases, however, it was the kahal itself that
engaged in tax evasion through tinkering with the population register.

82. *PVAA*, no. 297 [1671]. The precaution of the bribe, one assumes, was to
counter a similar ploy by the malefactor.

83. *PML*, no. 213 [1628]; cf. Rosman, "Magnates," pp. 153–54.

84. Binyamin Cohen, "Hareshut havoievodit," 15, cites the case of Lwów,
where the shtadlan until the mid-seventeenth century, was a non-Jew. *PML*, no.
147 [1628] instructs each kahal to meet the delegates at the Sejmiki and distrib-
ute gifts to them prior to their departure for the national Sejm in Warsaw, to
insure the delegates' support in forthcoming legislative activity. Even in minor
matters, it was common for Jewish communities to seek the intercession of an
influential non-Jew. The kehilla of Vilna in 1718 prevailed on the bishop to write
to the deacon of Novogrod and ask him to lower the rate of interest on loans to
the kehilla, *AVK* 13, no. 52.

85. *RIN* 1, no. 1071 quoted in Weinryb, *Poland*, p. 150.

86. *PVAA*, nos. 153 [1627]; 173 [1637–38]; 193 [1644]; 205 [1649]; 231 [1657];
234 [1658]; 236, 237 [1659]; 257, 258 [1666]; 262 [1667]; 346, 348 [1678]; 261
[1730]; 642 [1739]; 993 [1757]. *PML*, nos. 10 [1623]; 147, 206 [1628]; 269 [1632];
390, 394, 398, 399 [1639]; 475 [1650]; 691 [1673]; 772 [1678]; 855, 858 [1691];
1,000, 1,014 [1761]; and pp. 284, 289 (verdict of Lęczyca Court, 1681) and 291–
92 (verdict of Chomsk Court, 1652). Cf. N.M. Gelber and I. Halperin, "Va'ad
arb'a aratsot bashanim 1739–1753," *Zion* 2, (1937), 154–57, 172. A mid-seven-

teenth-century Responsum (*Sefer bet Hillel* of R. Hillel b. Naftali-Hirsh of Vilna, *Yoreh de'a*, no. 157) notes that it was standard practice for the Vilna shtadlanim to appear at the Lithuanian High Court (Tribunal), see Ben-Zion Katz, *Lekorot hayehudim berusia, polin velita* (Berlin: 1899), p. 13, doc. 10. The same work was done in the Karaite community by the *voit* (Meier Balaban, "Hakaraim befolin," *Ha-Tekufa*, no. 25 (1929), 472–73).

87. Baron, *SRH* 16, p. 95; idem, *Jewish Community* 2, pp. 115–16; Weinryb, *Poland*, p. 149.

88. The role of the court purveyor Marcus (Mordecai) Nikiel (Nekel) as chief syndic of Polish Jewry is mentioned in *PVAA*, nos. 254 [1665]; 257, 258 [1666]; 276 [1669].

89. From the Poznań *pinkas*, quoted in J. Perles, "Geschichte der Juden in Posen," *MGWJ* 14 (1865), 85 n. 10.

90. *PVAA*, no. 621 [1730]. The shtadlan of Vilna in the last half of the eighteenth century was paid 16 to 25 zlotys per week in addition to expenses. He was exempted from taxes and given a house by the kahal. Klausner, *Toledot hakehilla*, p. 136. Cf. *PVAA*, no. 258 [1666], the confirmation in office of Moshe b. Mordecai Nekel; and *PML*, no. 206 [1628], the appointment of Yeshaya of Vilna, Dr. Beirakh of Brest Litovsk, and Mordecai of Lomaz; and PML p. 301: the appointment of Haim b. Yosef of Vilna as shtadlan for the Lithuanian Council; the community regulation of Poznań no. 263 [1715], in I. Halperin, ed., *Takanot vehitmanuyot bekehillot yehudiot bameiot 17–18* (Jerusalem: 1962–63), p. 19.

91. *PML*, nos. 39, 81 [1623]. Cf. Klausner, *Vilna*, p. 11, on the authority of the shtadlan in Vilna.

92. This opinion of R. Meir b. Gedalia of Lublin (late sixteenth to early seventeenth century) was reported by R. Avraham Shrentzel's in his own Responsum, in *Sheelot uteshuvot eitan haezraḥi* (Ostroha: 1795), quoted in Ben-zion Katz, *Lekorot hayehudim*, doc. 12, p. 14, and in S. Assaf, *Ha'onshin*, p. 124. R. Meir's view is also reflected in his own Responsum, in which he urged a community to use its own discretion in the ransoming of a criminal. See *Sheelot uteshuvot . . . hagaon . . . R. Meir . . . milublin* (Venice: 1619), no. 15.

93. *PML*, no. 39 [1623].

94. *PML*, no. 433 [1647].

95. For example, see *AVK* 28, nos. 256 (28 September 1646), 268 (18 December 1646), 279 (19 October 1648), 300 (18 April 1660), 305 (23 July 1660), 306 (31 July 1660), 312 (17 December 1660), 316 (27 May 1663), 323 (20 March 1666), 326 (29 March 1666); *AVK* 29, nos. 23 (6 November 1669), 58 (28 May 1680), 68 (4 December 1680), 69 (8 December 1680).

96. Weinryb, *Texts and Studies*, pp. 49, 59; idem, "Beitrage zur Finanzgeschichte der juedischen Gemeinden in Polen," *HUCA* 16 (1941), 204–13; cf. *PVAA*, no. 342 [1674]; Mahler, *Toledot*, pp. 357–58.

97. Perles, "Geschichte," 176–77 n. 18. Salaries for communal officers represented 4,000 zlotys out of a total expenditure of 23,000 zlotys.

98. For example, *PVAA,* nos. 849 [ca. 1592]; 109 [1623]; 153 [1627]; 193 [1644]; 277 [1670]; 368 [1678]; 392 [1681]; 405 [1683]; 793 [1761]; and pp. 169–70 n. 13; *PML,* pp. 278–89, litigations between the Lithuanian Council and the Polish Four Lands Council, 1678–81; Mann, *Texts and Studies* 2, pp. 630–32.

99. *PML,* nos. 147 [1628], 827 [1687]; *PVAA,* nos. 353 [1676]; 392 [1681]; 433 [1687]; 639, 640 [budgets of the council 1739–40]; app. 962 [expenses of 1726]. Cf. Frenk, *Ha'ironim,* p. 48; Raphael Mahler, "A budzhet fun vad arba arotsoys in 18-tn yorhundert," *Yivo bletter* 15, no. 1/2 (1940), 73–81. Baron points out that the often prolonged litigations between the Jewish communities and city councils, generally involving the sending of delegations of lobbyists to the *Sejmiki* and royal tribunals, also required prodigious sums. Baron, *SRH* 16, p. 294.

100. Published in Weinryb, *Texts and Studies,* p. 54.

101. Mahler, "A budzhet," p. 74.

102. Halperin, *Yehudim,* pp. 266–76.

103. Rosman, "Magnates," p. 440; Binyamin Cohen, "Hareshut havoie-vodit," pp. 30–32.

Chapter 2

1. The theoretical problems raised by the use of the terms *tradition, modernity,* and *modernization* are too well known to require a lengthy exposition here. As critics have pointed out, the attempt by social and political analysts (especially in the 1960s and early 1970s) to define modernization and tradition in universally acceptable terms through imposing a preset dichotomy of mutually exclusive criteria and through the isolation of quantifiable variables was flawed by its teleological leveling of sociohistorical differences. Tradition and modernity are patently abstract generalizations and, therefore, unsuited for use as surgical analytical instruments. The use of these terms remains valid, I believe, if this pitfall is avoided and if neither term is construed as an absolute category. Moreover, whereas the use of strictly defined ideal-type patterns to define traditional and modern societies and polities has been criticized in particular when applied to the analysis of societies undergoing the early stages of rapid social change *today*—because the use of a prescriptive evolutionary model would seem to prejudge the outcome—in the case of a process of change that reached known conclusions in the past, this problem clearly does not apply. Among some of the more useful theoretical discussions of this issue in general and as it relates to Jewish history are: Samuel P. Huntington, "The Change to Change: Modernization, Development and Politics," *Comparative Politics* 3 (April 1971), 283–322; David E. Apter, *The Politics of Modernization* (Chicago/London: 1965), pp. v–xv, chaps. 1–3; C.S. Whitaker, Jr. *The Politics of Tradition* (Princeton, N.J.: 1970), pp.3–14; Edward Shils, *Tradition* (Chicago/London: 1981); Jacob Neusner, "From Theology to Ideology: The Transformation of Judaism in Modern

Times," in Kalman Silvert, ed., *Churches and States: The Religious Institution and Modernization* (New York: 1967), pp. 13–48; S.N. Eisenstadt, "Post-traditional Societies and the Continuity of Tradition," *Daedalus* 102, no. 1 (Winter 1973), 1–27.

2. The document was published by Israel Halperin in *Kiryat sefer* 12 (1935); it also appears on pp. 137–38 of his *Yehudim*.

3. The two communities and the two rabbis were rivals for prestige and hegemony, so their cooperation in such an agreement reflects the gravity of the situation and was probably calculated to lend weight to the decision. This cooperation was particularly important because the previous two incumbents in the council chair had been Żolkiew men, when in the past the seat had generally gone to leaders from the district's senior city, Lwów. Halperin suggests that the united front presented here by Lwów and Żolkiew may have been directed against a new rival, the kahal of Brody. See *Yehudim*, pp. 136–37.

4. In 1750 Brody unilaterally—and rather presumptuously, given its junior standing in the province—named a parnas for the council. Żolkiew lodged a protest with the Polish authorities and in concert with the Lwów and the Tysmienica kehalim attempted to boycott council sessions called by the upstart chairman; but they apparently did not succeed in unseating him (Halperin, *Yehudim*, p. 137).

5. The text appears in *PVAA*, app. 81 (pp. 76–77) and is translated in no. 825.

6. Rosman, "Magnates," pp. 420–21.

7. Halperin, *Yehudim*, p. 153 (based on a document published in 1903 by the Vilna University Library).

8. On this period and attitudes to the Jewish question—a hotly debated public issue—see, Mahler, *Toledot*, pp. 440–56; Dubnow, "Evreiskaia pol'sha v epokhu poslednykh razdelov," *ES* 4 (1911), 441–63; idem, *History* 1, pp. 270–91; N.M. Gelber, "Die Juden und die Judenreform auf dem vierjährigen Seim," in Ismar Elbogen et al., eds., *Festschrift zu Simon Dubnows siebzigstem Geburtstag* (Berlin: 1930), pp. 136–53; Valerian Kalinka, *Der vierjährige Polnische Reichstag, 1788 bis 1791* (Berlin: 1898) bk. 2 pp. 341–46; bk. 5 pp. 503–4.

9. Dubnow, *History* 1, pp. 272–74; Mahler, *Toledot*, p. 447.

10. The pamphlet, written while Shimon b. Ze'ev-Wolf was imprisoned by the opposing side in the Vilna conflict, was entitled, "The Prisoner of Nieśwież [Nesvizh] to the Sejm Now in Session, on the Need for Reform of the Jews" (*Wiezień w Nieświeżu do Stanów Sejmuiacych o potrzebie Reformy Żydów*), and is available in Israel Klausner's Hebrew translation appended to his essay, "Hamaavak hapenimi," *He-'Avar* 19 (1972), 54–73.

11. Mahler, *Toledot*, pp. 451–56; Dubnow, "Evreiskaia pol'sha," 449–50; Gelber, "Judenreform," p. 141.

12. The kahal was abolished in Poland in 1822, twenty-two years before such action took place in the Russian Pale of Settlement. See, N.M. Gelber, "Sheelat hayehudim befolin bishnot 1815–1830," *Zion* 13–14 (1948–49), 124–25; Shatzky, *Geshikhte fun yidn* 1, pp. 270–75.

13. Avraham Braver, *Galitsia viyehudeha* (Jerusalem: 1965), pp. 179–81; M. Balaban, "Perekhod pol'skikh evreev pod vlast' avstrii: galitsiskie evreii pri Marii Terezii i Iosif II," *ES* 6 (1913), 289–307; N.M. Gelber, "Oblastnoi ravvinat' v galitsii (1776–86 g.)," *ES* 7 (1914), 305–17; Trebitsch, *Korot ha'itim,* pt. 2 pp. xix–xx. (Trebitsch's work, a history of Europe from 1741–1801, was originally published in Brünn [Brno] in 1801.)

14. There is an extensive literature on the early growth of Hasidism in Poland and White Russia and on the opposition it aroused. Major historical works include Dubnow's *Toledot hahasidut* 3d ed. (Tel-Aviv: 1974 [1930–31]); and M. Wilensky's collection of primary sources, *Hasidim umitnagdim: letoledot hapulmus shebeineihem bashanim 5532–5575 [1772–1815]*, 2 vols. (Jerusalem: 1970 [henceforth Wilensky 1 and Wilensky 2]). Other important studies will be referred to in the course of the discussion. The Vilna rabbinate–kahal controversy was briefly described by Fuenn in *Kirya neemana,* pp. 24–26, 138–44; and subsequently studied in detail by I. Zinberg (Tsinberg), "Milhemet hakahal beharav haaharon bevilna," *He-'Avar* 2 (1918), 45–64; and in Zinberg's "Di makhloykes tsvishn di roshey hakohol un dem rov in vilne in der tsveyter helft 18tn yorhundert," in YIVO *Historishe shriftn* 2, pp. 291–321. The definitive history of the affair is Klausner's *Vilna,* which is based on court archives in Vilna and the journal kept by R. Shmuel b. Avigdor. Cf. Klausner's article, "Hamaavak hapenimi," *He-'Avar* 19 (1972), 54–73.

15. Dubnow, *Toledot hahasidut,* pp. 107–8; Dinur, *Bemifneh hadorot,* pp. 84–85, 140–41, 147–59. The fact that the Hasidim organized themselves in independent congregations "is but a further sign of the victory of [Hasidism], since it succeeded in effect in prying the Jewish masses loose from the authority of the existing social institutions and reorganized them in a new organizational framework . . .; [a victory] which was predicated on the social and moral disintegration of the Jewish system of self-government" (Dinur, p. 227).

16. Jacob Katz, *Tradition and Crisis,* pp. 230, 241–43.

17. S. Ettinger, review of Jacob Katz, *Masoret umashber* in *Kiryat sefer* 35, no. 1 (1959); idem, "The Hassidic Movement—Reality and Ideals," in H.H. Ben-Sasson and S. Ettinger, eds., *Jewish Society Through the Ages* (New York: 1973; originally published 1969), pp. 252–65.

18. Chone Shmeruk, "Mashma'uta hahevratit shel hashehita hahasidit," *Zion* 20 (1955), 47–72.

19. Ibid.; and Halperin, *Yehudim,* pp. 333–39 ("Yahaso shel r. Aharon hagadol mikarlin klapei mishtar hakehillot").

20. Ze'ev Greis, "Sifrut hahanhagot hahasidit mehamahatsit hashniya lamea ha-18 ve'ad shenot hashloshim lamea ha-19," *Zion* 46 (1981), 198–236 (esp. 230–36). As further evidence of conformity and socioreligious solidarity between Hasidim and non-Hasidim, Halperin finds a uniformity of responses to such crises as reports of impending government limitations on Jewish marriages, despite geographic, political, and ideological divisions (*Yehudim,* p. 309).

21. Dubnow, *Toledot hahasidut,* pp. 107–69, 242–89; Wilensky 1, pp. 28–31; Iulii Gessen, "K istorii religioznoi bor'by sredi evreev v kontse 18 i v nachale 19

v.," *Voskhod,* no. 1 (1902), 116–35; no. 2, 59–90; Wolf Zeev Rabinowitsch, *Lithuanian Hasidism* (New York: 1971), pp. 22–62; Weinryb, *Poland,* chap. 12.

22. A collection of the bans and proclamations was printed at Olexieniec, near Brody, in Volhynia, under the title *Zamir 'aritsim veḥarvot tsurim;* also found in Dubnow, *Chasidiana* (St. Petersburg: suppl. to *He-'Avar* 2 [1918]; repr. Jerusalem: 1969); Wilensky 2, pp. 27–69.

23. "Evildoers," that is, the Jacob Frank messianic sect in Poland and Bohemia-Moravia active in the 1750s and 1760s.

24. "The crown is removed from us," that is, the authority associated with the councils.

25. Dubnow, *Toledot haḥasidut,* p. 120; Wilensky 1, p. 46.

26. Wilensky 1, p. 72.

27. Dubnow, *Toledot haḥasidut,* pp. 138ff.; Wilensky 1, pp. 101–21; Gessen, "K istorii religioznoi bor'by," 120. The four communities who joined the ban were Grodno, Brest Litovsk, Slutsk, and Pinsk.

28. Rabinowitsch, *Lithuanian Hasidism,* p. 26; Dubnow, *Toledot haḥasidut,* pp. 244–48; Weinryb, *Poland,* pp. 289–90.

29. Klausner, *Vilna,* pp. 30–31.

30. Ibid., pp. 31–32. Klausner was able to see a copy of the letter in the Vilna State Archive. The letter also called for an emergency tax to pay for the proposed delegation. Both activities—the unauthorized tax and the proposed conference—were, of course, illegal. Cf. Weinryb, *Poland,* p. 291.

31. Klausner, *Vilna,* p. 32; Dubnow, *Toledot haḥasidut,* pp. 257–63; Weinryb, *Poland,* p. 292; Gessen, "K istorii religioznoi bor'by," 59–61. Avraham Ber Gottlober (*Zikhronot umasa'ot* [Jerusalem: 1976] 1, pp. 142–43) states that R. Shneur-Zalman and twenty-one others were accused of being agents of Napoleon; seven of these together with R. Shneur-Zalman were sent off to St. Petersburg, but the Hasidim were able to secure the release of the seven when they reached Riga.

32. Klausner, *Vilna,* pp. 33–36; Gessen, "K istorii religioznoi bor'by," pp. 62–67.

33. Klausner, *Vilna,* pp. 37–43. The open conflict between the two sides—including a further denunciation and arrest of R. Shneur-Zalman (1800)—continued until 1802. The details are fairly well known, particularly the events of 1800–1801, as documented by Dubnow's collection of state papers, "Vmeshatel'stvo russkago pravitel'stva v antikhasidskuiu bor'bu (1800–1801)," *ES* 3 (1910), 84–109, 253–82.

34. The public nature of this conflict is fortunate for the historian because many documents relating to the case were preserved, including court archives and a dossier kept by R. Shmuel b. Avigdor. The notoriety of the affair drew a great deal of scholarly attention, but no one has linked the episode to a larger pattern in which what occurred in Lithuanian Jewry from the 1770s to the 1790s can be recognized as being relatively unexceptional, given the structure of Jewish politics at the time.

35. Klausner, *Vilna,* pp. 50–82; Israel Zinberg (Tsinberg), "Milḥemet haka-halbeharav haaḥaron bevilna," *He'Avar* 2 1918), 53–57. For the text of R. Shmuel's contract, see Fuenn, *Kirya neemana,* pp. 138–40.

36. Massalski willingly aided R. Shmuel and the Jews of Antokol in his own political interest, which was contrary to that of Radziwiłł. The bishop was in a strong position to make demands of the Vilna kahal as he had held Vilna Jewry's communal debt, which was considerable, since 1777 (it took eighteen years to liquidate). See Klausner, *Vilna,* pp. 93–94.

37. Zinberg, "Milḥemet hakahal," 58; Klausner, *Vilna,* pp. 97, 112–18.

38. In addition to the signatures of 280 tailors, goldsmiths, coppersmiths, furriers, and other craftsmen, the signatures of 95 merchants and 72 members of the community's electoral assembly (out of a total of 180 assembly members) were affixed to the powers-of-attorney (Klausner, *Vilna,* p. 123).

39. A self-made expert on legal matters, Shimon b. Ze'ev-Wolf drafted peti-tions and helped prepare the cases of fellow Jews to be conducted through Polish and Lithuanian courts by non-Jewish lawyers. He subsequently became a mem-ber of the kahal board and was himself charged with fiscal irregularities during the later 1790s when the Hasidim renewed their battle with Vilna kahal. See Klausner, *Vilna,* p. 293; idem, "Hamaavak hapenimi," pp. 59, 63. He came to wider public notice because of his pamphlet in favor of abolishing the kahal system, see n. 10.

40. The documents relevant to the wojewoda's verdict and the subsequent complaints and countersuits appear in *AVK,* 29, *Akty o evreiakh,* no. 231 (29 November 1785), pp. 463–65: decree of the Vilna wojewoda deposing R. Shmuel b. Avigdor; no. 234 (19 July 1786), pp. 472–74: the royal letter of protection to the Jewish petitioners of Vilna; no. 233 (16 February 1786), pp. 467–77: suit filed in royal court by "Vilna Jews living in the jurisdiction of the bishop"; and generally, nos. 235–40, pp. 474–80). Cf. Bershadskii, *Litovskie evreii,* pp. 49–54.

41. Klausner, *Vilna,* pp. 143–45; *AVK,* no. 233 (16 February 1786).

42. For the complaint filed by two Jewish merchants of Vilna on 12 February 1788 against the Vilna kahal's violent response to this incident, see Jacob Shatzky, "Arkhivalia: tsu der geshikhte fun der rabonim-makhloykes in vilne tsum sof 18tn yorhundert," in YIVO *Historishe shriftn* 1 (Vilna: 1929, cols. 717–38; cf. Klausner, *Vilna,* pp. 167, 183, 226–44, 271. During the investigation of this affair, R. Elijah, the Vilna Gaon, was arrested.

43. Klausner, *Vilna,* pp. 153–57, 167, 210, 254, 259.

44. Ibid., pp. 255, 274–81, 287; idem, "Hamaavak hapenimi," 59–73; Zin-berg, "Di makhloykes," 316–17; Mahler, *Toledot,* pp. 448–49.

45. Dubnow, *History* 1, p. 276; Klausner, *Vilna,* pp. 292–93; Zinberg, "Di makhloykes," 317.

46. "Fun di vilner arkhivn: der bunt minsker 'amkho' kegn kohol in 1777," in YIVO *Historishe shriftn* 2, pp. 608–11; Mahler, *Toledot,* pp. 395–415; Weinryb, *Poland,* p. 285; P. Marek, "Vnutrennaia bor'ba v evreistve v 18 veke," *ES* 12 (1928), 102–78.

47. Isaac Levitats, *The Jewish Community in Russia, 1777–1844* (henceforth Levitats) (New York: 1943), 1, pp. 22–45; John Klier, "The Origins of the Jewish Minority Problem in Russia, 1772–1812," (Ph.D. diss., University of Illinois, 1981; S. Ettinger, "Hayesodot vehamegamot be'itsuv mediniut hashilton harusi klapei hayehudim 'im ḥalukat polin," *He-'Avar* 19 (1972), 20–34; idem, "Takanat 1804," *He-'Avar* 22 (1977), 87–110; Azriel Shochat, "Hahanhaga bekehillot rusia 'im bitul hakahal," *Zion* 42 (1977), 143–233; idem, *Harabanut mita'am*. Russian legislation is cited from the *Complete Compendium of the Laws* (*Polnoe sobranie zakonov rossiiskoi imperii* [henceforth *PSZ¹* or *PSZ²* to denote first or second series, followed by a volume number and the number of the law]).

48. *PSZ¹*, vol. 28: 21,547.

49. *PSZ²*, vol. 10: 8054.

50. *PSZ²*, vol. 19 (pt. 1): 18,546. In administratively separate Poland, the kahal was abolished in 1822.

51. In 1811 and 1817 the kahal was further obligated to guarantee the accuracy of Jewish population records: *PSZ¹*, vol. 31: 24,635; vol. 34: 26,805.

52. S.A. Bershadskii, "Polozhenie o evreiakh 1804 goda," *Voskhod*, no. 1 (1895), 82–103; no. 6 (1895), 45–63; Levitats 1, pp. 30–34; Klier, "Origins," pp. 229–72; Ettinger, "Takanat 1804," 87–102; Michael Stanislawski, *Tsar Nicholas I and the Jews: The Transformation of Jewish Society in Russia, 1825–1855* (Philadelphia: 1983), pp. 8–9; Dubnow, *History* 1, chap. 9; pp. 335–45. On earlier legislative precedents and policy statements regarding the kahal and *bet din,* see Levitats 1, pp. 24–29; Klier, "Origins," pp. 306, 311–19; Yehuda Slutsky, "Letoledot hayehudim berusia besof hamea ha-18: shalosh te'udot," *He-'Avar* 19 (1972), 74–78.

53. Klier, "Origins," p. 241. The Hasidic rebbe R. Nahman of Bratslav was considerably preoccupied with the matter of the threatened *punktn* (points, i.e., of the law), as reported by his scribe and disciple, Nathan Sternhertz in *Sefer ḥayei mohaRan* (Jerusalem: 1962), pp. 7, 9, 11, 56; cf. Arthur Green, *Tormented Master: A Life of Rabbi Nahman of Bratslav* (University, Ala.: 1979), pp. 140–41. A meeting to discuss the matter among leading Hasidic figures was held in Berdichev (see chap. 3, n. 50).

54. Lestchinsky estimated that about 30 percent of the Jews of Eastern Europe were directly dependent on the rural sector (chiefly innkeeping and other forms of leasehold [*arenda*] on gentry estate revenue), see *Matsavam hakalkali shel hayehudim beeiropa hamizraḥit vehamerkazit* (Tel-Aviv: 1935), pp. 35–36. This is confirmed by Kh. Korobkov's data on Zhitomir in 1789, see "Ekonomicheskii rol' evreev v pol'she v kontse 18 v.," *ES* 3 (1910), 377.

55. E. Tcherikover, "Der arkhiv fun Shimon Dubnov: Di kamf fun di baleymelokhes kegn kohol in kaydan in 1815," in YIVO *Historishe shriftn* 2, pp. 588–91.

56. David Fajnhauz, "Konflikty społeczne w śród ludności żydowskiej na litwie i białorusi w pierwszej polowie 19 w.," *BZIH*, no. 52 (1964), 8–15 (Rus-

sian docs.). Cf. Yehuda Slutsky, "Sikum 'agum," *He-'Avar* 19 (1972), 13. On official involvement in kahal elections, see, for example, "Protokol fun kehille-valn," YIVO *Historishe shriftn* 2, p. 577.

57. Gessen, "K istorii religioznoi bor'by," 59–89; Dubnow, "Vmeshatel'stvo russkago pravitel'stva," 84–109, 253–82; Rabinowitsch, *Lithuanian Hasidism,* pp. 58–61; Klausner, "Hamaavak hapenimi," 63; idem, *Vilna,* pp. 33–36, 293; Weinryb, *Poland,* pp. 293–94.

58. Mahler, *Divrei yemei yisrael: dorot aharonim* (Merhavia, Israel: 1955) 2, pp. 157–61; Gelber, "Sheelat hayehudim," *Zion* 13/14 (1948–49), 109–25; Shatzky, *Geshikhte fun yidn* 1, pp. 270–71; Isaiah Warszawski, "Yidn in kongres-poyln (1815–1831)," in YIVO *Historishe shriftn* 2, p. 323.

59. Max Erik, "Vegn sotsialn mehus fun Aksenfelds shafn," *Tsaytshrift* 5 (1931), 137–45, 162–65; Israel Zinberg (Tsinberg). *A History of Jewish Litera-ture* (Cincinnati/New York: 1978) 11, chap. 5 (esp. pp. 141, 144–48).

60. Shaul Ginsburg, *Historishe verk* 1, p. 20. The Vilna kahal was unprepared to assume this responsibility and the idea of a Yiddish newspaper fell through.

61. See Eliezer Dillon's letter to the Minsk kahal in 1817, published in *Pe-rezhitoe* 4 (1913), 188–91 (David Maggid, "Iz moego arkhiva: k istorii evreiskikh deputatov v tsarstvovanie Aleksandra I"); Salo Baron, "Herem vilna vehamem-shalot haadirot," *Horev* 12 (1956), 62–69; *Bikkurei ha'itim* 1821, p. 233. Baron read the text of the ban in a German translation in the Prussian state archives before the Second World War. I am indebted to Dr. Shaul Stampfer who drew my attention to Baron's article.

62. The most recent reconsideration of the subject, which clears up certain older misconceptions, is that of Stanislawski, *Tsar Nicholas I,* chap. 1. The literature on this topic is particularly extensive, including memoirs, monographs, and documentary studies. For some of the documentation relating to the inaugu-ration of the draft in Jewish communities, see H. Aleksandrov, "Fun arkhiv fun minsker kohol," *Tsaytshrift* 1 (1926), 239–49. On the conscription administra-tion after 1844, see Shochat, "Hahanhaga," 181–84. Cf. Tcherikover, "Heha-mon hayehudi."

63. See chap. 3 n. 42; Y.L. Levin, "Zikhronot vera'ayonot," *Sefer hayovel le-Nahum Sokolov* (Warsaw: 1904, pp. 354–59; A.J. Paperna, "Kaafikim bane-gev," *Sefer hayovel le-Nahum Sikolov* (Warsaw: 1904), p. 441; idem, "Iz nikolaevskoi epokhi," *Perezhitoe* 2 (1910), 42–49; A.S. Friedberg, "Zikhronot miyemei ne'urai," *Sefer hashana* 3 (1902), 84–88. For an apologia for the rabbis and kahal establishment, see Lifschitz, *Zikhron Ya'aakov* (Frankfurt am Main: 1924), vol. 1, pp. 106–27 (hereafter *ZY* 1). On *Megilla 'efa* (Kearny, N.J.: 1904) by S.I. Landsberg, see Zinberg, *History* 11, p. 26 n. 17; A.B. Gottlober, "Hagizra vehabeniya," *Haboker or* (1879), 782. The text, mistakenly identified as a manuscript of I.B. Levinsohn's was published by Ephraim Deinard (Kearny, N.J.: 1904). Gottlober claims that it was read aloud in the streets of many Volhynian towns.

64. PSZ^2 vol. 10: 8,054.

65. Cf. PSZ^2 vol. 13: 10,895; Levitats 1, p. 37; Stanislawski, *Tsar Nicholas I,* pp. 35–38.

66. On censorship, see chap. 4 herein. On the schools law of 1842, see Levitats 1, p. 74; Stanislawski, *Tsar Nicholas I,* p. 76; PSZ^2 vol. 17: 15,771. On the rabbinate, see Azriel Shochat, *Mossad harabanut mita'am* (Haifa: 1975–76), pp. 9–40. Such a rabbinical registrar, one Shraga b. Isaac, was appointed in Pruzany in 1838 "in accord with the order of our lord the Tsar," and all the Jews in the town and its environs were solemnly warned not to fail to register the birth of any child, male or female, with the "poll-register rabbi." Anyone violating this regulation would "not only be fined by the kahal . . . but also [would be] treated as a violator of the law of the state [i.e., turned over to the civil authorities]," (*Pinkes fun der shtot pruzhene* [Pruzany, Plnd.: 1930], p. 125).

67. Stanislawski (*Tsar Nicholas I*) is clearly correct in his reading of the enormous impact of the conscription law of 1827, but we differ on the question of the situation prior to that time, which he describes as static (p. 33), but which I believe to have been dynamic. The *political* transformation of Jewish society in Eastern Europe began in mid-eighteenth century Poland and was quite advanced by 1827. See p. 57 in the present volume.

68. R. Yitzhak-Ayzik, *Sheelot uteshuvot 'ateret Yitzhak* (Jerusalem: 1925), p. 51a, cited in Shochat, "Hahanhaga," 159.

69. Levitats 1, pp. 80, 82; Iulii Gessen, *Evreii v rossii,* (Petrograd: 1916), pp. 45, 446–48; idem, "Zabytyi obshchestvennyi deiatel': zapiska kuptsa feigina na imia imp. Nikolaia I," *ES* 4 (1911), 394–402.

70. PSZ^2 vol. 19 (pt. 1): 18,546.

71. Especially by Levitats, Shochat, and Stanislawski (*Tsar Nicholas I,* p. 126); cf. Alexander Zederbaum in *Kol mevasser,* no. 18 (1870), and Kalman Shulman, *Havatselet hasharon* 1 (1861), 42.

72. For a portrait of a Jewish "dictator" who reigned in Bialystok from 1850 until almost 1910, see A.S. Hershberg, "Di fuftsik-yorike hershaft fun Yehiel-Ber Volkovsky iber bialystoker kehille," in Y. Mark, ed., *Pinkes bialystok* (New York: 1949) 1, pp. 249–68.

73. Dubnow, *History* 1, pp. 290–91; Mahler, *Toledot,* pp. 453–54.

74. Levitats 1, pp. 87–89.

75. Reference is to the partition of Poland.

76. Hillel b. Ze'ev-Wolf, *Hillel ben shahar* (Warsaw: 1804), p. 22b.

77. On Zeitlin, see Shmuel Zitron, *Shtadlonim* (Warsaw: 1926), pp. 28–51; Fuenn, *Kirya neemana,* pp. 271–73; S.Y. Hurwitz, "Sefer hayai (zikhronot)," *Ha-Shiloach* 40 (1923), 3–7.

78. Iulii Gessen, "Deputaty evreiskago naroda pri Aleksandra I," *ES* 2 (1909), 18; idem, *Istoriia evreiskago naroda v rossii* 1 (Leningrad: 1927), p. 322; Levitats 1, pp. 95–96; Klier, "Origins," pp. 239–41, 244, 325.

79. Peretz, a wealthy contractor with connections in the Russian admiralty, was a familiar St. Petersburg figure. Nevakhovich, engaged by Zeitlin as tutor for Peretz, accompanied the latter to St. Petersburg and served as translator for

the government on at least one occasion, that of R. Shneur-Zalman's second imprisonment. Both he and Peretz later converted to Christianity. See Zitron, *Shtadlonim,* pp. 38–61, 65–67; S. Ginsburg, *Meshumodim in tsarishn rusland* (New York: 1946), pp. 34–53; Levitats 1, p. 97; and Ben-Zion Katz in *He-'Avar* 2 (1918), 197–201 (introduction to *Kol shav'at bat yehuda*). Notkin, also a contractor for the army, was active in public affairs in prepartition Poland and had promoted Jewish reform proposals that centered on the establishment of agricultural colonies and manufacturing projects for Jews. He was also involved in obtaining R. Shneur-Zalman's release in 1801 and in establishing the Jewish community of St. Petersburg. See Zitron, *Shtadlonim,* pp. 68–89; Hillel-Noah Maggid Steinschneider, *'Ir vilna,* pp. 242–44; Mordecai Levin, *'Erkei ḥevra vekhalkala baideologia shel tekufat hahaskala* (Jerusalem: 1975), pp. 186, 216, 235; Mazeh, *Zikhronot* 2, p. 70.

80. *Vopl' dshcheri iudeiskoi [The Lament of the Daughter of Judea]* was translated into Hebrew (or, more probably, published in the original Hebrew from which the Russian version was made) and entitled *Kol shav'at bat yehuda* (Shklov: 1804); reprinted in *He-'Avar* 2 (1918), n. pag. The Hebrew version was dedicated to Neta Notkin. The pamphlet will be discussed in chap. 3. Kochubei was a principal member of the Committee for the Amelioration of the Jews appointed under Alexander I.

81. *Kol shav'at,* pp. 6, 11, 32–33.

82. Statute on the Jews, 1804, art. 34.

83. Gessen, "Deputaty," 20–21; idem, *Istoriia* 1, pp. 318ff.; Dubnow, *History* 1, pp. 347–49.

84. Gessen, "Deputaty," 21. Foreign Minister Budberg objected to Kochubei's entire proposal, rejecting any possible connection between the Jews of Russia and Napoleon's ostensible ploy to rally all Jews to his flag. Kochubei's position was credited by Alexander, however, at least in part: He sent Senator Alekseev on an inspection tour of the western provinces to investigate.

85. Ibid.; Dubnow, *History* 1, p. 349; Levitats 1, p. 98.

86. Predictably, they recommended the suspension or abrogation of the main points of the 1804 statute adversely affecting the status quo in Jewish life. The Popov Commission, which took these reports into account, submitted its own report in 1812. It recommended the postponement of the remaining expulsions as well as some other measures asked for by the Jews, including a restoration of the ḥerem. The report remained unimplemented, but further expulsions from the villages were, indeed, postponed. See Gessen, "Deputaty," p. 23; Levitats 1, p. 98; Dubnow, *History* 1, pp. 352–55.

87. Gessen, "Deputaty," 22–24; cf. Shaul Ginsburg, *Otechestvennaia voina 1812 goda i russkie evreii* (St. Petersburg: 1912), p. 85.

88. David Maggid, "Iz moego arkhiva: k istorii evreiskikh deputatov," 181–86 (doc. 1); N. Steinschneider, *'Ir vilna,* pp. 146–48 n. 3; Levitats 1, pp. 99–100.

89. Gessen, "Deputaty," 198–201.

90. "K istorii evreiskikh deputatov," p. 185.

91. Ibid., pp. 186–88 (Dillon's letter of December 1816, doc. 2); Levitats 1, pp. 100–101.

92. Gessen, "Deputaty," pp. 27–29, 196–97; *Voskhod* no. 1 (January 1905), 75ff.; Levitats 1, pp. 102–3; PSZ[1] vol. 24: 27, 106.

93. Gessen, "Deputaty," pp. 203–6; Levitats 1, p. 104. On Sonnenberg's activities in St. Petersburg, see Zitron, *Shtadlonim,* pp. 103–23; idem, on Dillon, pp. 125–37.

94. "A kol-koyrey fun Tiktiner kehille vegn der gzeyre fun geyrush un vegn a baratung fun yidishe kehilles," in YIVO *Historishe shriftn* 2, docs. sec. (doc. 2), pp. 573–74.

95. Published by Gessen, "Zapiska vilenskago kagala o nuzhdakh evreiskago naroda (1833 g.)," *ES* 4 (1911), 107–8.

Chapter 3

1. See, for example, the Hebrew and German ode ("Lob und Danklied der Judengemeinde zu Mohilow beim Einzuge Ihrer Kayserlichen Majestät Katharina II") presented to Catherine the Great in 1780 while she was traveling in White Russia: see P. Kon in YIVO *Historishe shriftn* 1, cols. 753–60. Cf. H. Borodiansky, "Di loyblider lekoved Katerine II un zeyere mekhabrim," in YIVO *Historishe shriftn* 2, pp. 531–37, including similar odes presented by the Jews of Polotsk and Shklov at that time. On the basis of internal evidence and comparative material, Borodiansky asserts that the Shklov ode was written by Naftali Hirsch (Herz) Wessely and translated into German by Moses Mendelssohn.

2. Fuenn, *Kirya neemana,* p. 198.

3. RIN 3, docs. 2412–35; P. Kon, "A yidishe shtim tsum oyfshtand 1794 in vilne," *Yivo bletter* 4, no. 2 (1932), 134–48; Jacob Shatzky, *Kultur-geshikhte fun der haskole in lite* (Buenos Aires: 1950), pp. 37–40; Yosef Kermish, "Yehudei varsha bemered Koshchushko," *Sefer hayovel le-N.M. Gelber* (Tel-Aviv: 1963), pp. 221–29.

4. On Polish-Lithuanian Jews involved in assisting or involuntarily commandeered for supply service to the Napoleonic forces, see Azriel Frenk, *Yehudei polin biyemei milḥamot Napoleon* (Warsaw:1912–13), pp. 46–55; *AVK* 38, *Otechestvennaia voina 1812 g.,* docs. 277, 301, 469, 525, 606, 642, 659, 719, 801; P. Kon, "Yidn in dinst fun poylishn general Dombrowski," in YIVO *Historishe shriftn* 1, cols. 764–66. S. Posener, "Un Sanglant cauchemar de guerre," *L'Univers israélite* (August 1934), p. 291, offers arguments against the popular belief that Vilna Jews had been rabidly anti-French. Rare individual Polish Jews served in combat forces, this judging from one rabbinic responsum related to a problem of divorce; the soldier in question, however, deserted and reportedly went over to the Russian side, see Avraham Zvi-Hirsh b. Eliezer of Piotrków, *Sheelot uteshuvot berit Avraham* (Dyhrenfurth: 1819), *Even ha'ezer,* no. 70. For a good general discussion on varying Jewish attitudes in Poland in 1812, see

Shatzky, *Geshikhte fun yidn* 1, pp. 210–24. On Jewish attitudes in the period of 1807–11, see Frenk, *Yehudei polin*, pp. 9, 12–14, 18.

5. Ginsburg, *Otechestvennaia voina,* pp. 29–31, quotes extensively from the text of the synod's proclamation; cf. Gessen, *Istoriia* 1, pp. 337–38. A copy of the text is in the Central Archive for the History of the Jewish People (Jerusalem), file no. RU 33.

6. On Jewish support for Russia, see esp. Ginsburg, *Otechestvennaia voina,* pp. 36–37, and chaps. 5–7, 10; idem, *Historishe verk* 1, pp. 183–211; *AVK* 38, docs. 255, 270, 297, 824; Dubnow, *History* 1, pp. 355–59.

7. Dubnow, *History* 2, p. 14; S. Beilin, "Iz istoricheskikh zhurnalov: (4) otzyv velikago kniazia Nikolaia Pavlovicha o evreiakh," *ES* 4 (1911), 589–90. In 1827 a report prepared by Nikolai Novosil'tsev (deputy to the tsar's brother, Grand Duke Constantine) for Tsar Nicholas's consideration in connection with subjecting Russian Jews to military conscription similarly recalled the Jews' "constant" loyalty and service; see Dubnow, "Kak byla vvedena rekrutskaia povinnost' dlia evreev v 1827 g.," *ES* 2 (1909), 260. Novosil'tsev, however, was reportedly bribed by the Jews.

8. The text was published by Gessen, "Zapiska vilenskago kagala," *ES* 4 (1911), 99.

9. On the involvement of Polish Jews in the 1830–31 uprising, see Shatzky, *Geshikhte fun yidn* 1, pp. 306–30; N.M. Gelber, "Di yidn in Kalish un der oyfshtand in yanuar 1830–1831," *Lodzer visnshaftlekhe shriftn* 1 (1938), 258–66; idem, (ed.), *Hayehudim vehamered hapolani: zikhronotav shel Ya'akov Halevi Levin miyemei hamered hapolani bishnat 1830–1831* (Jerusalem: 1952), Introduction: pp. 16–29. Yaakov Halevi Levin's memoir itself, however, is not at all sympathetic to the Poles. In *ZY* 1, pp. 29–31, 55–56, Lifschitz, though not himself a witness to the events, also stresses the sufferings of the Jews at the hands of the Poles, the quandary faced by habitually law-abiding Jews when put under pressure by the Polish landowning gentry, and the bombast of Polish patriotic ambitions. On Polish propaganda among Jews in Lithuania, see S. Levin, "Tsum onteyl fun di litvishe yidn in oyfshtand fun 1831," *Yivo bletter* 2, no. 3 (1931), 222–33.

10. Shatzky, *Geshikhte fun yidn* 1, pp. 237–38, 242–44; Mahler, *Divrei yemei yisrael* 2, bk. 1 pp. 153, 155, 157; Gelber, "Sheelat hayehudim," 106–7; Raphael Mahler, "A Jewish Memorandum to the Viceroy of the Kingdom of Poland, Paskiewicz," in Saul Lieberman, ed., *Salo Baron Jubilee Volume* (Jerusalem: 1974) 2, pp. 669–96.

11. Shmuel Ettinger, "The Jews at the Outbreak of the Revolution," in Lionel Kochan, ed., *The Jews in Soviet Russia Since 1917* (Oxford/New York: 1972), p. 24; idem, "Jews and Non-Jews in Eastern and Central Europe Between the Wars," in Bela Vago and George Mosse, eds., *Jews and Non-Jews in Eastern Europe, 1918–1945* (New York/Jersualem: 1974), p. 4.

12. A thorough examination of how this theme surfaced in nineteenth-century Hebrew and Yiddish maskilic literature was made by Israel Bartal,

"Halo-yehudim veḥevratam besifrut 'ivrit veyidish bemizraḥ eiropa bein ha-shanim 1856–1914," Ph.D. diss., The Hebrew University: 1980.

13. Milton Gordon, *Assimilation in American Life: The Role of Race, Religion and National Origins* (New York/Oxford: 1964). Behavioral assimilation refers to the adoption by minority group members of social and cultural norms from the majority society, a process that need not be accompanied by the acceptance of such minority members into the majority society.

14. Steven J. Zipperstein, "Haskalah, Cultural Change, and Nineteenth-Century Russian Jewry: A Reassessment," *Journal of Jewish Studies* 35, no. 2 (1983), 191–207; idem, *The Jews of Odessa: A Cultural History, 1794–1881* (Stanford, Calif: 1985), in which Zipperstein demonstrates the interrelationship between Haskalah per se and broader processes of socioeconomic change in the particular setting of Odessa.

15. Haim b. Yitzhak, *Sefer ruaḥ Ḥaim: beur 'al masekhet avot* (Vilna: 1858), p. 37.

16. "Dokumenty i soobshcheniia," *Perezhitoe* 1 (1909), 15.

17. Jacob b. Isaiah Mazeh, *Zikhronot* (Tel-Aviv: 1936) 2, p. 32.

18. I. Iakhinson, ed., *Sotsial-ekonomisher shteyger ba yidn in rusland in 19 y.h.* (Kharkov: 1929), pp. 68–70. On Shklov's economic importance, see Israel Zinberg (Tsinberg), "Shklov i ego 'prosvetiteli' kontsa 18 veka," *ES* 12 (1928), 19. On the economic significance of smuggling among Jewish merchants in Eastern Europe, see Philipp Friedman, "Wirtschaftsliche Umschichtungsprozesse und Industrialisierung in der polnischen Judenschaft 1800–1870," in Salo W. Baron and Alexander Marx, eds., *Jewish Studies in Memory of George A. Kohut* (New York: 1935), pp. 203, 213–16; Bernard Weinryb, *Neueste Wirtschaftsgeschichte der Juden in Russland und Polen von der 1. polnischen Teilung bis zum Tode Alexanders II (1772–1881)*, 2d rev. ed. (Hildesheim, W. Ger./New York: 1972), pp. 40–42; Ginsburg, *Historishe verk* 1, p. 241.

19. As Baron points out, the ḥerem prohibited smuggling goods "in secret and stealth" but said nothing on the subject of merchandise imported openly with the agreement of corrupt Russian officials, which was the general case. The Prussian Interior Ministry was informed that in a short time, the petty merchants who had had to hide even from the Russian officials, for lack of the means to pay kickbacks, would "hopefully" learn to form partnerships and thus be able to resume business as usual! Baron, "Ḥerem vilna," 65–66, see especially the diplomatic dispatch to the ministry reproduced on 66–68. An indication of the importance of Jewish merchants in the international trade between Germany and Poland (and Russia) in the late eighteenth to early nineteenth centuries is given by the following figures: At the Leipzig fair (which took place three times a year), Jewish traders constituted 89 percent of all Polish merchants in 1790, 93 percent in 1796, and 98 percent in 1811, see Kh. Korobkov, "Uchastie evreev vo vneishnei torgovle pol'shi," *ES* 4 (1911), Table 3.

20. PSZ^1 vol. 40: 30,402, 30,581; and PSZ^2 vol. 8: 6,223; vol. 13: 11,088; vol. 14: 12,201, 13,003; vol. 18: 16,767; vol. 19: 17,503; vol. 25: 23,835; vol. 26: 24,975;

vol. 27: 26,327; vol. 32: 32,513. A campaign of support for the Jews expelled from the border areas was begun among Jews in Germany, and the Prussian ministries were concerned as well. See: Jacob Jacobson, "Eine Aktion für die russischen Grenzjuden in den Jahren 1843/44," in Ismar Elbogen, ed., *Festschrift zu Simon Dubnows siebzigstem Geburtstag* (Berlin: 1930), pp. 237–50.

21. Lifschitz, *ZY* 1, p. 25.

22. Isaac Ber Levinsohn, *Te'uda beyisrael* (Vilna: 1828), p. 183; idem, *Di hefker-velt,* 3d ed. (Warsaw: 1903), p. 31; Israel Aksenfeld, *Di genarte velt* (written ca. 1842), published in his *Verk,* edited by M. Wiener (Kiev/Kharkov: 1931) 1, p. 313; cf. Wiener's introductory essay, "Vegn Aksenfelds pyeses," p. 17. In 1833 Wolf Tugendhold published a novella *Der Denunziant* (Hebrew, *Hamoser, o sof resh'a,* 1847, trans. Menaham Benditsohn) that purported to relate a true incident involving informers and contraband. In fact, it was a defense of honest Jewish tradesmen and of the honor of Judaism.

23. Levinsohn, *Te'uda beyisrael,* p. 183.

24. Yehuda Leon Rosenthal, ed., *Ḥevrat marbei haskala beyisrael* 2, p. 120 (St. Petersburg: 1890 [henceforth: *Toledot OPE*]).

25. As recorded in the biographical section appended to Levi-Yitzhak's collected sermons, *Kedushat Levi,* ed. Zvi Elimelekh Kalish (New York: 1972, p. 154).

26. Simon Dubnow, "Iz khroniki mstislavskoi obshchiny," *Voskhod,* no. 9 (1899), 33–59; idem, "Mipinkasei kehillat mstislav: ma'aseh nisim sheir'a bishnat 5604," *He-'Avar* 1 (1918), 65–75; Iulii Gessen, " 'Mstislavskoe buistvo' po arkhivnym materialam," *Perezhitoe* 2 (1910), 54–77; S. An-sky, "Iz legend o mstislavskom dele," *Perezhitoe* 2 (1910), 248–57; A. Druyanov, "Ma'aseh amstislev," *Reshumot,* o.s., 4 (1926), 287–94 (as told by Israel Isser b. Avraham-Abba Smilak in 1922; trans. from Yiddish); Tcherikover, "Hehamon hayehudi," *Zion* 4 (1939), 156–57; Ginsburg, *Historishe verk* 3, pp. 243–72; idem, "Vi azoy men shraybt bay unz geshikhte," *Tsukunft* 44 (November 1939), 665.

27. Gessen, "Mstislavskoe buistvo," 74; Dubnow, "Mipinkasei kehillat mstislav," 71.

28. Dubnow, "Mipinkasei kehillat mstislav," 65. This account tallies with that of Smilak, who reports that the hue and cry was raised by Rachel Frumkin, whose charitable activities in the town supported one third of the population.

29. Dubnow, "Mipinkasei kehillat mstislav," 69–70; Gessen, "Mstislavskoe buistvo," 66–67; Ansky, "Iz legend o mstislavskom dele," 249–57.

30. On the background of the Jewish legal attitude to bearing arms in medieval and early modern times, se I.Z. Kahane, *Meḥkarim besifrut hateshuvot* (Jerusalem: 1973), pp. 164–78.

31. Shlomo Vind, *Rabbi Yehezkel Landau, toledot ḥayav* (Jerusalem: 1961), pp. 22–23, 115–16; cf. Aryeh-Leyb Gelman, *Ha-Nod'a biyhuda umishnato* (Jerusalem: 1961), pp. 128–29.

32. N.M. Gelber, "Korot hayehudim befolin mereishit ḥalukata ve'ad milḥemet ha'olam hasheniya," in Israel Halperin, ed., *Beit yisrael befolin* (Jerusa-

lem: 1948), p. 112; Dubnow, *Toledot hahasidut,* p. 239; Mahler, *Divrei yemei yisrael,* 1, bk. 3 pp. 80–81; Arthur Eisenbach, "Les droits civiques des juifs dans le royaume de pologne," *REJ* 3, no. 1–2 (1964), 26–27; Warszawski, "Yidn in kongres-polyn," p. 322; Frenk, *Yehudei polin,* pp. 44–47.

33. Dubnow, "Kak byla vvedena," *ES* 2 (1909), 256–65, quotes an internal government memorandum dealing, in part, with Jewish lobbying efforts against implementation of the conscription decree (see esp. pp. 258–60 on the efforts of Mordecai Leybovitch, a rabbi of Grodno province, and a known Jewish agent in St. Petersburg).

34. The petition cited in n.8.

35. Three manuscript copies of the talk, written shortly after the death of R. Dov-Ber, served as the basis for the version that was recently published in the anthology *Migdal 'oz,* ed. Yehoshua Mondshain (Kfar Habad, Israel: 1980), pp. 399–407. (I shall cite it as "Maamar haadmor haemtsa'i.") I am indebted to Dr. Michael Silber of The Hebrew University who brought it to my attention. The trustworthiness of the text is probably fairly high, given the circumstances and even allowing for later additions or changes, it should at the very least be taken as a reflection of trends of thought current in Liubavich circles in the late 1820s and early 1830s.

36. "Maamar haadmor haemtsa'i," pp. 400–407.

37. See the excellent summary of the issue in Stanislawski, *Tsar Nicholas I,* pp. 25–34; also see chap. 2 herein, p. 50.

38. Lifschitz, *ZY* 1, pp. 119–20; see generally pp. 106–27.

39. Tcherikover, "Hehamon hayehudi"; Ettinger, "The Jews at the Outbreak of the Revolution," p. 24.

40. Ginsburg, "Vi azoy men shraybt bay unz geshikhte," pp. 663–65; Stanislawski, *Tsar Nicholas I,* pp. 32, 106, 127–29; David G. Roskies, *Against the Apocalypse: Responses to Catastrophe in Modern Jewish Culture* (Cambridge, Mass.: 1984), p. 60.

41. See Ginsburg, *Historishe verk* 1, pp. 242–43; Stanislawski, *Tsar Nicholas I,* pp. 26, 129. One of those who protested kahal inscription procedure and was imprisoned when the kahal of his town charged him with disloyalty to the state was Rabbi Yom-tov Lipman Heilperin (Israel Eisenstadt and Shmuel Wiener, *Da'at kedoshim* [St. Petersburg: 1897–98], vol. 1, p. 29). The theme appears in literature as well, prominently so in Israel Aksenfeld's *Der ershter yidisher rekrut* (ca. 1837), Peretz Smolenskin's *Kevurat hamor* (1873), and G. Bogrov's *Poimannik* (1874), where smuggling is involved as well.

42. Ginsburg, *Historishe verk* 1, pp. 242, 247–49; Stanislawski, *Tsar Nicholas I,* pp. 129–31. Of the four specific cases of open petition mentioned by Stanislawski, three occurred in the early 1850s.

43. Steinschneider, *'Ir vilna,* p. 148 n. 1; cf. *Perezhitoe* 4 (1913), 185.

44. Shaul Stampfer, "Shalosh yeshivot litaiot bamea hatesh'a esreh," Ph.D. diss., The Hebrew University: 1981, p. 11; based on account published in *Ha-Melitz,* no. 6 (1881).

45. Stanislawski, *Tsar Nicholas I,* p. 137.

46. *Sefer ruaḥ Ḥaim* (Vilna: 1858), p. 8.

47. A.B. Gottlober, *Zikhronot umasa'ot* 1, p. 170.

48. *Kedushat Levi,* p. 23a.

49. Ibid., pp. 23b, 24a–24b, 25a, 43a.

50. Israel Halperin, "Rabbi Levi-Yitzhak mibardichev ugezerot hamalkhut beyamav," in Halperin, ed., *Yehudim,* pp. 340–47; Gottlober, *Zikhronot umasa'ot* 1, pp. 173–78. Contradictions in Gottlober's account make dating difficult, as Halperin argues.

51. Lifschitz, *ZY* 1, pp. 27–28; cf. Stampfer, "Shalosh yeshivot," pp. 13–14. Lifschitz notes that "Aunt Leah's" influence did have some success, though not in the matter of military conscription. Admiral Greig, her husband, served on a law commission early in Nicholas I's reign, where he reportedly spoke in favor of allowing Jewish merchants to trade in the Russian interior (ibid., pp. 28–29). On Alexei Samuilovich Greig (1775–1845), see entry in *Entsiklopedicheskii slovar',* 9(a), p. 606.

52. Ginsburg, *Historishe verk* 1, pp. 97ff.; Stanislawski, *Tsar Nicholas I,* p. 130; Dubnow, *History* 2, p. 121; and see the official report of the investigation, published by Dubnow in "Delo o evreiskom samosude v podolii (1838–40 g.)," *Perezhitoe* 1 (1908), docs. pp. 1–6.

53. Gessen, "Deputaty," 28.

54. Margaliot, *Dubna rabbati,* p. 16.

55. Ibid., pp. 18–19; the Rabbinical Commissions will be discussed later. Landau was one of those chosen by the Vilna community to speak with Baron Günzberg (in 1873) about interceding on behalf of the traditional *melamdim* whose livelihood was threatened by the education laws that required secular learning for all teachers in Jewish schools. Landau did not, in fact, go to St. Petersburg, however, owing to his lack of proper travel documents at that time (Lifschitz, *ZY* 2, p. 128).

56. Shimshon Dov Yerushalmi, "Va'adot uve'idot harabbanim berusia," *He-'Avar* 3 (1955), p. 87; *Evreiskaia entsiklopedia* (hereafter *EE*) 10, cols. 492–93; Ginsburg, *Historishe verk* 1, p. 90.

57. Shlomo Barukh Nisenboym, comp. *Sefer lekorot hayehudim belublin* (Lublin: 1899), p. 127.

58. On his role in defending the Jewish community of Staryi Konstantinov when it was accused of fomenting unrest over the institution of military conscription in 1827, see Zitron, *Shtadlonim,* pp. 297–98. On the struggle between him and the maskilim of Kiev and Volhynia, see chap. 4 herein.

59. Lilienthal's controversial role in the 1841–45 period as the chief Jewish promoter of state-sponsored Haskalah has been treated extensively by Stanislawski, *Tsar Nicholas I,* pp. 72–82; Immanuel Etkes, "Parashat hahaskala mita'am vehatemura bema'amad tenu'at hahaskala berusia," *Zion* 43 (1978), 264–313 (esp. pp. 280–99); Dubnow, *History* 2, pp. 50–59; Zinberg, *History* 11, pp. 75–93; Greenberg, *Jews in Russia* 1, pp. 34–40; and M. Morgulis, "K istorii

obrazovaniia russkikh evreev," in M. Morgulis, *Voprosy evreiskoi zhizni* (St. Petersburg: 1889), pp. 1–71. Contemporaries' reports appear in Benjamin Mandestamm, *Ḥazon lamo'ed* (Vienna: 1877), pt. 2; Gottlober, *Zikhronot umasa'ot* 2, pp. 127–45; and Lilienthal's own "My Travels in Russia," in David Philipson, *Max Lilienthal, American Rabbi: Life and Writings* (New York: 1915), pp. 159–367; Max Lilienthal's *Maggid yeshu'a, maggid leveit ya'akov teshu' atam uleveit yisrael 'ezraṭam: mikhtav shaluaḥ le'adat yisrael*, S.Y. Fuenn, trans. (Vilna: 1842).

60. Etkes, "Hahaskala mita'am," 294–95; Stanislawski, *Tsar Nicholas I*, p. 77; Lilienthal, "My Travels," pp. 344–50; Stampfer, "Shalosh yeshivot," pp. 35–36; Lifschitz, *ZY*, pp. 82–83.

61. The anonymous article appeared in *Israelitische annalen*, no. 6 (1841), and the entire episode is described by Saul Ginsburg, based on the Third Section's archives he researched, see "Menahem Mendl Liubavicher un di regirung," in his *Historishe verk* 1, pp. 63–74.

62. Memorandum to Benckendorff, quoted by Ginsburg, *Historishe verk* 1, pp. 72–73. The surveillance was, in fact, put into effect and was lifted only in 1847, on the recommendation of the Mogilev-Vitebsk governor-general, Count Golitsyn (ibid., p. 74).

63. *PSZ²*, vol. 19(pt. 1): 18,420.

64. As Morgulis put it, in rather more complacent terms, "There were those who regarded with suspicion the conservative character of the commission, given the identity of the majority of its members, and voiced serious concern over the satisfactory conclusion of its labors; but [what was accomplished] proved in the end to have reflected the foundations laid by the state" ("K istorii obrazovanniia," p. 61).

65. Stanislawski, *Tsar Nicholas I*, p. 80; Haim Meir Hilman, *Beit rebbi* (Berdichev: 1901–2), pt. 3, chap, 3, pp. 9–18, on the conference generally; pp. 19–20 on the concessions claimed by R. Menaham-Mendl.

66. Lifschitz, *ZY* 1, pp. 101–2. Lifschitz, though only five years old at the time, claimed to have retained vivid memories of R. Yitzhak's arrival; he was later told of R. Yitzhak's reply, which he did not witness.

67. Etkes, "Hahaskala mita'am," 299 n. 134. (The testimony is that of the popular maskilic writer, Ayzik Mayer Dik, in a letter to Yaakov Katznelson.) Both versions could, of course, be true.

68. *PSZ²*, vol. 23(pt. 1): 22,276.

69. Ibid., pars. 7, 9. Living expenses in St. Petersburg were to be paid from the Jewish *korobka* (kosher meat tax) fund, out of which all Jewish communal budgets were paid (par. 10). The budget came to 3,700 rubles, including a secretary, translator, and other aides.

70. Ibid., pars. 12, 13. Discussions were to be held in Russian, and recorded (pars. 16, 17).

71. Shimshon Dov Yerushalmi, "Va'adot uve'idot," 86–94; Morgulis, "K istorii obrazonvaniia," pp. 148–51; Levitats 2, p. 103.

72. Shimshon Dov Yerushalmi, "Va'adot uve'idot," 88; Morgulis, "K istorii obrazovaniia," pp. 151–49; D. Natanson, ed., *Sefer hazikhronot, divrei yemei ḥayei . . . Yitkhak Ber Levinsohn* (Warsaw: 1875), pp. 95–98 (Seltzer to Levinsohn); *Ha-Maggid,* no. 15 (22 April 1858) 60.

73. The French precedent of 1806–7 was one of the considerations of the framers of the Russian law of 1848 according to Morgulis ("K istorii obrazovaniia," pp. 149–50) and Seltzer, in his letter to I.B. Levinsohn (see nn. 82, 90).

74. See pp. 80, 118–19, 141 in this volume.

75. Klausner, *Toledot hakehilla,* pp. 42–43, 136; Steinschneider, *'Ir vilna,* p. 207; Zitron, *Shtadlonim,* pp. 8–13; Fuenn, *Kirya neemana,* pp. 222–23. On the ambiguous position of Maytes in the Vilna rabbinate controversy, see Klausner, *Vilna,* pp. 124–25. According to Fuenn, who quotes the tombstone inscription, Maytes died in 1807. Zitron, however, reports that the Vilna Gaon was still alive at the time of Maytes's death, making 1797 the last possible year of Maytes's life. (In the Hebrew date, this is a difference of only one letter; Fuenn may therefore be in error.)

76. Gessen, "Deputaty," p. 17.

77. "He [Yozel Günzburg] ran the *otkup* like a mini-government. Under him were ten province chiefs who were enormously wealthy in their own right. . . . Almost all of them conducted themselves with ostentatious, overbearing pride, and tyrannized the province, as the district chiefs [under them] did in each district" (Lifschitz, *ZY* 2, p. 55).

78. Feigin to Benckendorff, doc. 1 in Gessen, "Zabytyi obshchestvennyi deiatel'," *ES* 4 (1911), 394–95. Cf. *EE* 15, cols. 198–99.

79. Gessen, "Zabytyi," doc. 2: "Zapiska Feigina ob oblegkhenii polozheniia evreiskago naroda . . . ," *ES* 4 (1911), 396.

80. Ibid., pp. 396–97, 400–401. In his cover letter to Benckendorff, Feigin alluded to the recent ritual murder investigation at Velizh as an alarming sign of deterioration in the Jews' security and dignity. On the Velizh case, see: Dubnow, *History* 2, pp. 72–84; Ginsburg, *Historishe verk* 3, pp. 191–241.

81. Comparable examples are the memorandum of the Vilna kahal of 1833 (cited in nn. 8, 34) and the memorandum of the Polish Jewish leaders to Paskiewicz in 1832 (see n. 10):

> [N]ous venons . . . soumettre l'exposé des torts, vexations et persécutions que nous avons éprouvées de la part des autorités adminitratives. . . . Que l'Israélite ne soit point condamné pour être né dans la religion de Moïse, à passer sa vie dans la misère, qu'il soit traité . . . à l'égal des autres habitants du pays, . . . qu'il soit admit à la jouissance des lois sociales, en un mot, que l'Israéliite soit envisagé comme un homme par le Gouvernement." (Mahler, "A Jewish Memorandum," pp. 685, 696).

82. Seltzer to Levinsohn (26 Tammuz [1852]), in Natanson, *Sefer hazikhronot,* p. 95.

83. Ibid., p. 96.

84. Lifschitz, *ZY* 1, p. 168.

85. Seltzer to Levinsohn, *Sefer hazikhronot,* p. 96.
86. Ibid., pp. 96–97.
87. D. Z[eltser], "Lipman Zeltser, iz semeinikh vospominanii," *ES* 4 (1911), 294.
88. Lifschitz, *ZY* 1, p. 169. Lifschitz mistakenly identifies the date of the Gomel petition as 1851. It is clear from Seltzer's account that the subject of the request was the double conscription, which was not ordered until 1852 (Seltzer to Levinsohn [1 Shevat (1853)], *Sefer hazikhronot,* p. 97). The petition of the "trustees of the Jewish communities of the provinces of Mogilev, Minsk and Vitebsk" and Nicholas's response to it are also mentioned in the petition of 1854 submitted by Yozel Günzberg and eleven other Jewish notables to Nicholas; excerpts published by Tcherikover, "Fun di rusishe arkhivn: 1. gvirim-shtadlonim un di gzeyres fun rekrutchine un 'razriadn,' " YIVO *Historishe shriftn* 1, cols. 784–87; the full text is found in Azriel Shochat, "Legezerot hagiyusim shel Nikolai harishon (reshit shtadlanuto shel habaron Gintsburg)," in *Sefer Shalom Sivan* (Jerusalem: 1979), pp. 315–18. On Isaac Zelkind of Monastyrshchina (1787–1880), see *EE* 7, cols. 719–20; S.Y. Hurwitz, "Sefer ḥayai," p. 4 n. 2. Zelkind was married to a granddaughter of Yehoshua Zeitlin.
89. D. Z[eltser] "Lipman Zeltzer," 293; *Ha-Maggid,* no. 27 (10 July 1872), 319–320; *Ha-Shahar* 3 (1872), p. 333.
90. Seltzer to Levinsohn (1852), Natanson, *Sefer hazikhronot,* p. 98: "Although the patrician [*gvir*] R. Zisl Rapoport of Minsk was chosen as the fifth member, he has not come and he will not be coming [to St. Petersburg]."
91. Yerushalmi, "Va'adot uve'idot," p. 87.
92. *Ha-Maggid,* no. 36 (13 September 1859), 147.
93. *Ha-Maggid,* no. 41 (25 October 1859), 162–63.
94. *EE* 13, col. 308.
95. *Ha-Karmel,* no. 39 (14/26 March 1869), 305; cf. *Ha-Melitz,* no. 16 (17/29 April 1869), 112–14.
96. Lifschitz, *ZY* 2, p. 188.
97. Ibid., pp. 21, 188.
98. I am indebted for the phrase *a shadow government* in the Russian Jewish connection to Dr. Shaul Stampfer, who gave me the benefit of his own thoughts on this matter.
99. On the background and implementation, see Stanislawski, *Tsar Nicholas I,* pp. 155–60; K. Hodoshevich, "Der 'razbor' fun der yidisher bafelkerung vitebsker gubernye," *Tsaytshrift* 6 (1930), 139–45; Dubnow, *History* 2, pp. 142–43.
100. The effort was limited to Lithuania and White Russia (Lifschitz, *ZY* 1, p. 167).
101. Lifschitz, *ZY* 1, p. 166.
102. Ibid., p. 167. The partial success of the plan that was later claimed by one of the participants consisted in the bribe given to the secretary of the Ministry of Internal Affairs (see n. 84).

103. Ibid., p. 169. Stanislawski (*Tsar Nicholas I,* p. 184) notes correctly that in demanding ten Jewish recruits per thousand males rather than seven, Nicholas was bringing the Jewish quota up to the already-existing level for the lower gentry and townsmen of the western provinces. Stanislawski implies thereby that although the act constituted a new burden for the Jews, it was not, in fact, a case of deliberate discrimination. Yet the higher quota was a punitive measure imposed on the non-Jewish sector in 1831 (earlier than Stanislawski indicates) in response to the widespread support manifested among them for the Polish uprising of that year, and it was rescinded in 1853, whereas the higher quota remained in effect for the Jews and was exacted on a yearly rather than the biannual basis practiced elsewhere in the empire. These facts were brought out by Shochat ("Legezerot hagiyusim," pp. 309–10) in 1979. Stanislawski's comment that "no historians picked up [the higher quota for non-Jews in the provinces of the Pale] and checked the legal sources that were at their disposal" needs qualification.

104. Three letters were written by R. Menahem-Mendl Schneersohn, by R. Yosef of Slutsk, and by R. Gershon Tanhum of Minsk; these were also signed by six heads of the Minsk community. They appear in Lifschitz's biography of R. Isaac Elhanan Spector, *Toledot Yitzhak* (Warsaw: 1896), pp. 55–57, and were given to Lifschitz by Meshulam-Faivl Friedland's son (*ZY* 1, p. 171).

105. Lifschitz, *ZY* 1, p. 172. R. Schneerson also kept political agents in St. Petersburg—one R. Yudl Rakishker and a Mr. Pompianskii (ibid.).

106. On bribery to prevent opening a school, see *Pinkes . . . pruzhine,* p. 163; *Toledot OPE* 2, pp. 78, 89 (report on Berdichev by Dr. Rothenberg, June 1864). On the phenomenon of double budgeting and its uses, see Shochat, "Hahanhaga," p. 195; on secret taxes or siphoning of funds, see *Ha-Melitz,* no. 1, 1870, 1–2, and no. 3, 1870, 21; Haim Tchernowitz, *Masekhet zikhronot* (New York: 1954), p. 67; and Lifschitz, *ZY* 2, p. 186. The routine maintenance of unofficial rabbis and unauthorized synagogues in New Russia was reported to the provincial authorities in 1856 by Marcus Gurovich, the "learned Jew" of the governor-general's office, after undertaking two extensive field studies (1854, 1856). Major parts of his report appear in O.M. Lerner's *Evreii v novorossiiskom krae,* see esp. pp. 74–77.

107. Lifschitz, *ZY* 2, pp. 95–96.

108. *Di takse, oder di bande shtot baley-toyves,* Act IV, Scene 1 (p. 56 in Abramovich, *Alle shriftn* 1 [New York: 1910]).

109. An uncredited story told by Lifschitz makes this point explicit: a *rosh kahal* who became an informer as he drew closer and closer to the local officials was summoned by the town rabbi and told that *dina demalkhuta dina* did not apply to the laws of a kingdom that was worse than Sodom and that he could not use that principle in his defense (*ZY* 1, pp. 61–62).

110. Lifschitz, *ZY* 1, pp. 59–60.

111. As per Mapu's letters (*Mikhtevei Avraham Mapu,* ed. Ben-Zion Dinur [Jerusalem: 1970]), cited by Bartal, "Halo-yehudim vehevratam," p. 48.

112. Ibid.

Chapter 4

1. Vital, *Origins of Zionism,* p. 43.
2. Vasilii V. Popugaev, "O blagopoluchii narodnykh tel," in I. Shchipanov, ed., *Russkie prosvetiteli ot Radishcheva do dekabristov* (Moscow: 1966) 1, p. 289.
3. Ivan Berend and György Ranki, *The European Periphery and Industrialization, 1780–1914* (Cambridge/Budapest: 1982), p. 27.
4. *Ha-Maggid,* no. 8, 1860, p. 29.
5. "Hagizra vehabeniya," (from *Haboker or* 3, 1868) in Gottlober *Zikhronot umasa'ot* 2, p. 27.
6. On modernist Jewish educational and cultural innovations in Vilna prior to the 1840s, see Shatzky, *Kultur-geshikhte,* pp. 50–57, 63–77, 85–103; on the 1830–60 period, pp. 110–50. On Odessa as an exceptional social setting prior to 1840 see Zipperstein, *Jews of Odessa,* pp. 3, 36–55. Even in the less cosmopolitan towns of the interior, there were isolated individuals whose acquisition of new professional skills and secular education set them apart from the surrounding majority. The first Jewish pharmacy in Volhynia, for example, was opened in Berdichev in 1785, the year in which R. Levi-Yitzhak became rabbi there, see Baruch Karo, *Ha'ir berdichev* (Tel-Aviv: 1951), p. 8.
7. Gottlober, *Zikhronot umasa'ot* 1, pp. 243–48.
8. *Minḥat bikkurim,* quoted by Zinberg from the manuscript in the former OPE collection in Leningrad, see Zinberg, *History* 11, p. 42.
9. Yona b. Amitay [pseud.], *Maggid emet* (Leipzig: 1843), p. 4.
10. Margaliot, *Dubna rabbati,* pp. 23–24. Erter wrote to Leybush Glozberg in Dubno.
11. Lilienblum to J.L. Gordon, 13 July 1869, in *Igerot M. L. Lilienblum le-Y. L. Gordon* (Jerusalem: 1968), pp. 72–73.
12. Ibid., p. 74; cf. Moshe Leib Lilienblum, *Ḥatot ne'urim: ketavim autobiografiim* (Jerusalem: 1970), pp. 138–53.
13. Judah Leib Gordon, *Igerot Yehuda Leib Gordon* (Warsaw: 1894) 1, p. 155 (Gordon to Moshe Prozer).
14. See Ginsburg, *Historishe verk* 1, pp. 238–65 ("Fartsaytike yidishe mosrim").
15. Peretz Smolenskin built his novel *Kvurat ḥamor* entirely around the interplay of bribery, intimidation, informing, and vengeance in a quasifictitious Jewish community, Kshola (i.e., Shklov).
16. On the disputes that brought about state investigation of burial societies in Dubno in the 1850s and in Kherson in 1862, with the result that they became subject to a stricter mechanism of official supervision—a very good example in this period of internal dispute, informing, and civil suits dragged through Russian courts—see Margaliot, *Dubna rabbati,* p. 37; and Lerner, *Evreii v novorossiiskom krae,* pp. 92–93 (Gurovich's report of 1856 on *ḥevra kadisha* irregularities, submitted to Governor-General Stroganov).

17. For example, Shatzky states, "Precisely the most respected maskilim were the ones who had no confidence in their own influence and prestige, and viewed government intervention as the only practical way to bring reform into Jewish life" (*Kultur-geshikhte*, p. 110). Yaakov Lifschitz, who gets closer to the practical issue of power but is unable to view his maskilic opponents in anything approaching a balanced perspective, writes, "The free-thinking maskilim could not find a way to penetrate into the hearts of the people with their ideas. . . . [They] achieved their domination by brute force, the force of the government" (*ZY* 2, p.23). For a similar view, though from a different perspective, see Tcherikover, "Hehamon hayehudi," 150–69.

18. The Russian maskilim could also model their methods on those of their fellow maskilim across the border in Austrian Galicia who waged a relentless campaign against Hasidism through the medium of the state. See Raphael Mahler, *Der kamf tsvishn haskole un khasides in galitsye* (New York: 1942), esp. chap. 5 on Joseph Perl. Mahler attributes the recourse of maskilim in Galicia to the state only to their "outmoded" infatuation with enlightened absolutism (e.g., pp. 71ff.).

19. *RIN* 3, pp. 240–43; cf. Slutsky, "Shalosh te'udot," 78–80.

20. Indeed, informing against other maskilim was also not unheard of (see nn. 37, 71.)

21. See explicit references to the solicitation of state interference in favor of the Haskalah program as "informing" in Lifschitz, *ZY* 1, pp. 33–37, 62, 90–93; *ZY* 2, pp. 22–24, 85, 105–11.

22. Benjamin Mandelstamm, *Ḥazon lamo'ed*, pt. 2, p. 45.

23. M. Morgulis, "Iz moikh vospominanii," *Voskhod*, no. 2 (1895), 121–22; Zitron, *Shtadlonim*, pp. 301–6; *EE* 6, cols. 117–18.

24. Morgulis, "Iz moikh vospominanii," pp. 127–28; Zitron, *Shtadlonim*, pp. 299–300.

25. Stanislawski, *Tsar Nicholas I*, pp. 51–56, 106–9, 187–88.

26. Ibid., pp. 51–52, 58.

27. Gideon Katznelson, *Hamilḥama hasifrutit bein haḥaredim vehamaskilim* (Tel-Aviv: 1954), p. 168.

28. Moshe Rosensohn, *Milḥama beshalom* (Vilna: 1870), pp. 101–3. The pamphlet was subtitled, "The fight for peace . . . containing a defense of the sons of Joseph, upholders of the Torah of Moses, against their enemies and opponents, and demonstrating that anyone who sows wickedness and writes evil of them thereby sins against justice, against God, *against his king*, against the Torah and his own faith." (Emphasis added.)

29. Moshe Rosensohn, *Shelom mashuaḥ* (Vilna: 1870), pp. 40–47. The entire pamphlet is devoted to demonstrating the obligatory nature of the veneration of, and faithfulness to, the king in traditional Judaism.

30. Shochat, *Harabanut mita'am*, pp. 10, 12, 14, 44; Stanislawski, *Tsar Nicholas I*, pp. 37, 134. In addition to swearing that they would not permit any violation of the law to occur in the synagogue or in any religious ceremony, the

Notes

official rabbi was responsible for reporting any other violations and for making sure that all Jews under their instruction obeyed the laws. In 1856 they were also required to report any unlicensed private teachers (*melamdim*).

31. See Isaac Ber Levinsohn, *Te'uda beyisrael*, p. 157 n. 1; idem, *Beit haotsar* (Vilna: 1841), p. 293; and Lipps's report of 1837 to the Church authorities: "Tsenzura v tsarstvovanie Nikolaia I," *Voskhod*, no. 6 (June 1903), 133–34; Gurovich's report to Stroganov in 1856, in Lerner, *Evreii v novorossiiskom krae*, pp. 74–77; and "K voprosu o ravvinakh i koe-chto o proekte uchrezhdeniia ravvinskoi konsistorii," suppl. to *Ha-Karmel*, no. 38 (7 March 1869), 149; *Ha-Melitz*, no. 26 (1863), col. 404; Lifschitz, *ZY* 1, p. 176. One exception was R. Avraham Madievskii of Khorol (Poltava), who served as government rabbi and was named to the third St. Petersburg Rabbinical Commission in 1861–62.

32. Shochat, *Harabanut mita'am*, pp. 9–15.

33. "K voprosu o ravvinakh," 149.

34. Gessen reports on the early beginnings of the censorship of Jewish books that centered in Riga at the end of the 1790s and that enlisted the services of several multilingual Jews, in "K istorii tsenzury evreiskikh knig v rossii," (St. Petersburg: 1902), pp. 60–76.

35. A separate censor in Warsaw was responsible for the Polish provinces.

36. Wolf Tugendhold worked under the authority of Professor Lev Borovskii of Vilna University. It is Borovskii's imprimatur that appears on Hebrew books of the mid-1830s (e.g., see Levinsohn's *Efes damim* [1837], Günzberg's *Hamalakhut el Kaius Kaligula hakeisar hashlishi laromim me'et Yedidia haaleksandroni, hu Filon hayehudi* [1836], *Derasha mehaRamban migerona . . . lifnei hamelekh* [1836], and Holdhor's *Divrei shalom veemet* [1836]).

37. Seiberling was denounced by fellow maskilim for being too lenient with Hasidic books and was replaced with the convert Vladimir Feodorov (né Hirsh Grinboym)—a fascinating figure in his own right, discussed later. On Seiberling, see *EE* 15, col. 802; 7, col. 716. Seiberling also had to engage in a fruitless, running battle with the Kiev authorities over his residence permit in 1854–55; see his petitions in the documents section of *ES* 6 (1913), pp. 267–73, 276–78.

38. Stanislawski, *Tsar Nicholas I*, pp. 41–42, 58.

39. Just as under Alexander I, the censorship of Hebrew books had been assigned to professors of classical or oriental languages at the universities of Kiev and Vilna. See Gessen, "K istorii tsenzury evreiskikh knig," p. 76; Shatzky, *Kultur-geshikhte*, pp. 61–62; I.B. Levinsohn to Kiev professor Savitskii, in Natanson, *Sefer hazikhronot*, p. 65.

40. When Eliezer Zweifel, instructor of religion and Talmud at the Zhitomir rabbinical seminary, wanted to publish his empathetic study of Hasidism (*Shalom 'al yisrael*, published in segments in Kiev, Vilna, and Zhitomer between 1868 and 1873), his supervisor, Haim Selig Slonimskii, refused to give him censorship approval. Slonimskii wrote to the Kiev censor (Feodorev?) arguing that the book was opposed to enlightenment principles and thus against the state interest, and he recommended that Zweifel be sacked from his teaching post.

Zweifel managed to convince the Kiev authorities, however, that his book was of primary scholarly value. See A. Rubenstein's introduction to *Shalom 'al yisrael* (Jerusalem: 1972), p. 22. On the nature of author-censor relations within the maskilic camp, see Zinberg, *History* 12, pp. 167–68.

41. Shochat, *Harabanut mita'am,* pp. 17, 20; Gessen, *Istoriia* 2, pp. 81–82, 95–98.

42. *EE* 15, "*Uchonyi evrei,*" cols. 147–48.

43. S. Ginsburg, *Amolike peterburg* (New York: 1944), pp. 81–82. Mandelstamm was edged out owing to pressure by Daniel Khwolson; the latter became the ministry's chief Jewish advisor, although by that time he had converted. Mandelstamm's official replacement was Iosif Seiberling, formerly the censor in Kiev (see *EE* 7, col. 716; Shochat, "Kovets derushim be'arikhat Adam Hacohen Lebenson," *Meḥkarim betoledot 'am yisrael veeretz yisrael* 5 (1980), 257. Levitats states incorrectly that Mandestamm was not replaced (Levitats 2, p. 102).

44. *EE* 13, cols. 591–92.

45. The *uchonyi evrei* was paid a salary out of the Jewish communities' meat *korobka* (*EE* 15, col. 148).

46. Lerner, *Evreii v novorossiiskom krae,* pp. 73–74.

47. Quoted in Lerner, ibid., pp. 74–79, 92–94.

48. Ibid., p. 109.

49. *Ha-Maggid,* nos. 15, 17 (1861); cf. Lifschitz, *ZY* 2, pp. 12–13.

50. *EE* 15, col. 148.

51. On Galicia and the role of Joseph Perl in particular, see Mahler, *Der kamf tsvishn haskole,* pp. 71ff.

52. A report on such presses was submitted to Nicholas I in 1827 by two converted Jews, Zandberg and Fodello, a part of which was published by Gessen, "K istorii evreiskikh tipografii: kreshchenye evreii Zandberg i Fodello," *ES* 2 (1909), 253–55. Nine presses are listed for Volhynia–Podolia and an equal number for Lithuanian–White Russian provinces (pp. 254–55).

53. "Tsenzura v tsarstvovaniia Nikolaia I," *Voskhod,* no. 6 (June 1903), 131 (excerpted from the longer historical account in *Russkaia starina* of that year); cf. S. Beilin, "Iz istoricheskikh zhurnalov: 1. tsenzura evreiskikh knig (1833–1842 g.)," *ES* 2 (1911), 417–18.

54. "Tsenzura," 131; Beilin, "Tsenzura evreiskikh knig," p. 417.

55. Ibid.; and Natanson, *Sefer hazihronot,* p. 65; cf. Stanislawski, *Tsar Nicholas I,* p. 41; Carmilly-Weinberger, *Censorship,* p. 117; Gessen, "Tsenzura," in *EE* 15, col. 799.

56. "Tsenzura," (*Voskhod* 1903) p. 132.

57. Lifschitz, *Toledot Yitzhak,* pp. 58–61; Steinschneider, *'Ir vilna,* pp. 21–27; Carmilly-Weinberger, *Censorship,* p. 195; H. Shapira, "Haaḥim Shapira," *Ha-Shiloach* 30 (1914), 541–54; Gottlober, *Zikhronot umasa'ot* 1, pp. 185–86.

58. Lifschitz, *Toledot Yitzhak,* pp. 58–59.

59. Ginsburg, *Historishe verk* 1, pp. 90–96. The participants in the Rabbini-

cal Commission on this occasion were Y.E. Landau of Dubno, R. Dr. Neumann of Riga, Herman Baratz of Kishinev, R. Avraham Madievskii of Poltava, and Y.Z. Rapoport of Minsk as well as the *uchonye evreii* Sh. Y. Fuenn, Moisei Berlin, and Iosif Seiberling.

60. I. Klausner, "Hagezerot 'al tilboshet hayehudim, 1844–1850," *Gal-Ed* 6 (1982), 11–13; Iulii Gessen, "Bor'ba pravitel'stva s evreiskoi odezhdoi v imperii i tsarstve pol'skom," *Perezhitoe* 1 (1908), docs. pp. 10–11; Ginsburg, "Redifes oyf yidishe bgodim," in *Historishe verk* 3, pp. 286–90.

61. Klausner, "Hagezerot," 14.

62. Fuenn to Stern, Ellul 5600 [1840], published in *Ha-Pardes* 3 (1896), 152.

63. Ibid., 150–51; Klausner, "Hagezerot," 15; Stanislawski, *Tsar Nicholas I*, p. 46; Ginsburg, "Redifes," p. 290.

64. Klausner, "Hagezerot, 14–15.

65. Ibid., pp. 15–16; Gessen, "Bor'ba," pp. 14–15.

66. *Ḥazon lamo'ed*, pt. 2, p. 45; Benjamin Mandelstamm had earlier written along similar lines to Max Lilienthal (ibid., p. 14).

67. Text in Gessen, "Bor'ba," pp. 12–14; and Klausner, "Hagezerot," app. B, pp. 22–24; cf. Shochat, "Hitrofefut hatsipiyot hameshihiot etsel rishonei hamaskilim berusia vehahathalot lesheifat hishtalvut bahevra harusit," *'Iyun uma'as* 2 (1981), 219; Ginsburg, "Redifes," pp. 290–91.

68. Fuenn, 18 May 1845, in Klausner, "Hagezerot," app. C p. 25. The tax on Jewish clothing was put into effect at the end of 1844. Cf. Ginsburg, "Redifes," p. 293.

69. Fuenn, 18 May 1845, p. 25; cf. Lifschitz, *ZY* 1, pp. 135–38, and *ZY* 2, p. 24; Ginsburg, "Redifes," pp. 301–2, 305–10. A later (1852) decree against traditional head-coverings for women elicited a number of petitions to the Russian government. Two of these are published in *ES* 8 (1913), 399–403: one by the rabbi and community notables of Zhitomir, the second by a group of Jewish women in Vilna.

70. Moisei Berlin, *Ocherk etnografii evreiskago narodonaseleniia v rossii* (St. Petersburg: 1861), pp. 11–12. I am indebted to my friend Mark Kiel who brought this book to my attention. It represents the first social-anthropological study of Russia's Jews.

71. Alexander Orbach, *New Voices of Russian Jewry: A Study of the Russian Jewish Press of Odessa in the Era of the Great Reforms, 1860–1871* (Leiden, Neth: 1980), pp. 129–30; Zinberg, *History* 12, p. 170; the text of Kovner's denunciation appears in S. Borovoi, "Novoe ob A. Kovnere," in *Evreiskaia mysl'* 2 (1926), 241–43.

72. *Igerot Yehuda Leib Gordon* 1, p. 186: Gordon to Dainov, 5 June 1873.

73. Ibid., p. 159: Gordon to Yehoshua Syrkin, 6 July 1870.

74. I.G. Orshanskii, "Mysli o khasidizma," *EB* 1 (1871), 99–101, and Landau, p. 101, note to Orshanskii's article.

75. Correspondence from Kherson, *Ha-Maggid,* no. 3 (1865), 18.

76. Nevakhovich, *Kol shav'at bat yehuda,* suppl. to *He-'Avar* 2 (1918), sepa-

rate pag., 10–34. The Russian version, *Vopl' dshcheri iudeiskoi,* was published in St. Petersburg in 1803; the Hebrew version was published in Shklov in 1804.

77. Ibid., 10–11, 34–36.

78. Ibid., 23.

79. Ibid., introduction.

80. Ibid.

81. Nevakhovich dissociated himself from Jewish-related activity several years later, however, and converted to Christianity.

82. Nevakhovich's "The Lament" was dedicated to Notkin.

83. On Levinsohn in general, see Iulii Gessen, "Smena obshchestvennykh techenii: I. B. Levinzon i dr. M. Lilienthal; Pervyi russko-evreiskii organ," *Perezhitoe* 3 (1911), 1–37; Israel Zinberg (Tsinberg), "Isak Ber Levinzon i ego vremia," *ES* 3 (1910), 504–41; idem, *History* 11, chap. 2 and pp. 53–74; Gottlober, *Zikhronot umasa'ot* 2, pp. 19–21, 104–17. Correspondence with and by Levinsohn appears in Natanson's *Sefer hazihronot* and in Natanson's *Beer Yitzhak* (Warsaw: 1899–1900).

84. *Beit yehuda* was completed in 1829.

85. *Zerubavel* was completed in 1853.

86. Levinsohn states this in his introduction to *Efes damim,* written in 1833 (p. 8); cf. Natanson, *Sefer hazihronot,* pp. 42–49, 64, 100–108.

87. Levinsohn, *Beit yehuda,* pp. 147–52; on the blood libel, pp. 131, 146, 330–31.

88. Seltzer to Levinsohn in Natanson's *Sefer hazihronot,* p. 97.

89. Ibid., p. 36.

90. *Chrona Izraelitów* (Warsaw, 1831). Levinsohn, *Efes damim,* p. 10.

91. *Netivot 'olam* was the Hebrew translation of *Old Paths,* an anti-Jewish polemic by the British missionary McCaul. The translation, which was published in 1838, was done by Stanislaw Hoga, a Polish Jew who converted to Christianity in 1825 and who was active in mission work in London after 1833. Hoga began his career as a translator for the Napoleonic forces in Poland in the War of 1812—ironically, the same position that Levinsohn filled for the Russian army at the time. In 1817 Hoga became a spokesman and shtadlan of Warsaw's Jewish Committee. Hoga returned to Judaism in 1845. On his biography, see Azriel Frenk, *Meshumodim in poyln* (Warsaw: 1923–24), pp. 38–110.

92. Levinsohn to Mandelstamm (ca. 1853), quoted in Natanson's *Sefer hazihronot,* p. 103.

93. Ibid., p. 127.

94. Levinsohn, *Yemin tsidkati,* which was written in 1837.

95. In the wake of the Damascus blood libel of 1840, *Efes damim* was translated into English at the urging of Sir Moses Montefiore. It was reissued in 1864 in Odessa. See Natanson, *Sefer hazihronot,* pp. 29–30, 32.

96. Levinsohn, *Efes damim,* pp. 8–10, 12.

97. Ibid., p. 12, n.

98. Ibid., p. 12.

99. Ibid., p. 15.
100. The communities were Vishnevitz, Dubno, and Ostra (Natanson, *Beer Yitzhak,* pp. 46–48); Natanson, *Sefer hazihronot* mentions Luck as well (p. 37).
101. Natanson, *Beer Yitzhak,* pp. 46, 48.
102. Ibid., p. 47.
103. Natanson, *Sefer hazihronot,* p. 66.
104. *Ha-Kerem* (Warsaw: 1887), ed. Eliezer Atlas, pp. 41–46; letters dated July–August 1856.
105. *O nekotorykh srednevekovykh obvineniiakh protiv evreev* (St. Petersburg: 1861); also in *Biblioteka dlia chteniia* nos. 164–65, 1861 (repr. 1880).
106. Margaliot, *Dubna rabbati,* p. 19; Stanislawski, *Tsar Nicholas I,* pp. 144–46; Ginsburg, *Meshumodim,* pp. 251–63; "Iz perepiski A. B. Gottlobera," *ES* 3 (1910), 411–18; *EE* 16, cols. 423–25.
107. Vladimir Feodorov, "O talmude i vazhnosti ego," *Vestnik russkikh evreev,* nos. 14, 15, 18, 19 (1871); and as a separate publication (St. Petersburg: 1871).
108. Natanson, *Sefer hazihronot,* pp. 83–84; cf. Natanson's lauditory note about Grinboym/Feodorov, p. 83. On Feodorov, cf. Zinberg, *History* 12, pp. 134–38.
109. Moshe Mendelssohn, *Yerushalayim* (Feodorov trans., Vienna: 1876), published by Peretz Smolenskin (see *Ha-Shahar* 7 [1876], 456 n.).
110. M. Berlin, *Bugul'minskii talmudist* (St. Petersburg: 1862 [34 pp.]). I found a copy of this work at the National and University Library in Jerusalem bound at the back of Kolokov's *Zakony o evreiakh.*
111. Gottlober, *'Anaf 'ets 'avot* (Vilna: 1858), pp. 13, 19.
112. Ibid., pp. 73–77 and 78–79, respectively. The subscribers are listed by city in the book's front matter.
113. *Ha-Maggid,* no. 6 (1857), 24; no. 15 (17 March 1857), p. 59. The project never came to fruition.
114. M.A. Günzberg, *Hamalakhut el Kaius Kaligula,* Introduction, pp. 5–6. Note the similarity of his criticism here of the neglect by the Jews of their classical philosophers to his complaint (see n. 8) about the isolation suffered by contemporary maskilim.
115. Ibid., p. 4.
116. Ibid., pp. 4–5.
117. M.A. Günzberg, *Hamat damesek* (Königsberg: 1859–60), p. 39.
118. Ibid., pp. 43–44.
119. Ibid., pp. 66–67.
120. Ibid., p. 76.
121. Chone Shmeruk, "Hashem hamashma'uti Mordkhe-Markus—gilgulo hasifruti shel ideal hevrati," *Tarbitz* 29, no. 1 (1959), 76–98.
122. Gottlober, *"Di deputatn,"* published by Zinberg ("Fun Gottlobers literarishe yerushe") in *Tsaytshrift* 5 (1931), 43–46 (archival section).
123. Zinberg, *History* 11, p. 164.

Chapter 5

1. Stanislawski, *Tsar Nicholas I*, pp. 97–109, 187–88.

2. Ibid., pp. 108–9. I find his contention that the maskilim had by the 1850s grown "from a handful of disjointed [*sic*] individuals clustered in tiny enclaves on the borders of the Pale or in insulated anonymity in the largest cities . . . to a *well-coordinated movement* of several hundred adherents preaching their gospel to *thousands of committed students* throughout the Pale" overstated however (emphasis added). The degree to which the maskilim were able to coordinate activities was still very small even in the 1860s and, arguably, into the 1870s, and the solidarity and "security of numbers" of which he speaks (p. 108) does not seem to be corroborated by the perceptions of leading maskilim of the 1860s (see herein, chap. 4, nn. 7–9). How many of the students in the crown schools were particularly "committed" to anything is anyone's guess. The total number of students in the schools even in 1863 was just over 3,600 (see n. 14).

3. Minor to Y.L. Rosenthal, March 1864, in *Toledot OPE* 2, p. 19; also the letter of Sh. Y. Abramovich to the OPE board, September 1864, ibid., p. 80; and the letter of Volkoviskii, June 1865, ibid., p. 115; see the OPE's report of October 1866 on the reasons for the failure of the crown schools to attract a substantial number of pupils (ibid., pp. 89–92). The report was made by a special committee appointed to look into this question in late 1864 (ibid., p. 88). The inadequacy of the crown schools—partly because of their curriculum, partly because of unsuitable teachers, and partly because of the lack of suitable employment for many of the graduates—had been publicly pointed out by Vladimir Feodorov (Hirsh Grinboym) in the article published by the Kiev authorities in *Kievlianin*, no. 58 (1864). This aroused controversy among maskilim and elicited responses from leading maskilic figures, see *Toledot OPE* 2, pp. 73–75; Zinberg, *History* 12, pp. 134–38; Stanislawski, *Tsar Nicholas I*, pp. 144–46. For criticism of the seminaries by leading maskilim, see H.S. Slonimskii's letter of 1864, *Toledot OPE* 2, p. 23; minutes of Leon Rosenthal's remarks at the January 1867 meeting of the OPE (*Toledot OPE* 1, p. 43); and Leon Pinsker's remarks to the OPE Odessa branch in May 1868 (*Toledot OPE* 2, pp. 137–38). See also the proposal of Joachim Tarnopol for a better alternative, written in 1858, and modeled on West European rabbinical seminaries, *Opyt sovremennoi i osmotri-tel'noi reformy*, pp. 9–14.

4. Yehuda Slutsky, "Beit hamidrash lerabanim bevilna," *He-'Avar* 7 (1960), 47; idem, *Ha'itonut hayehudit-rusit bamea hatesh'a esreh* (Jerusalem: 1970): "The two rabbinical seminaries may be assigned particular value in the creation of the first nucleus of the Jewish-Russian intelligentsia" (p. 23).

5. In Russian, *Obshchestvo dlia rasprostranenia prosveshchenia mezhdu evreiami v rossii;* in Hebrew, known variously as *Ḥevrat mefitsei/marbei/haskala beyisrael beerets rusia.*

6. *Toledot OPE* 1, pp. 200–203. Of these, Joseph (Yozel) Günzberg pledged a yearly sum of 2,000 rubles for the society's budget. Eleven others,

including Günzberg's son Horace, pledged betweeen 100 and 500 rubles each. The remaining charter members each pledged 25 or 50 rubles. Later membership dues were fixed at: 500 rubles for members of the governing board, 100 rubles for "distinguished" members, 25 rubles for "trustee" members, and 10 rubles for "patron" members. Outstanding figures in the arts or scholarship might be coopted to the board or other membership categories without payment of the prescribed fee (ibid., p. 204).

7. Dr. Neumann was appointed second vice-chairman of the board. Three Odessa-based maskilim were among those appointed secretaries—Dr. Leon Pinsker and Dr. Emanuel Soloveitchik, the editors of *Sion* (also short-lived, 1861–62); and Joachim Tarnopol', originally Osip Rabinovich's collaborator in establishing *Razsvet*.

8. Tcherikover, *Istoriia obshchestva dlia rasprostranenia prosveshchenia mezhdu evreiami v rossii . . . 1863–1913 gg.*, ed. S. Ginsburg (St. Petersburg: 1913), app.

9. See the table of expenditures appended to *Toledot OPE* 2 (1864–84).

10. Calculated from the table of expenditures (see n. 9) and the table of income, *Toledot OPE* 2 (1864–84). The highest single area of educational support was in the field of medical studies (not including midwives): over 16,000 rubles. Rabbinical education (in Vilna, Zhitomir, and Breslau) accounted for over 7,500 rubles. Membership dues contributed only 27.7 percent of OPE's income but paid for 30.9 percent of the expenditures. The Günzbergs supplied 28 percent of expended funds and 25.8 percent of the income. Leon Rosenthal's contributions, made between 1872 and 1884, averaged 10 percent of total annual expenditure and 9.2 percent of income.

11. Rosenthal to board, 28 December 1863, *Toledot OPE* 2, pp. 3–5.

12. Gordon to board, March 1864, ibid., p. 24.

13. Ibid., pp. 12–13.

14. Ibid., p. 71: petition of February 1864. The OPE stated that there were 3,669 pupils in the crown schools. Cf. petitions of April 1866, ibid., p. 86.

15. Ibid., p. 111: petition to the Ministry of Internal Affairs.

16. Ibid., p. 7: Slonimskii to Rosenthal; *Toledot OPE* 1, p. 109 (March 1865).

17. *Toledot OPE* 2, p. 21: Orshanskii to board, January 1864; cf. p. 27, Orshanskii's follow-up letter of July 1864; *Toledot OPE* 1, p. 2: minutes of 1 February 1864.

18. *Toledot OPE* 2, p. 27: Tarnopol' to board, June 1864.

19. Ibid., pp. 30–31: Slonimskii to Rosenthal, March 1864.

20. Ibid., pp. 46–47; *Toledot OPE* 1, p. 9: minutes of 26 September, 1864.

21. *Toledot OPE* 2, pp. 50–51: David Meirovskii to board, October 1864.

22. Ibid., pp. 119–120: V. Vivodtsov & co. to the board, November 1865; and *Toledot OPE* 1, p. 27: minutes for 27 November 1865.

23. Among the many sins imputed to the Jews in the *Vestnik* was the allegation that they had actively supported the Polish revolt of 1863.

24. *Toledot OPE* 2, pp. 167–68.

25. Ibid., p. 168.

26. Ibid., pp. 168–69.

27. Ibid., pp. 169–72.

28. Ibid., p. 173

29. Ibid., pp. 174–75.

30. Ibid., p. 176; and minutes for 22 October 1866 (*Toledot OPE* 1, p. 38).

31. Nevertheless, in the course of his campaign against the Jewish community, Brafman was to point to the OPE specifically as a link in the clandestine "Jewish world brotherhood" along with the French Alliance Israélite Universelle.

32. *Toledot OPE* 2, pp. 200–201: OPE to Gedeonov, October 1868, and the latter's reply, 29 October (pp. 198–99): Lisitsin to Leon Rosenthal, August 1868. Aaron Lisitsin, a resident of Periaslav, had applied for such a position in February of that year and had been denied it on the grounds that he was a Jew (*Toledot OPE* 1, p. 65): minutes for 24 December 1869.

33. *Toledot OPE* 1, pp. 87–90, n.

34. Ibid., p. 97: minutes of 18 February 1873.

35. Ibid., pp. 93–94 n.

36. Lifschitz, *ZY* 2, pp. 124–26; cf. idem, *Toledot Yitzhak*, pp. 85–86.

37. *ZY* 2, p. 127; see the plan outlined by Mohilever in St. Petersburg in *Toledot OPE* 1, pp. 101–2.

38. Lifschitz, *ZY* 2, p. 128: on the episode, cf. *Ha-Ẓefirah*, no. 2 (1874), 11–12, citing J.L. Gordon's summary report on OPE's activities, which was issued at the end of 1873.

39. *ZY* 2, p. 127.

40. Tcerikover, *Istoriia*, app.; *Toledot OPE* 2, app.

41. *Ha-Ẓefirah*, no. 2 (1874), 11; no. 4 (1874), 31.

42. *Igerot Y. L. Gordon* 1, p. 146 (letter 78).

43. On the role of the traditional preacher in East European Jewish society, particularly on his role as social critic and second-level member of the rabbinic intelligentsia, see Ben-Sasson, *HVH*, pp. 90–129; cf. *PML*, no. 130 [1628], and *PVAA* no. 642 [1739]; Berakhia Beirakh, *Zer'a Beirakh*, pt. 2 (Amsterdam: 1662), *Ki tavo* (2), p. 28b; Berakhia b. Eliakim Getzl, *Zer'a Beirakh shlishi* (Frankfurt on the Oder: 1730), pp. a–b (Introduction).

44. Dinur, *Bemifneh hadorot*, pp. 261–64; Fuenn, *Kirya neemana*, pp. 177–79; Shatzky, *Kultur-geshikhte*, pp. 21–22.

45. The first, less complete edition, was published ten years earlier. The rather astonishing diversity of subject matter is listed on the title page in full detail.

46. Hurwitz, *Sefer haberit*, p. 1b.

47. See Katz, *Exclusiveness and Tolerance* (New York: 1961), pp. 156–68.

48. Hurwitz, *Sefer haberit*, pp. 162a, 164a; cf. pp. 162b–63a. Hurwitz also dwells on the social obligation of teaching a practical skill or trade to Jewish children, a stock item in later maskilic arguments in favor of Jewish economic reform. See, ibid., pp. 160b–161a.

49. Satanower, usually associated with the Galician Haskalah, spent some time in Shklov and his career spanned several countries. *Ḥeshbon hanefesh* was first published in Lemberg in 1808. On the book, see Zinberg, *History* 6, pp. 279–80; with particular reference to the book's influence on Israel Salanter and the musar movement, see Etkes, *R. Israel Salanter vereishita shel tenu'at harnusar* (Jerusalem: 1982), pp. 135–46.

50. Menahem Bendetsohn, *Higayon la'itim,* pt. 2 (Vilna: 1862), pp. 52–57; pt. 1 was published in Vilna in 1856.

51. In 1873 he became inspector of the teachers' seminary when the rabbinical program closed. His book of precepts was originally published in 1865 as Joshua Steinberg, *Or layesharim, mishlei ḥokhma umusar.* The 2d ed., slightly revised, was published as *Mishlei Yehoshu'a, lehair or layesharim* (Vilna: 1871) and was very popular.

52. Steinberg, *Mishlei Yehoshu'a,* pp. 151–53, and see generally, pp. 148–56.

53. See p. 9 of the Introduction to Eliezer Zweifel, *Shalom 'al yisrael.*

54. On Dainov see, *Toledot OPE* 1, pp. 69–70, 100; *Toledot OPE* 2, pp. 207–8; Lifschitz, *ZY* 2, pp. 62–64, 108, 189–94; *EE* 6, cols. 916–17; *Ha-Shahar* 5 (1874), pp. 329–47, 601–05; *Ha-Maggid,* no. 7, (1868) and no. 26 (1869); *Ha-Melitz* no. 23 (1868) and nos. 40–41 (1869). See Dainov's sermon of 1869, *Kevod melekh* (Odessa: 1869; Zhitomir: 1871), on the theme of loyalty to the tsar. There is virtually no difference between Dainov's sermon and the tract published by the Kovno Orthodox militants, *Shelom mashuaḥ* (Vilna: 1870). It is significant that the Orthodox, however, found a word to express the idea of the tsar's divine right (*mashuaḥ* [annointed]) that avoided the form *mashiah* (also annointed but connoting the Messiah). The maskilim did not hesitate to use *mashiah.*

55. There have been several major studies of the maskilic press: S. Zinberg's *Istoriia evreiskoi pechati v rossii* (Petrograd: 1915); S. Zitron's *Di geshikhte fun der yidisher presse fun yor 1863 biz 1889* (Vilna: 1923); Yehuda Slutsky's two volumes on the Russian-language journals, the first of which, *Ha'itonut hayehudit-rusit bamea hatesh'a esreh* (1970), covers the nineteenth century; and Orbach's *New Voices.* Of the two more recent studies, Slutsky's is limited by criteria of language and Orbach's by geography and time. Therefore in the survey of the press I have made, I decided to concentrate first on the Lyck-based *Ha-Maggid* and secondly on the Vilna *Ha-Karmel*—two of the important papers not covered by either Slutsky or Orbach—as well as on the press of the late 1870s.

56. *Ha-Maggid,* no. 3 (1856), 9.

57. *Ha-Maggid,* no. 17 (1867), 130–31.

58. *Ha-Melitz,* no. 3 (1869), 17.

59. Although published in Prussia, *Ha-Maggid* was subject to the review of the Russian censors in Vilna and St. Petersburg, otherwise it could not be imported and delivered promptly to subscribers in Russia—something on which the life of the paper depended. Silberman was therefore quite dependent on the

Russian authorities for approval. See *Ha-Maggid,* no. 1 (1856), and no. 17 (1857).

60. Silbermann to Y. Gurland, 18 October, 1859, published in *Reshumot* 2 (1922), 406.

61. *Ha-Maggid,* no. 6 (1860), p. 21.

62. Lifschitz, *ZY* 2, p. 42.

63. Ibid., pp. 42, 44. Because of his avid interest in the press, he became known as "Yankl Hamaggid."

64. Ibid., p. 25.

65. On the 1859 riot, see Orbach, *New Voices,* pp. 26–27; Zipperstein, *Jews of Odessa,* pp. 120–21; *Ha-Maggid,* suppl. to no. 22 (1859), 2pp.

66. Joachim Tarnopol', "Un journal israélite-russe," *Archives israélites* (April 1860), 193–98.

67. *Ha-Maggid* no. 13 (1860), 49.

68. Orbach, *New Voices,* pp. 32–37; *Razsvet,* no. 1 (1860): L. Levanda, "Neskol'ko slov o evreiakh zapadnago kraia rossii," 7–9; Slutsky, *Ha'itonut,* pp. 43–44; Levanda, "K istorii vozniknoveniia pervago organa russkikh evreev," *Voskhod,* no. 1 (1881), 143–45; *Razsvet,* no. 3 (1860), 37 and no. 6 (1860), 83.

69. *Ha-Maggid,* no. 30 (1860), 107; cf. no. 41 (1860), 163.

70. *Ha-Maggid,* no. 30 (1860), 120, and no. 38 (1860), 162.

71. *Ha-Maggid,* no. 31 (1860), 121–22, and no. 45 (1860), 177.

72. *Ha-Maggid,* no. 45 (1860), 178–79, and no. 46 (1860), 184. See also Silberman's editorials in nos. 46 and 47 (1860).

73. *Ha-Maggid,* no. 1 (1861).

74. Orbach, *New Voices,* pp. 40–42; *Razsvet,* no. 52 (1861) 827. *Razsvet*'s subscribership reached a maximum of 640, see Slutsky, *Ha'itonut,* p. 46.

75. Pro-Jewish articles by maskilim in the Russian press form an entire subliterature and are too numerous to cite specifically. In 1866–67, to give but one episode, Jewish responses to attacks on Jewry in the *Vilenskii vestnik* were published in that journal (no. 155 [1866]; no. 5 [1867]) and in the Russian supplement to *Ha-Karmel* (nos. 11, 12, 14, 19, 20, 22–25 [1866]).

76. *Ha-Maggid,* no. 22 (1869).

77. *Ha-Melitz,* no. 3 (1869); cf. *Ha-Maggid,* no. 10 (1869): "Let us hope that it, too [along with *Ha-Melitz*] will speak out in our favor and stop the mouths of our enemies from without." Its original name, *Posrednik,* was a direct translation of *Ha-Melitz* (mediator).

78. *Ha-Melitz,* no. 12 (1869); cf. *Den',* no. 48 (1870), 356.

79. Lifschitz, *ZY* 2, p. 96. Sir Moses Montefiore, hero of the Damascus affair and benefactor of many Jewish communities, visited Russia on the behalf of his Russian brethren several times and was treated like royalty.

80. Ibid., p. 98.

81. The article, by the brother of Yaakov Lifschitz, appeared in *Ha-Levanon,* suppl. to no. 26 (1870), 201–6.

82. Lifschitz, *ZY* 2, pp. 118–20; first published in *Ha-Kol,* no. 13 (1879), cols.

185–86. Orbach (*New Voices,* pp. 60, 68, 70) notes that Zederbaum did in fact play the part of the old-style shtadlan in his dealings with the government. His fellow maskilim, however, tended to find his methods repellent.

83. *Milhama beshalom o milhemet hashalom, misifrei marbei shalom, kolel hitnatslut benei Yosef mahzikei torat Moshe neged soneihem . . .* (Vilna: 1869–70), pp. 22–23.

84. *Ha-Karmel,* no. 1 (1868), 1–2. Emphasis added.

85. *Ha-Karmel,* no. 1 (1868), 1.

86. Zinberg, *History* 12, p. 170.

87. See *Ha-Maggid,* no. 31 (1867) 242; and Silberman's letter to H.J. Gurland (5 Adar-sheni 1867), published in *Reshumot* 2 (1922), 407.

88. *Ha-Maggid,* no. 1 (1863), 1–2.

89. *Ha-Maggid,* nos. 16, 17 (1860); ibid., no. 1 (1863), p. 2.

90. *Ha-Maggid,* no. 1 (1863), 2.

91. *Ha-Maggid,* nos. 8, 12, 13, 14, 17, 18, 19 (1869); ibid., nos. 36, 37 (1869).

92. *Ha-Maggid,* no. 20 (1869); contd. in nos. 21–28 (1869).

93. *Ha-Karmel,* no. 15 (1868), 113.

94. *Ha-Karmel,* no. 21 (1868), 161. Yet when Fuenn believed a conflict to be not one of pure principle, but one of politics, he urged the public to avoid disunity through disciplined obedience to notables and scholars. This was his position on the disputed reelection of Zalkind Minor to the post of rabbi in Minsk; see ibid., no. 39 (1869), p. 305.

95. *Ha-Melitz,* no. 25 (1868), 181–82.

96. Lifschitz, *Toledot Yitzhak,* p. 58.

97. Bernard Susser, "On the Reconstruction of Jewish Political Theory," in Sam Lehman-Wilzig and Bernard Susser, eds., *Comparative Jewish Politics (1): Public Life in Israel and the Diaspora* (Ramat-Gan, Isr.: 1981).

98. L. Levanda, "Goriachee vremia," pt. 2, *EB* 2 (1872), 34.

99. J.L. Gordon, *Kitvei Yehuda Leib Gordon* (Tel-Aviv: 1960), vol. 2, pp. 98–99: (Zedekiah): "What vanity they speak, who say there is a God / Almighty, omnipotent and supreme judge. / Where is His judgment? / . . . But what sin, what crime have I committed? / Only that I did not submit to Jeremiah . . . whose counsel was to accept shame, slavery, surrender? / . . . Was it personal arrogance that led me to do what I have done, / that I tried to break the yoke of Babylon? / Was it not my people's honor and liberty that I cherished? / . . . And what would this priest from 'Anatot have had us do? / 'Do not bear arms on the Sabbath.' / Was that a time for festivals and sabbaths?"

100. Ibid., p. 100.

101. Max Lilienthal, *Maggid yeshu'a.* The German text was translated by Shmuel Yosef Fuenn (see Gottlober, *Zikhronot umasa'ot* 2, p. 129 n. 4).

102. Ibid., pp. 10–11.

103. Gottlober, *Zikhronot umas'aot* 2, p. 137.

104. Mordecai Aaron Günzberg [Yonah b. Amitai, pseud.], *Maggid emet* (Leipzig: 1843), pp. 4–7.

105. *Mikhtevei Avraham Mapu*, pp. 14–15: Mapu to Günzburg, 13 February 1857.

106. Ibid., p. 14.

107. *Ha-Maggid*, no. 6 (1857), 24.

108. Lilienthal left Russia abruptly in 1845, never to return. On his probable motives, see Stanislawski, *Tsar Nicholas I*, pp. 85–96.

109. *Ha-Maggid*, no. 5 (1860), 19.

110. Ibid.

111. "Der seym," originally printed in Zhitomir in 1869, is published in A. Friedkin and Z. Raizen, eds., *A. B. Gottlobers yidishe verk* (Vilna: 1927), pp. 76–77 (vol. 2 of the editors' *A. B. Gottlober un zayn epokhe*). The poem was originally written in 1842. See Friedkin and Raizin's introduction, p. xiv; and Zinberg, *History*, 11, p. 164.

112. Friedkin and Raizen, *A.B. Gottlobers yidishe verk*, pp. 24–27.

113. *Razsvet*, no. 15 (1860), 236. A similar theme was struck years later by Alexander Zederbaum, in *Ha-Zefirah* no. 14 (1877): The Jews are unable to act politically or juridically against their vilifiers because they have no collective status. "Private individuals cannot demand satisfaction on behalf of the collective, of which they are only single members, and the collective has no official existence." Both passages are also cited by Shochat, "Hahanhaga," pp. 228–29, 231.

114. *Ha-Maggid*, no. 24 (1863): "Davar be'ito, 'ikva demeshiha."

115. Ibid., 189.

116. Whereas in 1856–60 *Ha-Maggid* had included articles extolling Jewish notables on an average of one every seven weeks (and *Ha-Zefirah* of 1862, once every three weeks)—constituting 100 percent of all mention of notables—in 1869 criticism of notables' inaction in *Ha-Maggid* led to a drop in pro-notable comments, these now constituting only 87 percent of all mention of notables. The same proportion is observed in *Ha-Melitz* of 1868. The more conservative *Ha-Karmel* was pro-notable 90 percent of the time in 1868.

117. For example, Silbermann in *Ha-Maggid*, no. 20 (1869), 153–54; no. 21, 161–62; no. 22, 170; cf. *Ha-Melitz*, no. 42 (1869), 289.

118. *Ha-Karmel*, no. 3 (1868), 18.

119. Ibid.

120. Ibid., no. 4 (1868), 25. The reference is to conflicts between Hasidim and non-Hasidim in Shklov and Moscow, see *Ha-Karmel*, no. 2 (1868), 12; and (on Moscow), *Ha-Melitz*, no. 8 (1869), 58.

121. *Ha-Melitz*, no. 9 (1868), 67.

122. *Ha-Melitz*, no. 9 (1868), 69. On the Vilna Commission, see pp. 142–44.

123. See *Ha-Maggid*, no. 7 (1868); cf. Lifschitz, *ZY 2*, p. 70.

124. *Ha-Maggid*, nos. 13, 14, 16–19 (1868); nos. 8, 15, 25 (1869).

125. *Ha-Karmel*, nos. 2, 5 (1868); cf. Katznelson, *Hamilḥama hasifrutit*, pp. 69–71; Seymour Siegel, "The War of the *Kitniyot*," in Arthur Chill, ed., *Perspectives on Jews and Judaism: Essays in Honor of Wolfe Kelman* (New York: 1978), pp. 383–93.

126. *Ha-Karmel,* nos. 7, 9 (1868).
127. *Ha-Karmel,* no. 13 (1868), 100; no. 14 (1868), 106.
128. *Ha-Karmel,* no. 9 (1868), 66.
129. *Ha-Karmel,* suppl. to no. 8 (1869), 10. On Levinsohn, see Kressel, *Leksikon hasifrut ha'ivrit* 2, cols. 208–9.
130. *Ha-Karmel,* no. 12 (1869), 90–91.
131. *Ha-Karmel,* no. 131 (1869), 98–99. For a similar opinion on both counts see Zvi-Hirsh Jonathansohn's "News from Kovno," in *Ha-Melitz,* no. 49 (1868), 364.
132. *Ha-Karmel,* no. 14 (1869), 106–7.
133. *Ha-Maggid,* no. 17 (1869): "'Al devar matsav benei yisrael berusia vetikuno."
134. Ibid.
135. *Ha-Maggid,* no. 28 (1869), 217–18.
136. *Ha-Maggid,* no. 27 (1869), 209–10.
137. Ibid. Salanter at this time was living in Klaipėda (Memel) on the Prussian side of the Lithuanian border. On Salanter's reputation among Lithuanian Jewry at this time, see Etkes, *R. Israel Salanter* (Jerusalem: 1982), pp. 256–57, 260–62, 275–76.
138. Silbermann in *Ha-Maggid,* nos. 21–23, 26 (1869).
139. *Ha-Maggid,* no. 48 (1869), 383–84. On the idea of a consistory, see the Russian supplement to *Ha-Karmel,* no. 38 (1869), 149–51. Margolies was a private tutor in the home of Ezekiel Jaffe in Kovno. He later took up the position of rabbi in a town in Grodno province but feel afoul of Orthodox opinion there and after only two years fled to New York; see, *EE* 10, col. 622; *Encyclopedia Judaica* 11, cols. 959–60; *He-Asif* 4 (1887), 72–74.
140. *Ha-Melitz,* no. 42 (1869), 288–89.
141. *Den',* nos. 8, 11 (1870); cf. Slutsky, *Ha'itonut,* pp. 39, 62, 78–81.
142. Slutsky, *Ha'itonut,* pp. 78–79; *Den',* no. 1 (1870), 11, and no. 12 (1870), 202; *Razsvet* (St. Petersburg), nos. 20, 22–24, 28 (1870); *Nedel'naia khronika voskhoda,* no. 14 (1892), 371.
143. David Feinberg, "Zikhronot," *He-'Avar* 4 (1956), 26–36; Slutsky, *Ha'itonut,* 78–79. For a similar view of St. Petersburg Jewry as a flagship community, see S. Mandelkern, "Letters from St. Petersburg," *Ha-Melitz,* no. 42 (1868), 307.
144. Levitats 2, pp. 193–94. Jacob Brafman and his book, *Kniga kagala,* inspired an entire antisemitic genre, whose reincarnations are circulated to this day. J.L. Gordon's response on behalf of the OPE appeared in *EB* 4 (1873), pp. 284–91, and in *Golos,* no. 156 (1876). Cf. Tcherikover, *Istoriia,* p. 94.
145. *Ha-Melitz,* no. 45 (1869), 310, and nos. 2–4, 6–9, 13, 17 (1878); *Den',* nos. 2, 4, 11, 21 (1870); and *Ha-Maggid,* no. 41 (1870), 323; no. 5, 34; no. 6, 42. Also P. Rabinovich, "Geon Ya'akov," *Knesset yisrael* 2 (1887), cols. 159–60; S. An-sky, "Evreiskaia delegatsiia v vilenskoi komissii 1869 goda," *ES* 5 (1912), 187–201; Iulii Gessen, "Vilenskaia komissiia po ustroistvo byta evreev," *Pe-*

rezhitoe 2 (1911), 306–11; M. Knorozovskii,"Eshcho o vilenskoi komissii 1869 goda," *Perezhitoe* 3 (1912), 385–92; Lifschitz, *ZY,* 2, pp. 113–14. Gessen published a group photograph taken of the Jewish delegates in *Perezhitoe* 4, following p. 320.

146. *Ha-Melitz,* no. 24 (1868), 174. The Jewish participants at the time were Lev Levanda, Jonah Gerstein, Asher Wahl, and Yaakov Barit.

147. *Ha-Melitz,* no. 45 (1869), col. 310; no. 2 (1878), cols. 29–32; no. 3 (1878), cols. 49–52; minutes of the session of 11 October 1869 are found in *ES* 5, 190–95.

148. As reported in *Ha-Melitz,* no. 4 (1878), cols. 69–70.

149. Minutes [Vilna conimession] . . . no. 7 (pp. 197–99) and petition of the delegates to Potapov are found in *ES* 5, 200–201; *Ha-Melitz,* no. 9 (1878), cols. 179–80; no. 13, cols. 249–51; no. 17, cols. 321–23; no. 45 (1869), 311; Rabinovich, "Geon Ya'akov," p. 160.

150. Israel Bartal, "Halo-yehudim vehevratam," pp. 15–22, 45–51; cf. Bartal, "Bein haskala radikalit lesotsializm yehudi," PWCJS 8 (1984), *Panel Sessions: Jewish History,* pp. 16–17. The tendency was less pronounced in Yiddish literature, Bartal argues.

151. Bartal, "Halo-yehudim vehevratam," pp. 90–95, 130–31. Compare the simliar views of Aron Liberman, expressed in 1873 in the pages of the nationalist journal, *Ha-Shahar* cited in Frankel, *Prophecy and Politics,* p. 32.

152. Abramovich, *Di kliatshe,* in *Gesamlte shriftn fun Mendele Moykher Sforim* (New York: 1910) 1, p. 54.

153. Ibid., pp. 50–51.

154. Ibid., p. 54.

155. Ibid., p. 89.

156. Abramovich, *Di takse,* p. 59 (in the same edition as above).

157. Idem, *Di kliatshe,* pp. 79–80.

158. *Ha-Melitz,* no. 16 (1870), 121–22.

159. Gottlober to H.J. Gurland, 2 December 1866, published in *Reshumot* 2 (1922), 420–21.

160. Serialized in Gottlober's journal, *Haboker or,* 1876–78; repr. in 2 vols. Jerusalem: 1974, with an introduction by Gershon Shaked.

161. Braudes, *Hadat vehahaim* 2, pp. 194–195.

162. On the genesis of the new St. Petersburg *Razsvet,* see Slutsky, *Ha'itonut,* pp. 105–111.

163. David Gordon, "Beshuva venahat tivashe'un," *Ha-Maggid* 1863; S.Z. Shechter, " 'Hamaggid' vera'ayon shivat ziyon beshnot hashishim shel hamea ha-19," *Mehkarim betoledot 'am yisrael veeretz yisrael* 5 (1980), 219–30; Vital, *Origins,* pp. 11–12.

164. Upgrading the Vilna and Zhitomir rabbinical schools into Western-style seminaries (on the Breslau model) would have meant creating a more sophisticated, university-level curriculum. Although the maskilic proponents of the idea continued to press for the establishment of such an institution for Russian Jews,

the regime in 1873 downgraded the existing rabbinical schools, transforming them into teachers' seminaries. In effect, the state and the maskilim were working at cross purposes. See Shochat, *Harabanut mita'am,* pp. 70–101, 134–43.

165. On the entire episode, see Shlomo Braiman, "Pulmus hatikunim badat basifrut ha'ivrit beemts'a hamea ha-19," *He-'Avar* 1 (1952), 115–31; Haim Hamiel, "Bein haredim lemaskilim berusia beshnot ha-60 veha-70," *Sinai* 59, no. 1/2 (1966), 76–84; Katznelson, *Hamilhama;* Shochat, *Harabanut mita'am,* pp. 20–21, 61–63, 70–104, 134–43; Slutsky, "Beit hamidrash lerabanim bevilna," *He-'Avar* 7 (1960), 29–48. On Lilienblum, see his essays, "Orhot hatalmud" and "Nosafot lehamaamar orhot hatalmud" (in installments, *Ha-Melitz,* 1868 and 1869); Zalman Epstein, *Moshe Leib Lilienblum—shitato vehelekh mahshevotav besheelot hadat* (Tel-Aviv: 1935); Haim Hamiel, "Pulmus M. L. Lilienblum," *Sinai* 60, no. 5/7 (1967), 299–310; Lilienblum, *Ketavim autobiografiim;* Zipperstein, *Jews of Odessa,* 141–42.

166. See the discussion of the famine and the battle in the press over Passover consumption of *kitniot* (legumes), n. 20; and Tarnopol', *Opyt sovremennoi i osmotritel'noi reformy,* p. 7.

167. Peretz Smolenskin, "'Am 'olam," in his collected essays, *Maamarim* (Jerusalem: 1925) 1, p. 28 (originally serialized in *Ha-Shahar* beginning with 3 [1872]). It should be noted that Smolenskin began his public career as an itinerant preacher, a role in which he had to conceal his maskilic thinking (see Arthur Hertzberg, ed., *The Zionist Idea* [New York: 1971], p. 143).

168. See Smolenskin, n. 167 and *Maamarim* 2, pp. 141–47; Frankel, *Prophecy and Politics,* p. 82; Vital, *Origins,* pp. 46–47.

169. Frankel, *Prophecy and Politics,* pp. 28–44, 53; Bartal, "Bein haskala radikalit lesotsializm yehudi," PWCJS 8 (1984), pp. 13–20; M. Mishkinsky, ed., *A. S. Liberman: katavot umaamarim be'Vperyod', 1875–1876* (Tel-Aviv: 1967).

170. This was so much taken for granted that Nahum Sokolov, writing in 1879, attempted to shock his readers by denying the existence of a true "public opinion" in Jewish society, equating public opinion with consensus: *Ha-Kol,* no. 61 (1879), cols. 899–903.

171. Abramovich, "Ma na'aseh?" (What Is to Be Done? The title is borrowed from the Russian critic Chernyshevsky), *Ha-Melitz,* no. 1 (1878), cols. 3–8 and no. 2, cols. 31–36.

172. Ibid., cols. 5–6.

173. Ibid., cols. 31–32, 36.

174. Dan Miron and Anita Norich, "The Politics of Benjamin III," in M. Herzog et al., eds., *The Field of Yiddish: Studies in Language, Folklore and Literature, Fourth Collection* (Philadelphia: 1980), pp. 27–33, 43–44, 64–76.

175. See, for example, Zederbaum, in *Ha-Melitz,* no. 30 (1868), col. 221; Abraham Uri Kovner, "Ruah haim," *Ha-Karmel,* nos. 24, 26 (1867).

176. "Auto-emancipation," (1882) in Hertzberg, *Zionist Idea,* pp. 182, 198: "[The Jews are] a nation long since dead. With the loss of their fatherland, the Jews . . . fell into a state of decay which is incompatible with the existence of a

whole and vital organism. . . . The lack of national self-respect and self-confidence, of political initiative and of unity, are the enemies of our national renaissance."

177. Mordecai b. Hillel Hacohen, "Tikva nikhzeva," *Ha-Kol,* no. 30, (1879), cols. 449–50. On the expectation that emancipation was just around the corner, see, for example, Nahum Sokolov, "Hayehudim beyihus hashitot hamediniot," *Ha-Melitz,* no. 19 (1878), col. 371; Lifschitz, *ZY* 2, pp. 203–4.

178. M.L. Lilienblum, "Petah tikva," *Ha-Kol,* no. 22 (1878), col. 157. The last remark is a parody of the traditional adage that, without Torah, the Jews are like a body without a soul. Lilienblum was equally dismissive of the Jewish knowledge of wealthy lay leaders: ibid., cols. 157–58.

179. Hacohen, "Tikva nikhzeva," *Ha-Kol,* no. 33 (1879), cols. 493–95. On the bitterly contested election in Kovno, see Lifschitz, *ZY* 2, p. 206. On the role of nonrabbinic figures in the Rabbinical Commissions generally, see Morgulis, "K istoriia obrazovaniia," p. 193.

180. The other members were Y.Y. Kaufman of Odessa, Meyer Levin of Minsk, Hirsh Shapira of Kovno, Zalman Liubich of Grodno, and Dr. A.A. Harkavy. See Yerushalmi, "Va'adot uve'idot," p. 87.

181. "Correspondence from St. Petersburg," (I.B. Halevi Ish Hurwitz), *Ha-Maggid,* no. 8 (1879), p. 61.

182. *Ha-Maggid,* no. 11 (1879), p. 84; *Ha-Melitz,* no. 4 (1879), col. 71 and cf. no. 10, col. 202.

183. "Petersburger Briefe," *Allgemeine Zeitung des Judenthums,* no. 10 (4 March 1879), 147–50; no. 13 (25 March 1879), 193–95, 203.

184. Hacohen, "Tikva nikhzeva," col. 496; Lifschitz, *ZY* 2, pp. 207–8; Yerushalmi, "Va'adot uve'idot," p. 88.

185. Hacohen, "Tikva nikhzeva," col. 450.

186. Morgulis, "Divrei ish 'ivri la'ivrim bemikhtav 'et 'ivri," *Ha-Melitz,* no. 5 (1878), cols. 89–95.

187. Ibid., cols. 89, 92–95. The theme of disorder and the need for a new communal form was also struck by Morgulis in Russian, in 1880: "Vozmozhno-li i sleduet-li predostavit' evreiam pravo samoupravleniia obshchestvennymi delami?" *Razsvet,* nos. 18–20 (1880). Reprinted in his anthology, *Voprosy evreiskoi zhizni,* pp. 458–482; see esp. his conclusion, p. 482.

188. Morgulis, "Divrei ish 'ivri," cols. 89–90.

Conclusion

1. Frankel, *Prophecy and Politics,* pp. 51, 57, 61, 74–79.

2. Jewish autonomy was the political goal of several Jewish parties at the turn of the twentieth century and in the interwar period. Political autonomy within the larger socialist movement as well as cultural autonomy for the Jews within a multinational socialist state were goals pursued by the Jewish Workers'

Bund. The *Folkspartei*, led by the historian Simon Dubnow, was a liberal party committed to the idea of national-cultural autonomy for Jews. After 1906 the Zionist movement in Russia also supported the demand for national-cultural autonomy for Jews in the diaspora. The idea was partly put into effect in inter-war Poland and Lithuania and to some extent elsewhere in East Central Europe, in accordance with the Minority Rights treaties agreed to at the Versailles Peace Conference of 1919.

3. See, for example, the consideration of Zionism as an absolute faith of a minority with the sanction to lead the majority against its will in comments by Anita Shapira (*Totalitarian Democracy and After* [Jerusalem: 1984], pp. 354–60); and ibid., Jonathan Frankel, "Democracy and Its Negations: On Polarity in Jewish Socialism," pp. 329–341.

4. Shlomo Zalman Landa and Yosef Rabinovich, comps., *Sefer or laye-sharim, yair divrei meorot hagedolim ḥavat da'at kedoshim neged hasitna hatsiyonit* (Warsaw: 1900), pp. 23–24.

5. "Purim is keyn yontef, fiber—keyn krenk," in Y.L. Peretz, *Alle verk* (New York: 1947), 8, p. 118.

6. See Zvi Gitelman, *Jewish Nationality and Soviet Politics. The Jewish Sections of the CPSU, 1917–1930* (Princeton, N.J.: 1972); Mordecai Altshuler, *Hayevsektsia bivrit hamo'atsot, 1918–1930: bein leumiut lekomunizm* (Tel-Aviv: 1980–81); Ezra Mendelsohn, *The Jews of East Central Europe Between the World Wars* (Bloomington, Ind.: 1983); Jonathan Frankel, "The Paradoxical Politics of Marginality," in Jonathan Frankel, ed., *Studies in Contemporary Jewry* 4 (New York/Oxford: 1988), pp. 3–21.

Bibliography

Primary Sources or Sources Used as Primary Documents

Abramovich, Shalom. "Ma na'aseh?" *Ha-Melitz,* no. 1 (1878), no. 2, (1878).
————. *Alle shriftn.* New York: Hebrew Publishing Co., 1910.
Abravanel, Isaac. *Ma'ayanei hayeshu'a.* Jerusalem/Tel-Aviv: Abravanel Books/ Elisha, 1960. (Originally published Amsterdam, 1661.)
Aksenfeld, Israel. *Y. Aksenfelds verk.* Edited by M. Wiener. Kiev/Kharkov: Institut far yidisher kultur ba der ukraynisher akademye—Melukhe farlag "Literatur un kunst," 1931.
Akty izdavaemye vilenskoiu komissieiu dlia razbora drevnykh aktov, vol. 13, *Akty glavnago litovskago tribunala* (Vilna: 1886); vols. 28/29, *Akty o evreiakh* (Vilna: 1902); vol. 37, *Otechestvennaia voina 1812 g.,* (Vilna: 1912)
Aleksandrov, H. "Fun arkhiv fun minsker kohol," *Tsaytshrift* 1 (1926), 239–49.
An-sky, S. "Iz legend o mstislavskom dele," *Perezhitoe* 2 (1910), 248–57.
————. "Evreiskaia delegatsiia v vilenskoi komissii 1869 goda," *ES* 5 (1912), 187–201.
Assaf, Simha. *Ha'onshin aharei hatimat hatalmud.* Jerusalem: Hapoel Hatzair, 1922.
Avraham Zvi-Hirsch b. Elazar. *Sheelot uteshuvot berit Avraham.* Dyhrenfurth: 1819.
Beilin, S. "Iz istoricheskikh zhurnalov: (4) otzyv velikago kniazia Nikolaia Pavlovicha o evreiakh," *ES* 4 (1911), 589–90.
Benditsohn, Menahem. *Higayon la'itim.* Vilna: 1856–62.
Berakhia Beirakh b. Isaac. *Zer'a Beirakh,* pt. 1. Cracow: 1646; pt. 2, Amsterdam: 1662.

Berakhia b. Eliakim Getzl. *Zer'a Beirakh shlishi.* Frankfurt on the Oder: 1730.

Bergmann, J. "Aus dem Briefen Abraham Bedersi's," *MGWJ* 42 (1898), 507–17.

Berlin, Moisei. *Ocherk etnografii evreiskago narodonaseleniia v rossii.* St. Petersburg: 1861.

———. *Bugul'minskii talmudist.* St. Petersburg: 1862.

Bogrov, G. "Poimannik," *EB* 4 (1874), 1–110.

Borodiansky, H. "Di loyblider lekoved Katerine II un zeyere mekhabrim." In YIVO *Historishe shriftn* 2 (Vilna: 1937), pp. 531–37.

Bottomore, Thomas B., ed. *Karl Marx. Early Writings.* New York: McGraw-Hill, 1964.

Braiman, Shlomo, ed. *Igerot M. L. Lilienblum le-Y.L. Gordon.* Jerusalem: Magnes, 1968.

Brann, M. "Additions à l'autobiographie de Lipman Heller," *REJ* 21 (1890), 272–77.

Braudes, Reuven Asher. *Hadat vehaḥaim.* Jerusalem: Mossad Bialik, 1974.

Dainov, Zvi-Hirsh. *Kevod melekh.* Odessa: 1869 and Zhitomir: 1871.

Darshan, David. *Shir hama'alot le-David. Ketav hitnatslut ledarshanim,* trans. and annotated by H.G. Perelmuter. Cincinnati, Ohio: Hebrew Union College Press, 1984.

Dinur, Ben-Zion. *Yisrael bagola: mekorot ute'udot,* 2 vols. Tel-Aviv and Jerusalem: Dvir and Mossad Bialik, 1959–71.

Druyanov, A. "Ma'aseh amstislev," as told by Israel-Isser b. Avraham Abba Smilak (Yiddish). *Reshumot,* o.s., 4 (1926), 287–94.

Dubnow, Simon. "Iz khroniki mstislavskoi obshchiny," *Voskhod,* no. 9 (1899), 33–59.

———. "Delo o evreiskom samosude v podolii (1838–40 g.)," *Perezhitoe* 1 (1908), docs. pp. 1–6.

———. "Vmeshatel'stvo russkago pravitel'stva v antikhasidskuiu bor'bu (1800–1801)," *ES* 3 (1910), 84–109, 253–82.

———. "Mipinkasei kehillat mstislav: ma'aseh nisim sheir'a bishnat 5604," *He'Avar* 1 (1918), 63–79.

———. *Chasidiana.* Jerusalem: 1969 (originally published as a supplement to *He-'Avar* 2 [1918]).

———. ed. *Pinkas medinat lita.* Berlin: Ayanot, 1925.

———. "Fun mayn arkhiv," *Yivo bletter* 1, no. 5 (1931), 404–7.

Emden, Jacob. *'Edut be-Ya'akov.* Altona: 1756.

Ephraim of Lentschütz. *'Ir giborim.* Basle: 1580.

———. *Oraḥ ḥaim.* Lublin: 1595.

———. *'Olelot Efraim.* Lublin: 1600.

Fajnhauz, David. "Konflikty społeczne w śród ludności żydowskiej na litwie i białorusi w pierwszej polowie 19 w.," *BZIH,* no. 52 (1964), 8–15.

Feinberg, David. "Zikhronot," *He-'Avar* 4 (1956), 26–36.

Feodorov, Vladimir. "O talmude i vazhnosti ego," *Vestnik russkikh evreev,* nos.

14, 15, 18, 19 (1871) (reprinted as a separate publication [St. Petersburg: 1871]).

Finkelstein, Louis, ed. *Jewish Self-Government in the Middle Ages,* 2d ed. New York: Feldheim, 1964.

Flusser, David, ed. *Sefer Yossipon.* Jerusalem: Merkaz Zalman Shazar, 1978.

Friedberg, A.S. "Zikhronot miyemei ne'urai," *Sefer hashana* 3 (1902), 84–88.

Friedkin, A., and Z. Raizen, eds., *A. B. Gottlobers yidishe verk,* vol. 2, *A. B. Gottlober un zayn epokhe,* Vilna: Kletzkin, 1927.

Fuenn, Shmuel Yosef. *Kirya neemana: korot 'adat yisrael be'ir vilna,* 2d rev. ed. Vilna: Funk, 1915.

"Fun di vilner arkhivn: der bunt fun minsker 'amkho' kegn kohol in 1777." In YIVO *Historishe shriftn* 2 (Vilna: 1937), pp. 608–11.

Ganz, David b. Shlomo. *Sefer tsemaḥ David lerabbi David Ganz.* Edited by Mordecai Breuer. Jerusalem: Magnes, 1983.

Gelber, N.M., ed. *Hayehudim vehamered hapolani: zikhronotav shel Ya'akov Halevi Levin miyemei hamered hapolani bishnat 1830–1831.* Jerusalem: Mossad Bialik, 1952.

――――, and Israel Halperin. "Va'ad arb'a aratsot bashanim 1739–1753," *Zion* 2 (1937), 154–84, 333–46.

Gessen, Iulii. "Bor'ba pravitel'stva s evreiskoi odezhdoi v imperii i tsarstve pol'skom," *Perezhitoe* 1 (1908), docs. pp. 10–18.

――――. " 'Mstislavskoe buistvo' po arkhivnym materialam," *Perezhitoe* 2 (1910), 54–77.

――――. "Zapiska vilenskago kagala o nuzhdakh evreiskago naroda (1833 g.)," *ES* 4 (1911), 96–108.

――――. "Zabytyi obshchestvennyi deiatel': zapiska kuptsa Feigina na imia imp. Nikolaia I," *ES* 4 (1911), 394–402.

Goldberg, Jacob. *Jewish Privileges in the Polish Commonwealth.* Jerusalem: Israel Academy of Sciences and Humanities, 1985.

Gordon, Judah Leib. *Igerot Yehuda Leib Gordon,* 2 vols. Warsaw: 1894.

――――. *Kitvei Yehuda Leib Gordon,* 2 vols. Tel-Aviv: Dvir, 1959–1960.

Gottlober, Avraham Ber. *'Anaf 'ets 'avot.* Vilna: 1858.

――――. *Mizmor letoda.* Zhitomir: 1866.

――――. *Zikhronot umasa'ot.* 2 vols. Jerusalem: Mossad Bialik, 1976.

Günzberg, Mordecai Aaron. *Hamalakhut el Kaius Kaligula hakeisar hashlishi laromim me'et Yedidia haaleksandroni, hu Filon hayehudi.* Vilna: 1836.

――――. *Maggid emet.* Leipzig: 1843.

――――. *Ḥamat damesek.* Königsberg: 1859–60.

Haberman, Abrham, ed., *Sefer gezerot ashkenaz vetsarfat.* Jerusalem: Tarshish, 1945.

Haim b. Yitzhak. *Sefer ruaḥ Ḥaim, beur 'al masekhet avot.* Vilna: 1858.

Halperin, Israel, ed. *Pinkas va'ad arb'a aratsot.* Jerusalem: Mossad Bialik, 1945–46.

216 *Bibliography*

———, ed., *Takanot vehitmanuyot bekehillot yehudiot bameiot 17–18.* Jerusalem: The Hebrew University, 1962–63.

Heller, Yom-tov Lipman. *Megilat eiva.* Breslau: 1836.

Hillel b. Ze'ev Wolf. *Hillel ben shaḥar.* Warsaw: 1804.

Hisdai, Yaakov, comp. *Sifrut haderush kemakor histori biyemei reishit haḥasidut.* Jerusalem: The Hebrew University, 1984.

Hodoshevich, K. "Der 'razbor' fun der yidisher bafelkerung vitebsker gubernye," *Tsaytshrift* 6 (1930), 139–45.

Holdhor, Reuven. *Divrei shalom veemet/Slova mira i pravdy.* Vilna: 1836.

Horn, Maurycy. "Regesty Dokumentów z Metryki Koronnej do Historii Żydów w Polsce," *ZBIH,* nos. 116–124 (1980–82).

Hurwitz, Judah b. Mordecai. *Tsel ma'alot.* Königsberg: 1764–65.

Hurwitz, Pinhas-Elijah b. Meir. *Sefer haberit.* Brünn: 1807.

Hurwitz, S.Y. "Sefer ḥayai (zikhronot)," *Ha-Shiloach* 40 (1923), 1–14.

I., Ya. "Bor'ba pravitel'stva s khasidizmom, 1834–1853 g.," *ES* 7 (1914), docs. pp. 90–102.

"Iz perepiska A. B. Gottlobera," *ES* 3 (1910), 283–92, 411–18.

Josephus Flavius. *The Jewish War.* Translated by H. St.J. Thackeray. London/Cambridge, Mass.: Heinemann/Harvard University Press, 1927.

Katz, Ben-Zion. *Lekorot hayehudim berusia, polin velita.* Berlin: Ahiasaf, 1899.

Khwolson, Daniel. *O nekotorykh srednevekovykh obvineniiakh protiv evreev.* St. Petersburg, 1861.

Knorozovskii, M. "Eshcho o vilenskoi komissii 1869 goda," *Perezhitoe* 3 (1912), 385–92.

Kon, P. "Fun di vilner arkhivn: (1) A loyb-lid fun der mohilever kehille lekoved Katerina II." In YIVO *Historishe shriftn* 1 (Vilna: 1929), cols. 753–60.

Korobkov, Kh. "Epizody iz epokhi Aleksandr I," *ES* 4 (1911), 581–87.

Kovner, Abraham Uri. "Ruaḥ ḥaim," *Ha-Karmel,* nos. 24, 26: 1867.

Kracauer, J. "Journal de Joselmann," *REJ* 16 (1888), 84–103.

Landa, Shlomo Zalman, and Yosef Rabinovich, comps. *Sefer or layesharim yair divrei meorot hagedolim ḥavat da'at kedoshim neged hasitna hatsiyonit.* Warsaw: M.I. Halter, 1900.

Landau, Asher Aaron. *Sefer ahavat hamelekh.* Breslau: 1832.

Landsberg, Shlomo Isaiah. *Megilla 'efa.* Kearny, N.J.: 1904. (Originally written in 1827.)

Lebenson, Adam Hacohen. *Kelil yofi.* Vilna: 1856.

———, ed. *Kovets derushim leshabatot ulemo'adim uleyemei ḥagei adoneinu hakeisar.* Vilna: 1863.

Lerner, O.M. *Evreii v novorossiiskom krae: istoricheskie ocherki.* Odessa: G. Levinson, 1901.

Leszcznyski, Anatol. "Żydzi ziemi bielskiej w dokumentach z 18 w.," *BZIH,* no. 117 (1981), 21–36.

Levanda, Lev. "Neskol'ko slov o evreiakh zapadnago kraia rossii," *Razsvet,* no. 1 (1860).

———. "Goriachee vremia," *EB* 2 (1872), 1–160.

Levi Yitzhak b. Meir of Berdichev. *Kedushat Levi.* Edited by Zvi Elimelekh Kalish. New York: Taryag, 1972 (republished ed. of Munkacz: 1939).

Levin, Y.L. "Zikhronot vera'ayonot," *Sefer hayovel le-Naḥum Sokolov.* Warsaw: Shuldberg, 1904, pp. 354–67.

Levinsohn, Isaac Ber. *Te'uda beyisrael.* Vilna: 1828.

———. *Efes damim.* Vilna: 1837.

———. *Beit yehuda.* Vilna: 1839.

———. *Beit haotsar.* Vilna: 1841.

———. *Zerubavel.* Odessa: 1863/Warsaw: 1875.

———. *Yemin tsidkati.* Warsaw: 1881.

———. *Di hefker velt,* 3d ed. Warsaw: Halter, 1903.

Lifschitz, Yaakov Halevi. *Toledot Yitzhak.* Warsaw: 1896.

———. *Zikhron Ya'akov,* 2 vols. Frankfurt am Main: 1924.

Lilienblum, Moshe Leib. *Ḥatot ne'urim: ketavim autobiografiim.* In *Ketavim autobiografiim,* ed. Shlomo Braiman. Jerusalem: Mossad Bialik, 1970,

———. *Igerot M.L. Lilenblum le-Y.L. Gordon,* ed. Shlomo Braiman. Jerusalem: Magnes, 1968.

Lilienthal, Max. *Maggid yeshu'a, maggid leveit ya'akov teshu'atam uleveit yisrael 'ezratam: mikhtav shaluaḥ le'adat yisrael.* Translated by S.Y. Fuenn. Vilna: 1842.

Maggid, David. "Iz moego arkhiva: k istorii evreiskikh deputatov v tsarstvovanie Aleksandra I," *Perezhitoe* 4 (1913), 181–91.

Mahler, Raphael. "A Jewish Memorandum to the Viceroy of the Kingdom of Poland, Paskiewicz," *Salo Baron Jubilee Volume.* Edited by Saul Lieberman. Jerusalem: American Academy for Jewish Research, 1974. 2, pp. 669–96.

Mandelstamm, Benjamin. *Ḥazon lamo'ed.* Vienna: 1877.

Mandelstamm, Leon. *Shnei perakim: 'al devar haḥov hamutal 'aleinu leehov ulekhabed et adoneinu hakeisar . . . 'Al devar ma'alat ukhevod he'amim hayesharim asher bizemaneinu.* St. Petersburg: 1856–57.

Mann, Jacob. *Texts and Studies in Jewish History and Literature,* 2 vols. Cincinnati, Ohio: Hebrew Union College Press, 1931.

Mapu, Avraham. *'Ayit tsavu'a.* Vilna: 1867.

Margaliot, Haim Wolf, comp. *Dubna rabbati.* Warsaw: Hatsefira, 1910.

Margalioth, Judah-Leyb. *Beit midot.* Dyhrenfurth: 1778.

. *Tal orot.* Pressburg: 1843.

Mazeh, Jacob b. Isaiah. *Zikhronot,* 2 vols. Tel-Aviv: Yalkut, 1936.

Meir of Lublin, *Sheelot uteshuvot.* Venice: 1619.

Mishkinsky, M. ed. *A. S. Liberman: katavot umaamarim be 'Vperyod' 1875–1876.* Tel-Aviv: Tel-Aviv University, 1976–77.

Mondshain, Yehoshua, ed. *Migdal 'oz.* Kfar Habad, Israel: Machon Liubavitch, 1980. (Cited in notes as "Maamar haadmor haemtsa'i.")

Morgulis, M. *Voprosy evreiskoi zhizni.* St. Petersburg, 1889.

———. "Iz moikh vospominanii," *Voskhod,* no. 2 (1895).

Natanson, D.., ed. *Sefer hazihronot, divrei yemei ḥayei . . . Yitzhak Ber Levin-sohn*. Warsaw: 1875.

――――. *Beer Yitzḥak*. Warsaw: Alafin, 1899–1900.

Neubauer, Adolf, and Moritz Stern. *Hebräische Berichte über die Judenverfol-gungen wahrend der Kreuzzüge*. Berlin: Leonard Simion, 1892.

Nevakhovich, Lev. *Kol shav'at bat yehuda*. Shklov: 1804; repr. in *He-'Avar* 2 (1918), separate pagination.

Nisenboym, Shlomo Barukh, comp. *Sefer lekorot hayehudim belublin*. Lublin: 1899.

Orshanskii, I. G. "Mysli o khasidizma," *EB* 1 (1871), 73–101.

Paperna, A.J. "Kaafikim banegev," *Sefer hayovel le-Naḥum Sokolov*. Warsaw: Shuldberg, 1904, pp. 440–50.

――――. "Iz nikolaevskoi epokhi." *Perezhitoe* 2 (1910), 1–53.

Pazdro, Zbigniew. *Organizacya i praktyka żydowskich sądów podwojewod-zinskich w okresie 1740–1772*. Lwow: Nakl. Fund. Konkurs, 1903.

Pinkes fun der shtot pruzhine. Pruzany, Poland: 1930.

Popugaev, Vasilii V. "O blagopoluchii narodnykh tel." In *Russkie prosvetiteli ot Radishcheva do dekabristov*, 1, edited by I. Shchipanov. Moscow: Mysl', 1966.

Rava, Yoel. "Protokol shel kinus va'ad gelil volin bishnat 1700 (ḥalukat mas hagulgolet)," *Gal-'Ed* 6 (1982), 215–28.

Regesty i nadpisi: svod materialov dlia istorii evreev v rossii (80 g.–1800 g.), 3 vols. St. Petersburg: Krais, 1913.

Rosensohn, Moshe. *Milḥama beshalom*. Vilna: 1870.

――――. *Shelom mashuaḥ*. Vilna: 1870.

Rosenthal, Yehuda Leon, ed. *Ḥevrat marbei haskala beyisrael*, 2 vols. St. Peters-burg: 1890. (Cited as *Toledot OPE*.)

Shatzky, Jacob. "Arkhivalia: tsu der geshikhte fun der rabonim-makhloykes in vilne tsum sof 18tn yorhundert." *YIVO Historishe shriftn* 1 (Vilna: 1929), cols. 717–38.

Shimon b. Zeev-Wolf. "Heasir benesvizh [*Więzién w Nieświęzu do Stanów Sejmuiacych o potrzebie reformy żydów*]," translated by Israel Klausner. *He-'Avar* 19 (1972), 64–73.

Shochat, Azriel. "Legezerot hagiyusim shel Nikolai harishon (reshit shtadlanuto shel habaron Ginzburg)." In *Sefer Shalom Sivan*. Edited by Avraham Even-Shoshan, et al. Jerusalem: Kiryat Sefer, 1979, pp. 315–318.

Shorr, M. "Materialy, dokumenty i soobshcheniia: (2) spetsial'nyie privilegii krakovskikh evreev (1549–1678)," *ES* 2 (1909), 223–245.

Slutsky, Yehuda. "Letoledot hayehudim berusia besof hamea ha-18: shalosh te'udot," *He-'Avar* 19 (1972), 74–78.

Smolenskin, Peretz. "Kevurat ḥamor," *Ha-Shaḥar* 3 (1873).

――――. *Maamarim*. Jerusalem: Dfus Hapoalim, 1925.

Sokolov, Nahum. "Hayehudim beyiḥus hashitot hamediniot," *Ha-Melitz, nos.* 18–19 (1878).

Steinberg, Yehoshu'a. *Mishlei Yehoshu'a, lehair or layesharim.* Vilna: 1871.

Steinschneider, Hillel-Noah Maggid. *'Ir vilna.* Vilna: Romm, 1900.

Sternhertz, Nathan. *Sefer ḥayei mohaRan.* Jerusalem: Vardi, 1962. (Originally published 1875.)

Tarnopol', Joachim. *Opyt sovremennoi i osmotritel'noi reformy v oblasti iudaizma v rossi.* Odessa: 1868.

————. "Un journal israélite-russe," *Archives israélites* (April 1860).

Tcherikover, E. "Fun di rusishe arkhivn: (1) gevirim-shtadlonim un di gzeyres fun rekrutshine un razryadn." In YIVO *Historishe shriftn* 1 (Vilna: 1929), cols. 784–87.

————. "Der arkhiv fun Shimon Dubnov." In YIVO *Historishe shriftn* 2 (Vilna: 1937), docs. sec.

Tishby, Isaiah. "Dapei geniza miḥibur meshiḥi-mist 'al gerushei sefarad uportugal," *Zion* 48 (1983), 55–102, 347–85.

Trebitsch, Abraham b. Reuben Hayyat. *Korot ha'itim,* 2d ed., with "Korot nosofot" by Jacob Blodek. Lemberg: 1851.

Tugendhold, Wolf. *Hamoser, o sof resh'a.* Translated by M. Benditsohn. Vilna: 1847.

ibn Verga, Shlomo. *Shevet yehuda.* Edited by Azriel Shochat. Jerusalem: Mossad Bialik, 1946.

Weinryb, Bernard. *Texts and Studies in the Communal History of Polish Jewry, PAAJR* entire volume 19 (1950).

Wilensky, M. *Ḥasidim umitnagdim: letoledot hapulmus shebeineihem bashanim 5532–5575 [1772–1815],* 2 vols. Jerusalem: Mossad Bialik, 1970.

Zinberg, Israel. "Fun Gottlobers literarishe yerushe," *Tsaytshrift* 5 (1931), 43–77.

Zweifel, Eliezer. *Shalom 'al yisrael.* Jerusalem: Mossad Bialik (Jerusalem: 1972). (Originally published Kiev/Vilna/Zhitomir: 1868–73.)

Secondary Sources

Agus, Irving. *Urban Civilization in Pre-Crusade Europe,* 2 vols. New York: Yeshiva University Press, 1965.

Aleksandrov, H. "Di yidishe bafelkerung in vaysrusland in der tsayt fun di tseteylungen fun polyn," *Tsaytshrift* 4 (1930), 31–83.

Almog, Shmuel. *Tsiyonut vehistoria.* Jerusalem: Magnes, 1982.

Altshuler, Mordecai. *Hayevsektsia bivrit hamo'atsot, 1918–1930: bein leumiut lekomunizm.* Tel-Aviv: Sifriat Poalim, 1980–81.

Ankori, Zvi. *Karaites in Byzantium.* New York: Columbia University Press, 1959.

Apter, David E. *The Politics of Modernization.* Chicago/London: University of Chicago Press, 1965.

Arendt, Hannah. *The Origins of Totalitarianism.* New York: Harcourt Brace Jovanovich, 1973. (Originally published 1951.)

———. *On Violence.* New York: Harcourt, Brace and World, 1969.

Baer, Yitzhak. "Don Yitzḥak Abravanel veyaḥaso el be'ayot hahistoria vehamedina," *Tarbitz* 8 (1936–37), 241–99.

———. "Sefer Yosippon ha'ivri." In *Sefer Dinaburg,* edited by Yitzhak Baer. Jerusalem: Kiriat Sefer, 1949.

———. "Hayesodot vehahatḥalot shel irgun hakehilla hayehudit biyemei habeinayim," *Zion* 15 (1950), 1–41.

———. *A History of the Jews in Christian Spain,* 2 vols. Philadelphia: Jewish Publication Society, 1966.

Balaban, M. "Pravovoi stroi evreev v pol'she," *ES* 3 (1910), 39–60, 161–91, 324–45.

———. "Perekhod pol'skikh evreev pod vlast' avstrii: galitsiskie evreii pri Marii Terezii i Iosif II," *ES* 6 (1913), 289–307.

———. "Hakaraim befolin," *Ha-Tekufa,* no. 25 (1929), 450–87.

Barit, M.I., *Toledot Yaakov, hu harav . . . Yaakov Barit hamekhuneh kovner.* (Vilna: 1883).

Baron, Salo W. *The Jewish Community,* 3 vols. Philadelphia: Jewish Publication Society, 1942.

———. *A Social and Religious History of the Jews,* 18 vols. New York/Philadelphia: Columbia University Press/Jewish Publication Society, 1952–84.

———. "Ḥerem vilna vehamemshalot haadirot," *Ḥorev* 12 (1956), 62–69.

———. *The Russian Jew Under Tsars and Soviets.* New York: Macmillan, 1964.

———. *Ancient and Medieval Jewish History.* New Brunswick, N.J.: Rutgers University Press, 1972.

Barry, Brian, ed. *Power and Political Theory.* London/New York: Wiley, 1976.

Bartal, Israel. "Halo-yehudim veḥevratam besifrut 'ivrit veyidish bemizraḥ eiropa bein hashanim 1856–1914." Ph.D. diss., The Hebrew University, 1980.

———. "Bein haskala radikalit lesotsializm yehudi." In *PWCJS* 8 (1984), *Plenary Sessions; Jewish History,* pp. 13–20.

Beinart, Haim. "Demuta shel haḥatsranut hayehudit bisefarad hanotsrit." In *Kevutsot elit ushekhavot manhigot betoledot yisrael uvetoledot he'amim.* Jerusalem: Israel Academy of Sciences and Humanities, 1966.

Bell, David V.J. *Power, Influence and Authority: An Essay in Political Linguistics.* New York/Oxford: Oxford University Press, 1975.

Ben-Sasson, Haim Hillel. "'Osher ve'oni bemishnato shel hamokhiaḥ r. Efraim ish lentshitz," *Zion* 19 (1954), 142–66.

———. *Hagut vehanhaga: hashkefoteihem haḥevratiot shel yehudei polin beshalhei yemei habeinayim.* Jerusalem: Mossad Bialik, 1959.

———. "Dor golei sefarad 'al 'atsmo," *Zion* 26 (1961), 23–64.

Berend, Ivan, and György Ranki. *The European Periphery and Industrialization, 1780–1914.* Cambridge: Cambridge University Press, 1982.

Berger, H. "Der Commentar des R. Benjamin b. Jehuda zu den Sprüchen," *MGWJ* 45 (1901), 138–65, 373–404.

Bernfeld, Shimon. *Toledot hareformatsion beyisrael.* Warsaw: Edelstein, 1908.

Bershadskii, S.A. *Litovskie evreii.* St. Petersburg: 1883.

———. "Polozhenie o evreiakh 1804 goda," *Voskhod,* no. 1, 82–103; no. 3, 69–96; no. 4, 86–109; no. 6, 33–63 (1895).

Bettan, Israel. "The Sermons of Ephraim Luntshitz," *HUCA* 8–9 (1931–32), 443–80.

Biale, David. *Gershom Scholem: Kabbalah and Counter-History.* Cambridge, Mass.: Harvard University Press, 1979.

———. *Power and Powerlessness in Jewish History.* New York: Schoken, 1986.

Blidstein, Gerald. "A Note on the Function of 'The Law of the Kingdom Is Law' in the Medieval Jewish Community," *Jewish Journal of Sociology* 15, no. 2 (1973), 213–19.

———. "On Political Structures—Four Medieval Comments," *Jewish Journal of Sociology* 22, no. 1 (1980), 47–58.

———. *'Ekronot mediniim bemishnat haRambam.* Ramat-Gan, Isr.: Bar-Ilan University, 1983.

Bogucka, Maria. "Towns in Poland and the Reformation," *APH* 40 (1979), 55–74.

———. "Les recherches polonaises des années 1969–1978 sur l'histoire des villes et de la bourgeoisie jusqu'au declin du 18 siècle," *APH* 41 (1980), 239–58.

Borovoi, S. "Novoe ob A. Kovnere," *Evreiskoe mysl'* 2 (1926), 241–43.

Braiman, Shlomo. "Pulmus hatikunim badat basifrut ha'ivrit beemts'a hamea ha-19," *He-'Avar* 1 (1952), 115–31.

Braver, Avraham. *Galitsia viyehudeha.* Jerusalem: Mossad Bialik, 1965.

Breuer, Mordecai. "Ma'amad harabanut behanhagatan shel kehillot ashkenaz bamea ha-15." In *PWCJS* 6 (1975), vol. 2, pp. 141–47.

———. "Hadiyun beshalosh hashevu'ot badorot haaharonim." In *Geula umedina.* Jerusalem: Defense Ministry Press, 1979, pp. 49–57.

Buber, Martin. *The Origin and the Meaning of Hasidism.* New York: Harper and Row, 1960.

Buber, Salomon. *Anshei shem.* Cracow: 1895.

Carmilly-Weinberger, Moshe. *Censorship and Freedom of Expression in Jewish History.* New York: Sepher Hermon Press/Yeshiva University Press, 1977.

Chadwick, Owen. *The Secularization of the European Mind in the Nineteenth Century.* Cambridge: Cambridge University Press, 1975.

Champlin, John, ed. *Power.* New York: Atherton, 1971.

Chazan, Robert. *Medieval Jewry in Northern France.* Baltimore, Md.: The Johns Hopkins University Press, 1973.

———. "Emperor Frederick I, the Third Crusade, and the Jews," *Viator* 8 (1977), 83–93.

Cherniavksy, Michael. *Prologue to Revolution*. Englewood Cliffs, N.J.: Pren-
tice-Hall, 1967.
Cohen, Binyamin. "Havoievoda betorat shofet hayehudim befolin hayeshana,"
Gal-'Ed 1 (1973), 1–12.
———. "Hareshut havoievodit vehakehilla hayehudit bameiot ha-16–18," *Gal-
'Ed* 3 (1976), 9–32.
Cohen, Gerson D. *Sefer Haqabbalah (The Book of Tradition) by Abraham Ibn
Daud*. Philadelphia: Jewish Publication Society, 1967.
———. "Messianic Postures of Ashkenazim and Sephardim," Leo Baeck Memo-
rial Lecture. New York: Leo Baeck Institute, 1967.
Cohen, Stuart, and Eliezer Don-Yehiya, eds. *Comparative Jewish Politics (2):
Conflict and Consensus in Jewish Political Life*. Ramat-Gan, Isr.: Bar-
Ilan University, 1986.
Dagani, Ben-Zion. "Hamivneh shel hahistoria ha'olamit ugeulat yisrael be'Tse-
maḥ David' lerabbi David Ganz," *Zion* 45 (1980), 173–200.
Dahl, Robert. "The Concept of Power," *Behavioral Science* 2 (1957), 201–15.
———. *Modern Political Analysis*, 3d ed. Englewood Cliffs, N.J.: Prentice-Hall,
1976.
Dinur, Ben-Zion. *Bemifneh hadorot: meḥkarim ve'iyunim bereishitam shel haze-
manim hahadashim betoledot yisrael*, Jerusalem: Mossad Bialik, 1971.
Dubnow, Simon. "Istoricheskii soobshcheniia: podgotovitel'nyia raboty dlia
istorii russkikh evreev: oblastnye kagal'nye seimy v voevodstve volin-
skom i v belorussii (1666–1764)," *Voskhod*, nos. 4, 12 (1894), 25–44.
———. "Va'ad arb'a aratsot befolin veyahaso el hakehillot." In *Sefer hayovel le-
Nahum Sokolov*. Warsaw: Shuldberg, 1904, pp. 250–61.
———. "Evreiskaia pol'sha v epokhu razdelov," *ES* 2 (1909), 3–16.
———. "Kak byla vvedena rekrutskaia povinnost' dlia evreev v 1827 g.," *ES* 2
(1909), 256–65.
———. "Evreiskaia pol'sha v epokhu poslednykh razdelov," *ES* 4 (1911), 441–
63.
———. *History of the Jews in Russia and Poland*, 3 vols. Philadelphia: Jewish
Publication Society, 1916.
———. *Nationalism and History: Letters on Old and New Judaism*. Edited by K.
Pinson. New York: Atheneum, 1970.
———. *Toledot hahasidut*, 3d ed. Tel-Aviv: Dvir, 1974 (Originally published
1930–31.)
Duker, Abraham. "The Tarniks (Believers in the Coming of the Messiah in
1840)." *Joshua Starr Memorial Volume*. New York: Jewish Social Stud-
ies, 1953, pp. 191–201.
Eisenbach, Artur. "Les Droits civiques des juifs dans le royaume de pologne,"
REJ 3 (1964), 19–84.
Eisenstadt, Israel, and Shmuel Weiner. *Da'at kedoshim*. 2 vols. St. Petersburg:
1897–98.
Elazar, Daniel J. "Jewish Political Studies as a Field of Inquiry," *Jewish Social
Studies* 36 (1974), 220–33.

————, ed. *Kinship and Consent: The Jewish Political Tradition and Its Contemporary Uses.* Ramat-Gan, Isr.: Turtledove, 1981.

Elazar, Daniel J., and Stuart Cohen. *The Jewish Polity: Jewish Political Organization from Biblical Times to the Present.* Bloomington: Indiana University Press, 1984.

Elbogen, Ismar. *Der jüdische Gottesdienst in seiner geschichtlichen Entwicklung.* Frankfurt am Main: J. Kaufman, 1931.

Elon, Menahem. *Hamishpat ha'ivri.* Jerusalem: Magnes, 1973.

Epstein, Zalman. *Moshe Leib Lilienblum—shitato vehelekh maḥshevotav besheelot hadat.* Tel-Aviv: Dvir, 1935.

Erik, Max. "Vegn sotsialn mehus fun Aksenfelds shafn," *Tsaytshrift* 5 (1931), 125–69.

Eshkoly, A.Z. *Hatenu'ot hameshiḥot beyisrael.* Jerusalem: Mossad Bialik, 1956.

Etkes, Immanuel. "Parashat hahaskala mita'am vehatemura bema'amad tenu'at hahaskala berusia," *Zion* 43 (1978), 264–313.

————. *R. Israel Salanter vereishita shel tenu'at hamusar.* Jerusalem: Magnes, 1982.

Ettinger, Shmuel. "Ma'amadam hamishpati vehaḥevrati shel yehudei ukraina bemeiot ha15–17," *Zion* 20 (1955), 128–52.

————. "Hayesodot vehamegamot be'itsuv mediniut hashilton harusi klapei hayehudim 'im ḥalukat polin," *He-'Avar* 19 (1972), 20–34.

————. "The Jews at the Outbreak of the Revolution." In *The Jews in Soviet Russia Since 1917,* edited by Lionel Kochan. Oxford/New York: Oxford University Press, 1972, pp. 14–28.

————. "The Hasidic Movement—Reality and Ideals." In *Jewish Society Through the Ages,* edited by H.H. Ben-Sasson and S. Ettinger. New York: Schocken, 1973, pp. 252–65. (Originally published 1969.)

————. "Jews and Non-Jews in Eastern and Central Europe Between the Wars: An Outline." In *Jews and Non-Jews in Eastern Europe, 1918–1945,* edited by Bela Vago and George Mosse. New York/Jerusalem: Wiley/Keter, 1974, pp. 1–20.

————. "Takanat 1804," *He-'Avar* 22 (1977), 87–110.

Evans, R.J.W. *Rudolf II and His World.* Oxford: Oxford University Press, 1973.

Frank, Moshe. *Kehillot ashkenaz uvatei dineihen.* Tel-Aviv: Dvir, 1937.

Frankel, Jonathan. *Prophecy and Politics: Socialism, Nationalism and the Russian Jews.* Cambridge: Cambridge University Press, 1981.

————. "The Crisis of 1881–82 as a Turning Point in Modern Jewish History." In *The Legacy of Jewish Migration: 1881 and Its Impact,* edited by David Berger. New York: Brooklyn College Press, 1983, pp. 9–22.

————. "Democracy and Its Negations—on Polarity in Jewish Socialism." In *Totalitarian Democracy and After: International Colloquium in Memory of Jacob L. Talmon.* Jerusalem: Israel Academy of Sciences and Humanities/Magnes, 1984, pp. 329–41.

Frenk, Azriel. *Yehudei polin biyemei milḥamot Napoleon.* Warsaw: Hatsefira, 1912–13.

————. *Ha'ironim vehayehudim befolin.* Warsaw: Hatsefira, 1921. (Repr. Jerusalem, 1969.)

————. *Meshumodim in poyln.* Warsaw: Freyd, 1923–24.

Freund, Richard A. *"Principia Politica:* The Political Dimensions of Jewish and Christian Self-Definition in the Greco-Roman Period." Ph.D. diss., Jewish Theological Seminary of America, 1982.

Friedman, Philipp. "Wirtschaftsliche Umschichtungsprozesse und Industrialisierung in der polnischen Judenschaft 1800–1870." In *Jewish Studies in Memory of George A. Kohut,* edited by Salo W. Baron and Alexander Marx. New York: Kohut Memorial Foundation, 1935.

Gekker (Hekker), Elena. "Evreii v pol'skikh gorodakh vo vtoroi polovine 18 veka," *ES* 6 (1913), 184–200, 325–32.

Gelber, N.M. "Oblastnoi ravvinat' v galitsii (1776–86 g.)," *ES* 7 (1914), 305–17.

————. "Die Juden und die Judenreform auf dem vierjährigen Seim." In *Festschrift zu Simon Dubnows siebzigstem Geburtstag,* edited by Ismar Elbogen et al. Berlin: Jüdischer Verlag, 1930, pp. 136–53.

————. "Di yidn in kalish un der oyfshtand in yanuar 1830–1831," *Lodzer visnshaftlekhe shriftn* 1 (1938), 258–66.

————. "Sheelat hayehudim befolin bishnot 1815–1830," *Zion* 13–14 (1948–49), 106–43.

————. "Korot hayehudim befolin mereishit ḥalukata ve'ad milḥemet ha'olam hasheniya." In *Beit yisrael befolin,* edited by Halperin. Jerusalem: World Zionist Organization, 1948.

Gelman, Aryeh-Leyb. *Ha-Noda biyhuda umishnato.* Jerusalem: He'asor, 1961.

Gessen, Iulii. "K istorii religioznoi bor'by sredi evreev i v kontse 18 i v nachale 19 v.," *Voskhod,* no. 1 (1902), 116–35; no. 2, (1902) 59–90.

————. "Deputaty evreiskago naroda pri Aleksandra I," *ES* 2 (1909), 17–29, 196–206.

————. "K istorii evreishkikh tipografii: kreshchenye evreii Zandberg i Fodello," *ES* 2 (1909), 253–55.

————. "Vilenskaia komissiia po ustroistvo byta evreev," *Perezhitoe* 2 (1910), 306–11.

————. "Smena obshchestvennykh techenii: I. B. Levinzon i dr. M. Lilienthal; Pervyi russko-evreiskii organ'," *Perezhitoe* 3 (1911), 1–59.

————. *Istoriia evreiskago naroda v rossii,* 2 vols. Leningrad: L. Ganzburg, 1927. (Originally published as *Evreii v Rossii* [Petrograd: 1916.])

Ginsburg, Shaul. *Otechestvennaia voina 1812 goda i russkie evreii.* St. Petersburgh: Razum: 1912.

————. *Historishe verk,* 3 vols. New York: Shaul Ginsburg Jubilee Committee, 1937.

————. "Vi azoy men shraybt bay unz geshikhte," *Tsukunft* 44 (November 1939), 662–65.

————. "Di haskole un ihre moderne kritiker," *Tsukunft* 45 (December 1939), 719–22.

————. *Amolike peterburg.* New York: CYCO, 1944.

————. *Meshumodim in tsarishn rusland.* New York: CYCO, 1946.

Gitelman, Zvi. *Jewish Nationality and Soviet Politics. The Jewish Sections of the CPSU, 1917–1930.* Princeton, N.J.: Princeton University Press, 1972.

Glatzer, N.N. "The Attitude to Rome in the Amoraic Period," in PWCJS 6 (1975), vol. 2, pp. 9–19.

Goldberg, Jacob. "Bein ḥofesh lenetinut: sugei hatelut hafeiudalit shel hayehudim befolin," in *PWCJS* 5 (1972), vol. 2, pp. 107–13.

————. *"De non tolerandis iudaeis:* On the Introduction of the Anti-Jewish Laws into Polish Towns and the Struggle Against Them." In *Sefer Raphael Mahler,* edited by S. Yeivin. Tel-Aviv/Merhavia: Sifriat Poalim, 1974, pp. 39–52.

————. "Poles and Jews in the 17th and 18th Centuries: Rejection or Acceptance," *Jahrbücher für Geschichte Osteuropas* 22 (1974), 248–82.

Goldscheider, Calvin, and Alan Zuckerman. *The Transformation of the Jews.* Chicago: University of Chicago Press, 1984.

Goodenough, Erwin. *The Politics of Philo Judaeus: Practice and Theory.* New Haven/London: Yale University Press, 1938.

Gordon, Milton. *Assimilation in American Life: The Role of Race, Religion and National Origins.* New York/Oxford: Oxford University Press, 1964.

Graff, Gil. *Separation of Church and State. Dina de-Malkhuta Dina in Jewish Law, 1750–1848.* University: University of Alabama Press, 1985.

Graetz, Michael. *Haperiferia hayta lamerkaz.* Jerusalem: Mossad Bialik, 1982.

Green, Arthur. *Tormented Master: A Life of Rabbi Nahman of Bratslav.* University: University of Alabama, 1979.

Greenberg, Louis. *The Jews in Russia: The Struggle for Emancipation,* 2 vols. New Haven, Conn.: Yale University Press, 1944 (Reissued New York: Schocken, 1976).

Greis, Zeev, "Sifrut hahanhagot haḥasidit mehamaḥatsit hasheniya lamea ha-18 ve'ad shenot hashloshim lamea ha-19," *Zion* 46 (1981), 198–236.

Grinwald, Itamar, "Mizriḥa leshki'a: ledemutan shel haeskhatologia vehameshiḥiut bayahadut." In *Hara'ayon hameshiḥi beyisrael: yom 'iyun leregel malat 80 shana le-Gershom Scholem.* Jerusalem: Israel Academy of Sciences and Humanities, 1982, pp. 18–36.

Hacker, Yosef. "Yisrael bagoyim betiuro shel R. Shlomo leveit Halevi misaloniki," *Zion* 34 (1969), 43–87.

————. "Khronikot ḥadashot 'al geirush hayehudim misefarad, sibotav vetotsaotav," *Zion* 44 (1980), 201–28.

Halperin, Israel. "Reishito shel va'ad medinat lita veyaḥaso el va'ad arb'a aratsot," *Zion* 3 (1938), 51–57.

————. *Yehudim veyahadut bemizraḥ eiropa.* Jerusalem: Magnes, 1968.

Hamiel, Haim. "Bein ḥaredim lemaskilim berusia beshnot ha-60 veha-70," *Sinai* 59, no. 1/2 (1966), 76–84.

————. "Pulmus M. L. Lilienblum," *Sinai* 60, no. 5/7 (1967), 299–310.

Hertzberg, Arthur, ed. *The Zionist Idea.* New York: Atheneum, 1971.

Hilberg, Raul. *The Destruction of the European Jews.* Chicago: Quadrangle, 1967.

Hilman, Haim Meir. *Beit rebbi.* Berdichev: 1901–2.

Horodetzky, S.A. "Rabbi Levi-Yitzhak berdichevskii," *ES* 1 (1909), 205–36.

———. *Lekorot harabanut.* Warsaw: Tushia, 1911.

Hundert, Gershon. "Security and Dependence: Perspectives on Seventeenth-Century Polish-Jewish Society Gained Through a Study of Jewish Merchants in Little Poland." Ph.D. diss., Columbia University, 1979.

———. "Jewish Urban Residence in the Polish Commonwealth in the Early Modern Period," *Jewish Journal of Sociology* 26, no. 1 (1984), 25–34.

Huntington, Samuel P. "The Change to Change: Modernization, Development and Politics," *Comparative Politics* 3 (April 1971), 283–322.

Iakhinson, I., ed. *Sotsial-ekonomisher shteyger ba yidn in rusland in 19 y.h.* Kharkov: Tsentraler farlag far di felker fun f.s.s.r., 1929.

Jacobson, Jacob. "Eine Aktion für die russischen Grenzjuden in den Jahren 1843/44." In *Festschrift zu Simon Dubnows siebzigstem Geburtstag,* edited by Ismar Elbogen et al. Berlin: Jüdischer Verlag, 1930.

Juster, Jean. *Les Juifs dans l'empire romain.* Paris: Geuthner, 1914.

Kahane, I.Z. *Meḥkarim besifrut hateshuvot.* Jerusalem: Mossad Harav Kook, 1973.

Kalinka, Valerian. *Der vierjährige Polnische Reichstag 1788 bis 1791,* 2 vols. Berlin: 1898.

Karo, Baruch. *Ha'ir berdichev.* Tel-Aviv: 1951.

Katz, Jacob. *Exclusiveness and Tolerance.* New York: Schocken, 1961.

———. *Tradition and Crisis: Jewish Society at the End of the Middle Ages.* New York: Schocken, 1971.

———. *Leumiut yehudit.* Jerusalem: Zionist Library, 1982.

Katznelson, Gideon. *Hamilḥama hasifrutit bein haḥaredim vehamaskilim.* Tel-Aviv: Dvir, 1954.

Kaufmann, David. "The Prayer Book According to the Ritual of England Before 1290," *JQR,* o.s., 4 (1892), 20–63.

———. "Jewish Informers in the Middle Ages," *JQR,* o.s., 8 (1896), 217–38.

Kermish, Yosef. "Yehudei varsha bemered Koshchushko." In *Sefer hayovel le-N. M. Gelber.* Tel-Aviv: Olameinu, 1963.

Klausner, Israel, *Toledot hakehilla ha'ivrit bevilna.* Vilna: Hakehilla ha'ivrit, 1938.

———. *Vilna bitekufat hagaon.* Jerusalem: Sinai, 1942.

———. "Hamaavak hapenimi bekehillot rusia velita vehatsa'at R. Shimon ben Volf letikunim," *He-'Avar* 19 (1972), 54–73.

———. "Hagezerot 'al tilboshet hayehudim, 1844–1850," *Gal-'Ed* 6 (1982), 11–26.

Kleinman, I.A. "Propovednik-buntonvik 18 veka," *ES* 12 (1928), 179–88.

Klier, John D. "The Jewish Question in the Reform Era Russian Press, 1855–1865," *Russian Review* 39, no. 3 (1980), 301–19.

————. "The Origins of the Jewish Minority Problem in Russia, 1772–1812." Ph.D. diss., University of Illinois, 1981.

————. *Russia Gathers Her Jews: The Origins of the "Jewish Question" in Russia, 1772–1825.* Dekalb, Ill.: Northern Illinois University Press, 1986.

Kohn, Hans. *Die politische Idee des Judentums.* Munich: Meyer and Jessen, 1924.

Kon, P. "Yidn in dinst fun poylishn general Dombrowski." In YIVO *Historishe shriftn* 1 (Vilna: 1929), cols. 764–66.

————. "A yidishe shtim tsum oyfshtand 1794 in vilne." In *Yivo bletter* 4, no. 2 (1932), 134–48.

Korobkov, Kh. "Ekonomicheskii rol' evreev v pol'she v kontse 18 v.," *ES* 3 (1910), 346–77.

————. "Uchastie evreev vo vneishnei torgovle pol'shi," *ES* 4 (1911), 19–39, 197–220.

Lamm, Zvi. "Defusim mesortiim vetahalikhei modernizatsia bayahadut," *Bitefutsot hagola* 73/74 (Summer 1975), 62–72.

Landman, Leo. *Jewish Law in the Diaspora: Confrontation and Accommodation.* Philadelphia: Jewish Publication Society, 1968.

Lasswell, Harold. *Power and Society.* New Haven/London: Yale University Press, 1950.

Lederhendler, Eli. "From Autonomy to Autoemancipation: Historical Continuity, Political Development, and the Preconditions for the Emergence of National Jewish Politics in Nineteenth-Century Russia." Ph.D. diss., The Jewish Theological Seminary of America, 1987.

Lehman-Wilzig, Sam, and Bernard Susser, eds. *Comparative Jewish Politics (1): Public Life in Israel and the Diaspora.* Ramat-Gan, Isr.: Bar-Ilan University, 1981.

Leibowitz, Yeshayahu. *Yahadut, 'am yisrael umedinat yisrael.* Jerusalem/Tel-Aviv: Schocken, 1979.

————. *Emuna, historia ve'arakhim.* Jerusalem: Akademon, 1982.

Lerner, Daniel. *The Passing of Traditional Society.* New York/London: Macmillan, 1958.

Lestchinsky, Jacob. *Dos yidishe ekonomishe lebn in der yidisher literatur: heft 1: Rival un Aksenfeld.* Warsaw: Kultur-lige, 1922.

————. *Matsavam hakalkali shel hayehudim beeiropa hamizrahit vehamerkazit.* Tel-Aviv: Shem, 1935.

————. *Hatefutsa hayehudit.* Jerusalem: Mossad Bialik, 1960.

Levanda, Lev. "K istorii vozniknoveniia pervago organa russkikh evreev," *Voskhod*, no. 6 (1881), 132–52.

Levin, Mordecai. *'Erkei hevra vekhalkala baideologia shel tekufat hahaskala.* Jerusalem: Mossad Bialik, 1975.

Levin, S. "Tsum onteyl fun di litvishe yidn in oyfshtand fun 1831," *Yivo bletter* 2, no. 3 (1931), 222–33.

Levin, Yitzhok. *Yidn in altn polyn.* Buenos Aires: Tsentral-farband fun poylishe yidn in argentine, 1962.

228 Bibliography

———. "Der kherem als eksekutiv-mitl fun vad arba arotsoys," *Yorbukh* 1 (1964), 76–109.

Levitats, Isaac. *The Jewish Community in Russia, 1772–1844.* New York: Columbia University Press, 1943.

———. *The Jewish Community in Russia, 1844–1917.* Jerusalem: Posner, 1981.

Levy, Marion J., Jr. *Modernization: Latecomers and Survivors.* New York: Basic Books, 1972.

Lewy, Guenter. *Religion and Revolution.* Oxford/New York: Oxford University Press, 1974.

Lukes, Steven. *Power: A Radical View.* London: Macmillan, 1974.

Lurie, I. "Kehillot lita vehakaraim: ha'arakhat misim 'al hakaraim ugeviatam bamea ha'16 veha-17," *He-'Avar* 1 (1918), 159–71.

Mahler, Raphael. "A budzhet fun vad arba arotsoys in 18tn yorhundert," *Yivo bletter* 15, no. 1/2 (1940), 73–81.

———. *Der kamf tsvishn haskole un khasides in galitsye.* New York: YIVO, 1942.

———. *Toledot hayehudim befolin ('ad hamea hatesh'a 'esreh).* Merhavia, Israel: Sifriat Poalim, 1946.

———. *Divrei yemei yisrael: dorot aharonim.* Merhavia, Israel: Sifriat Poalim, 1955.

———. *Hahasidut vehahaskala.* Merhavia, Israel: Sifriat Poalim, 1961.

Mair, Lucy. *Primitive Government.* Baltimore, Md.: Penguin, 1962.

Maor, Yitzhak. *Hatenu'a hatsiyonit berusia.* Jerusalem: Magnes, 1986.

Marek, P. "Krizis evreiskago samoupravleniia i khasidizm," *EB* 12 (1928), 45–101.

———. "Vnutrennaia bor'ba v evreistve v 18 veke," *ES* 12 (1928), 102–78.

Mark, Y., ed. *Pinkes bialystok.* New York: Society for the History of Bialystok, 1949.

Mendelsohn, Ezra. *Class Struggle in the Pale.* Cambridge: Cambridge University Press, 1970.

———. *The Jews of East Central Europe Between the World Wars.* Bloomington: Indiana University Press, 1983.

Miron, Dan, and Anita Norich. "The Politics of Benjamin III." In *The Field of Yiddish: Studies in Language, Folklore and Literature, Fourth Collection,* edited by M. Herzog et al. Philadelphia: Institute for the Study of Human Issues, 1980, pp. 1–116.

Mishkinsky, Moshe. *Reishit tenu'at hapo'alim hayehudit berusia: megamot yesod.* Tel-Aviv: Tel-Aviv University, 1980.

Nadav, Mordecai. "'Iyun bahitrahashuyot beshalosh kehillot befolin-lita biyemei milhemet hatsafon uleahareha," in *PWCJS* 8 (1982), pp. 89–96.

———. "Ma'asei alimut bein yehudim lelo-yehudim belita lifnei 1648," *Gal-'Ed* 7/8 1985), 41–56.

Nagel, Jack. *The Descriptive Analysis of Power.* New Haven, Conn./London: Yale University Press, 1975.

Neher, André. *David Ganz uzemano.* Jerusalem: Reuven Mass, 1982.

Netanyahu, Ben-Zion. *Don Isaac Abravanel.* Philadelphia: Jewish Publication Society, 1972.

Neuman, A.A. *The Jews in Spain.* Philadelphia: Jewish Publication Society, 1942.

Neusner, Jacob. *A History of the Jews in Babylonia,* vol. 2. Leiden, Neth.: Brill, 1966.

————. "From Theology to Ideology: The Transformation of Judaism in Modern Times." In *Churches and States: The Religious Institution and Modernization,* edited by K. Silvert. New York: American Universities Field Staff, 1967, pp. 13–48.

————. *There We Sat Down: Talmudic Judaism in the Making.* Nashville, Tenn./ New York: Abingdon, 1972.

————. *Messiah in Context: Israel's History and Destiny in Formative Judaism.* Philadelphia: Fortress Press, 1984.

Oakley, Frances. "Legitimation by Consent," *Viator* 14 (1983), 303–35.

Ogus, Ia. N. "Istoricheskii ocherk deiatel'nosti ravvinskoi komissii," *Rasvet,* nos. 1–2 (1880).

Olsen, Marvin, ed. *Power in Societies.* New York/London: Collier-Macmillan, 1970.

Opalinski, Edward. "Great Poland's Power Elite Under Sigismund III, 1587–1632," *APH* 42 (1980), 41–66.

Orbach, Alexander. *New Voices of Russian Jewry: A Study of the Russian Jewish Press of Odessa in the Era of the Great Reforms, 1860–1871.* Leiden, Neth.: Brill, 1980.

Parkes, James. *The Jew in the Medieval Community.* London: Soncino, 1938.

Perles, J. "Geschichte der Juden in Posen," *MGWJ* 14 (1865), 81–93, 121–36, 165–78, 205–16, 256–63.

Philipson, David. *Max Lilienthal, American Rabbi: Life and Writings.* New York: Bloch, 1915.

Posner, S. "Un Sanglant cauchemar de guerre," *L'Univers israélite* (August 1934).

Pospiech, Andrzej, and Wojciech Tygiclski. "The Social Role of Magnate Courts in Poland (From the End of the Sixteenth up to the Eighteenth Century," *APH* 43 (1981), 75–100.

Rabinovich, P. "Geon Ya'akov," *Knesset yisrael* 2 (1887), cols. 157–62.

Rabinowitsch, Wolf Zeev. *Lithuanian Hasidism.* New York: Schocken, 1971.

Rosenblum, Noah. "Lebeḥinat hashkafat 'olamo shel Adam Hacohen Lebenson," *Peraqim* 2 (1960), 151–67.

Roskies, David G. *Against the Apocalypse: Responses to Catastrophe in Modern Jewish Culture.* Cambridge, Mass.: Harvard University Press, 1984.

Rosman, Murray Jay. "The Polish Magnates and the Jews: Jews in the Sieniawski-Czartoryski Territories, 1686–1731." Ph.D. diss., Jewish Theological Seminary of America, 1982.

Schiper, Yitzhak. *Toledot hakalkala hayehudit,* 2 vols. Tel-Aviv: A.I. Stibl,
    1935–36.
Scholem, Gershom. *The Messianic Idea in Judaism and Other Essays.* New
    York: Schocken, 1971.
Schorsch, Ismar. "On the History of the Political Judgment of the Jew," Leo
    Baeck Memorial Lecture 20. New York: Leo Baeck Institute, 1977.
————. "The Emergence of Historical Consciousness in Modern Judaism," *Leo
    Baeck Institute Yearbook* 28 (1983), pp. 413–37.
Segre, Dan. "Colonization and Decolonization: The Case of Zionist and African
    Elites," *Comparative Studies in Society and History* 20, no. 1 (1980), 23–
    41.
Seltzer, Robert. "From Graetz to Dubnow: The Impact of the East European
    Milieu on the Writing of Jewish History." In *The Legacy of Jewish Migra-
    tion: 1881 and Its Impact,* edited by David Berger. New York: Brooklyn
    College Press, 1983, pp. 49–60.
Septimus, Bernard. *Hispano-Jewish Culture in Transition: The Career and Con-
    troversies of Ramah.* Cambridge, Mass.: Harvard University Press, 1982.
————. "Piety and Power in Thirteenth-Century Catalonia." In *Studies in Medi-
    eval Jewish History and Literature (1),* edited by Isadore Twersky. Cam-
    bridge, Mass.: Harvard University Press, 1979, pp. 197–230.
Shapira, H. "Haahim Shapira," *Ha-Shiloach* 30 (1914), 541–54.
Shatzky, Jacob. *Geshikhte fun yidn in varshe,* 3 vols. New York: YIVO, 1947.
————. *Kultur-geshikhte fun der haskole in lite.* Buenos Aires: Tsentral-farband
    fun poylishe yidn in argentine, 1950.
Shatzmiller, Yosef. "Litemunat hamahloket harishona 'al kitvei haRambam,"
    Zion 34 (1969), 126–38.
————. "Igrato shel R. Asher b.r. Gershom lerabbanei tsarfat mizeman ha-
    mahloket 'al kitvei haRambam," *Mehkarim betoledot 'am yisrael veeretz
    yisrael* 1 (1970), 129–40.
————. "Halikhatam shel yehudim le'arkhaot shel goyim beprovans biyemei
    habeinayim," in *PWCJS* 5 (1972), vol. 2, pp. 375–81.
Shilo, Shmuel. *Dina demalkhuta dina.* Jerusalem: Dfus Akademi, 1975.
Shils, Edward. *Tradition.* Chicago/London: University of Chicago Press,
    1981.
Shmeruk, Chone. "Mashma'uta hahevratit shel hashehita hahasidit," *Zion* 20
    (1955), 47–72.
————. "Hashem hamashma'uti Mordkhe-Marcus—gilgulo shel ideal hevrati,"
    Tarbitz 29, no. 1 (1959), 76–98.
Shochat, Azriel. *'Im hilufei tekufot.* Jerusalem: Mossad Bialik, 1960.
————. "Berurim befarashat hapulmus harishon 'al sifrei haRambam," *Zion* 36
    (1971), 27–60.
————. "Hahanhaga bekehillot rusia 'im bitul hakahal," *Zion* 42 (1977), 143–
    233.
————. *Mossad harabanut mita'am berusia.* Haifa: University of Haifa, 1975–
    76.

———. "Kovets derushim be'arikhat Adam Hacohen Lebenson," *Meḥkarim betoledot 'am yisrael veeretz yisrael* 5 (1980), 253–74.

———. "Hitrofefut hatsipiyot hameshiḥiot etsel rishonei hamaskilim berusia vehahatḥalot lesheifat hishtalvut baḥevra harusit," *'Iyun uma'as* 2 (1981), 205–26.

Siegel, Seymour. "The War of the Kitniyot." In *Perspectives on Jews and Judaism: Essays in Honor of Wolfe Kelman,* edited by Arthur Chiel. New York: Rabbinical Assembly, 1978, pp. 383–93.

Silver, D.J. *Maimonidean Criticism and the Maimonidean Controversy, 1180–1240.* Leiden, Neth.: Brill, 1965.

Simonsohn, Shlomo. *Toledot hayehudim beduksut mantuvah,* 2 vols. Tel-Aviv/Jerusalem: Tel-Aviv University/Ben-Zvi Institute, 1965.

Slutsky, Yehuda. "Beit hamidrash lerabanim bevilna," *He-'Avar* 7 (1960), 29–48.

———. *Ha'itonut hayehudit-rusit bamea hatesh'a 'esreh.* Jerusalem: Mossad Bialik, 1970.

———"Sikum 'agum," *He-'Avar* 19 (1972), 5–19.

Sonne, Yeshayahu. *Mi-Paulo harevi'i 'ad Pius haḥamishi.* Jerusalem: Mossad Bialik, 1954.

Sosis, I. "Natsional'nyi vopros v literature 60-kh godov," *ES* 8 (1915), 38–56.

———. "Period 'obruseniia': natsional'nyi vopros v literature kontsa 60-kh i nachala 70-kh godov," *ES* 8 (1915), 324–37.

———. "Na rubezhe dvukh epokh," *ES* 8 (1915), 324–37.

———. "Sotsyale kegnzatsn in yidishe kehilles in 16tn un 17tn yorhundert loyt rabonishe responsn," *Tsaytshrift* 1 (1926), 225–38.

Stampfer, Shaul. "Shalosh yeshivot litaiot bamea hetesh'a 'esreh." Ph.D. diss., The Hebrew University, 1981.

Stanislawski, Michael. *Tsar Nicholas I and the Jews: The Transformation of Jewish Society in Russia, 1825–1855.* Philadelphia: Jewish Publication Society, 1983.

———. "The Tsarist Mishneh Torah: A Study in the Cultural Politics of the Russian Haskalah." In *PAAJR* 50 (1983), 165–83.

Stern, Selma. *The Court Jew.* Philadelphia: Jewish Publication Society, 1950.

———. *Josel of Rosheim.* Philadelphia: Jewish Publication Society, 1965.

Stow, Kenneth. "Gishat hayehudim laapifiorut vehadoktrina shel haganat hayehudim bashanim 1063–1147," *Meḥkarim betoledot 'am yisrael veeretz yisrael* 5 (1980), 175–90.

Susser, Bernard. "On the Reconstruction of Jewish Political Theory." in *Comparative Jewish Politics (1): Public Life in Israel and the Diaspora,* edited by Sam Lehman-Wilzig and Bernard Susser. Ramat-Gan, Isr.: Bar-Ilan University, 1981, pp. 13–22.

Synan, E. *The Popes and the Jews in the Middle Ages.* New York: Macmillan, 1965.

Talmage, Frank, ed. *Disputation and Dialogue: Readings in the Jewish-Christian Encounter.* New York: Ktav, 1975.

Talmon, Jacob. *Political Messianism*. London: Secker and Warburg, 1960.
————. *The Origins of Totalitarian Democracy*. New York: Norton, 1970.
————. *The Myth of the Nation and the Vision of Revolution*. London/Berkeley and Los Angeles: Secker and Warburg/University of California Press, 1980.
Talmon, Yonina. "Pursuit of the Millennium: The Relationship Between Religious and Social Change," *Archives européenes de sociologie* 3, no. 1 (1962), 125–48.
————. "Millenarian Movements," *Archives européenes de sociologie* 7, no. 2 (1966), 159–200.
Tcherikover, E. *Istoriia obshchestva dlia rasprostranenia prosveshchenia mezhdu evreiami v rossii . . . 1863–1913 gg*, edited by S. Ginsburg. St. Petersburg: I. Fleitman, 1913.
————. "Hehamon hayehudi, hamaskilim vehamemshala biyemei Nikolai I," *Zion* 4 (1939), 150–69.
Tishby, Isaiah. "Hapulmus 'al sefer hazohar bemea hashesh 'esreh beitalia," *Peraqim* 1 (1967/68), 131–82.
Trunk, Isaiah. "The Council of the Province of White Russia," *YIVO Annual of Jewish Social Science* 11 (1956/57), 188–210.
Tsigelman, A. "'Iskei ḥakhirot shel yehudei polin ukesharam lehitehavut va'ad arb'a aratsot," *Zion* 47 (1982), 112–44.
Ullmann, Walter. *The Growth of Papal Government in the Middle Ages: A Study in the Relation of Clerical to Lay Power*. London: Methuen, 1970.
————. *The Church and the Law in the Early Middle Ages*. London: Varorium Reprints, 1975.
Urbach, Ephraim. *The Sages*. 2 vols. Jerusalem: Magnes, 1975.
Vind, Shlomo. *Rabbi Yehezkel Landau, toledot ḥayav*. Jerusalem: Da'at Torah, 1961.
Vital, David. *The Origins of Zionism*. Oxford/New York: Oxford University Press, 1980.
Warszawski, Isaiah. "Yidn in kongress-poyln (1815–1831)." In YIVO *Historishe shriftn* 2 (Vilna: 1937), pp. 322–54.
Weinryb, Bernard. "Beitrage zur Finanzgeschichte der juedischen Gemeinden in Polen," *HUCA* 16 (1941), 187–214.
————. *Neueste Wirtschaftsgeschichte der Juden in Russland und Polen von der 1. polnischen Teilung bis zum Tode Alexanders II (1772–1881)*, 2d rev. ed. Hildesheim, W. Ger./New York: Georg Olms, 1972. (Originally published 1934.)
————. *The Jews in Poland: A Social and Economic History*. Philadelphia: Jewish Publication Society, 1973.
Werblowsky, R.J. Zwi. "Messianism in Jewish History." In *Jewish Society Through the Ages*. Edited by Ben-Sasson and Ettinger. New York: Schocken, 1971, pp. 30–45.
Whitaker, C.S., Jr. *The Politics of Tradition*. Princeton, N.J.: Princeton University Press, 1970.

Wiener, M. "Vegn Aksenfelds pyeses." In *Y. Aksenfelds verk,* edited by M. Wiener. Kiev/Kharkov: Institut far yidisher kultur ba der ukraynisher akademye—Melukhe farlag "Literatur un kunst," 1931.

Wrong, Dennis. *Power: Its Forms, Bases and Uses.* Oxford: B. Blackwell, 1979.

Wyrobisz, Andrzej. "Small Towns in Sixteenth- and Seventeenth-century Poland," *APH* 34 (1976), 153–64.

Yerushalmi, Shimshon Dov. "Va'adot uve'idot harabanim berusia," *He-'Avar* 3 (1955) 86–94.

Yerushalmi, Yosef Haim. "The Lisbon Massacre of 1506 and the Royal Image in the Shebet Yehudah," *HUCA* suppl. 1 (1976).

Zeitlin, Hillel. *Haḥasidut leshitoteha uzerameha.* Warsaw: Sifrut, 1910.

Zeitlin, S. "Opposition to the Spiritual Leaders Appointed by the Government," *JQR,* n.s., 31 (1940–41) 287–308.

Z[eltser]., D. "Lipman Zeltser, iz semeinikh vospominanii," *ES* 4 (1911), 293–98.

Zimmer, Eric. *Harmony and Discord: An Analysis of the Decline of Jewish Self-government in Fifteenth-Century Central Europe.* New York: Yeshiva University Press, 1970.

Zinberg (Tsinberg), Israel. "Isak Ber Levinzon i ego vremia," *ES* 3 (1910), 504–41.

———. *Istoriia evreiskoi pechati v rossii.* Petrograd: 1915.

———. "Milḥemet hakahal beharav haaḥaron bevilna," *He-'Avar* 2 (1918), 45–64.

———. "Shklov i ego 'prosvetiteli' kontsa 18 veka," *ES* 12 (1928), 17–44.

———. "Di makhloykes tsvishn di roshey hakohol un dem rov in vilne in der tsveyter helft 18tn yorhundert." In YIVO *Historishe shriftn* 2 (Vilna: 1937), 291–321.

———. *A History of Jewish Literature,* 12 vols., edited and translated by Bernard Martin. New York/Cincinnati, Ohio: Ktav/Hebrew Union College Press, 1978.

Zipperstein, Steven J. "Haskalah, Cultural Change and Nineteenth-Century Russian Jewry: A Reassessment," *Journal of Jewish Studies* 35, no. 2 (1983), 191–207.

———. *The Jews of Odessa: A Cultural History, 1794–1881.* Stanford, Calif.: Stanford University Press, 1985.

Zitron, Shmuel. *Di geshikhte fun der yidisher presse fun yor 1863 biz 1889.* Vilna: Fareyn fun yidishe literatn un zhurnalistn in vilne, 1923.

———. *Shtadlonim.* Warsaw: Ahisefer, 1926.

Index

Index